Mark Odell, PhD
Charles E. Campbell, MEd

The Practical Practice
of Marriage and Family Therapy
Things My Training Supervisor
Never Told Me

Pre-publication
REVIEWS,
COMMENTARIES,
EVALUATIONS . . .

"*T*he Practical Practice of Marriage and Family Therapy: Things My Training Supervisor Never Told Me* reads like a series of conversations with a couple of seasoned mentors who have your best interests at heart. In this book, which is targeted at the recently graduated (or soon to be graduated) marriage and family therapist, Odell and Campbell seek to provide a comprehensive and thorough overview of the practical issues facing beginning marriage and family therapists. Writing in an informal, personal style, the authors overview a range of issues from examining one's values and agenda as a therapist, to finding a clinical position, handling paperwork and treatment planning, and

dealing with a host of ethical and treatment issues.

While there are plenty of books out there about therapy models or treatment approaches for a particular presenting problem, this is the first book, to my knowledge, that explores the nitty-gritty practical stuff one needs to consider before embarking on a career as a marriage and family therapist. I applaud Odell and Campbell for their efforts and feel that this book should be required reading in all MFT professional issues courses. Students ought to have this book firmly in hand as they leave graduate school and seek their fortune in the real world of clinical practice."

Mark White, PhD
Assistant Professor,
Department of Human L
and Family Studies,
Auburn University,
Auburn, AL

"**O**dell and Campbell provide a professional, yet friendly, account of what is important in the preparation of a therapist. All of the chapters are my favorites because each is crucial to the therapist as a professional working with clients experiencing pain and difficult life circumstances. As a teacher, supervisor, and clinician in the field of marriage and family therapy for over twenty years, it is clear to me that the authors have delineated what it means to be a marriage and family therapist. I particularly liked the emphasis on a client system that included the social context, as well as ways to address reluctant clients unwilling to accept (or apprehensive or unaware of) the involvement of other family members. More important, the book provides the reader with the answer to 'why' such an approach is crucial to problem resolution and successful behavior change. The steps for becoming a successful family therapist from theoretical competence, to license attainment, to case management, to personal values and dual relationship issues that confront ethical and legal challenges for the therapist, are all here. Once you attain such success, how to avoid clinical burnout and achieve a personally fulfilled life is a bonus. This text would be valuable for any practicum or internship experience, and whether the clinical trainee is beginning or advanced, the conversational and sometimes humorous writing style provides enjoyable as well as informative reading."

William H. Quinn, PhD
Professor and Director,
Clinical Research and Services,
Department of Child
and Family Development,
University of Georgia,
Athens, GA

"**R**eading this book is like having a friend with whom you can continue the stimulating conversations about family therapy that you had when you were a student. It is easy and enjoyable to read and loaded with concrete practical advice covering a wide range of issues one is likely to encounter. Excellent case vignettes with case notes and assessment examples from both a systemic and traditional (individual) therapy perspective (including DSM-IV diagnoses) are included. This book truly does cover topics that are often left out of graduate programs, but are nonetheless encountered in one's professional experiences."

Jerry Gale, PhD
Director,
Marriage and Family
Therapy Program,
University of Georgia,
Athens, GA

The Practical Practice
of Marriage
and Family Therapy
Things My Training Supervisor
Never Told Me

HAWORTH Marriage & the Family
Terry S. Trepper, PhD
Senior Editor

The Practical Practice of Marriage and Family Therapy
Things My Training Supervisor Never Told Me

Mark Odell, PhD
Charles E. Campbell, MEd

The Haworth Press
New York • London

The Haworth Press, Inc., 10 Alice Street, Binghamton, NY 13904-1580

Library of Congress Cataloging-in-Publication Data

Cover design by Marylouise E. Doyle.

Odell, Mark.
    The practical practice of marriage and family therapy : things my training supervisor never told me / Mark Odell, Charles E. Campbell.
      p. cm.
    Includes bibliographical references and index.
    ISBN 0-7890-0431-3 (alk. paper)
    1. Marital psychotherapy. 2. Family psychotherapy. I. Campbell, Charles E. II. Title. III. Title: Things my training supervisor never told me.
RC488.5.O34 1997
616.89'156—dc21
                                                97-19857
                                                  CIP

To my wife and soulmate Kelye, my gifts of a son Spenser
and daughter Shelby, and to my ever-dependable parents,
Jack and Gay.

—Mark Odell

To my wife and true companion, Lynn; to three of the people
in this world I admire most, my sons Noah, Kurt, and Scott;
and to the ones who have always been there for me,
my parents, Chuck and Janet.

—Charles Campbell

ABOUT THE AUTHORS

Mark Odell, PhD, has been a practicing clinician for ten years, and currently trains graduate students in the marriage and family therapy program at Bowling Green State University. He is also in private practice at the Center for Solutions in Brief Therapy in Sylvania, Ohio. A graduate of the University of Georgia, he is a Clinical Member and Approved Supervisor of the American Association for Marriage and Family Therapy (AAMFT) and a Licensed Marriage and Family Therapist. Dr. Odell has worked in inpatient, outpatient, and private agency settings.

Charles E. Campbell, MEd, is a therapist with over twenty years' experience. A Licensed Professional Clinical Counselor and a Clinical Member of the American Association for Marriage and Family Therapy (AAMFT), he is in private practice in Toledo, Ohio with Lutheran Social Services and is Lead Therapist for Firelands Counseling and Recovery Services in Fremont, Ohio. He is a graduate of Bowling Green State University, where he now teaches and trains graduate students in the marriage and family therapy program. He is also associated with the Department of Psychiatry, Medical College of Ohio, as a volunteer Clinical Instructor and member of the Associate Medical Staff. His professional experience includes work in public and private schools; community mental health counseling; private practice in individual, marriage, and family therapy; and agency consultation/supervision.

CONTENTS

Foreword

One of the biggest problems I have seen among students in all of the clinical disciplines is that they are not prepared for the realities of clinical work. Oh, I don't mean deciding which clinical intervention to use for what type of family exhibiting what type of problem. That sort of problem should be—and usually is—covered well during clinical training. What I mean are the nuts-and-bolts sorts of problems endemic to the *practice* of family therapy in the real world. For example, how do you integrate family therapy into the workings of an individual-therapy-oriented agency? Or, how can you do systemically oriented intakes, treatment plans, and discharge summaries when all of the forms are designed for individuals? What is the *real* scoop about insurance claims, managed care, and health maintenance organizations for family therapists?

The Practical Practice of Marriage and Family Therapy, by Mark Odell and Charles Campbell, was clearly written with the new family therapist in mind. It is not only written in a lively, conversational way (as an antidote to the four years of textbook reading most have just completed!), but it also is written with regard to the concerns of new therapists at the forefront. It is almost as if Odell and Campbell held a focus group of recently graduated clinicians, asked them what they wish they had been told about real-life clinical practice during their training, and then wrote their book to fill in the gaps. To that end, this book will make an excellent required text in either professional studies courses or in clinical practice.

Although *The Practical Practice of Marriage and Family Therapy* is mostly targeted to students and newly trained therapists, I believe more "seasoned" professionals will find this book extremely useful as well. Some of the authors' creative solutions to common dilemmas are refreshing and quite useful, even for us "old pros." For example, I found their chapters on values conflicts and dual relationships to be extremely timely, given the field's current concern with risk management.

I know both students and professionals will find this book as delightful and helpful as I did. I expect in the future to see this work on the bookshelves of many therapists, not unopened, but with that characteristic often-read, often-referred-to look.

Terry S. Trepper, PhD
Executive Editor
Haworth Marriage & the Family

Acknowledgments

We wish to acknowledge the people in our lives who have helped to make this book possible, either directly or indirectly. Our efforts here are the result of various experiences for each of us in several contexts. First and foremost, we have experienced many, many hours of psychotherapeutic work with clients that have helped us to come to some understanding of how that world often works. We wish to thank our clients for providing us with an education that is more complete than we ever could have learned in school. Second, our own training experiences in graduate school have given us a view of what it was like—and in many ways still is—to go through the "gauntlet" of training. Third, our experience as trainers and supervisors of therapists and graduate students has helped us to see what many budding professionals need in order to be just a bit more ready for "real world" practice. We want to thank them for helping us to see their needs and giving us an inkling of a way to begin to meet them. They have been valuable teachers for us and were the initial inspiration for the writing of this book. Finally, we would like to thank Terry Trepper, our editor, for his unflagging encouragement and consistently helpful input.

Each of us, however, has a few individuals to whom we would like to express our appreciation.

I would like to thank William Quinn for his continued and ongoing mentorship. He has shown me excellence in every aspect of professional work—in clinical treatment, in the classroom, in supervision and training, and in research. I would also like to acknowledge Karin Jordan for her encouragement over the years, as well as her colleagial spirit. I would like to thank my co-author, Charles "Chip" Campbell, for his encouragement and enthusiasm for this project and for his professional wisdom. Overall, he is one heck of a guy and a solid friend. Writing with him has been a lot of fun, too. I would also like to express my appreciation to Marc Dielman, a colleague and friend of impeccable quality, and to a couple of my other trainers/supervisors/scholars who made as much time as possible to tell me things I needed to hear: Carl Ridley, Greg Samples, Doris Hewitt, and Luciano L'Abate. Finally, I would like to thank my wife for allowing me the time and energy necessary to complete "the book," for her encouragement, and for being proud of me.

—Mark Odell

I would first like to acknowledge my co-author, Mark Odell, who was the prime instigator for this whole project. I wish to thank him for his wit, his wisdom, his writing and editing talents, and most of all, his friendship. I would also like to thank my good friend, fellow therapist, and peer supervisor for the last twenty years, Tom Fine, for always being there for me. Finally, I would like to acknowledge those therapists who have been my trainers and supervisors over the last twenty years. My heartfelt thanks go to my first graduate school professor, Bernard Rabin, for introducing me to psychotherapy; to Augustus Napier, David Keith, and the late Carl Whitaker for their inspirational teaching and training on family therapy; and to my most trusted supervisors over the years, James Guinan and Walling Mariea, who have always had the time to tell me the things I needed to hear.

—Charles Campbell

Introduction

The process of becoming a complete marriage and family therapist takes a considerable amount of time, certainly longer than just the time spent training in graduate school. It is a professional cliché today, nonetheless true, that the therapist is never finished with training. It is a lifelong process of gathering experience, new skills, and new ideas while honing what one already possesses to an ever sharper edge.

While this is a pedagogically appealing way to think about being a professional marriage and family therapist, it has obvious pragmatic limitations. It begs the question of when the therapist is ready. How much training is sufficient before the trainee is prepared adequately to practice? Philosophical debate aside, therapists of all disciplines in fact are considered ready to practice and given permission to do so by graduate schools, professional associations, and state licensing boards when they have completed a graduate course of study and fulfilled a clinical experience requirement of given length. To be honest, we do not have any serious bone to pick about this normative process, and we have heard little complaining from various mental health agencies and employers concerning their new hires. The process largely works.

This does not mean that it is ideal, however. We have found that newly minted therapists tend to enter the "real" practice world with a good repertoire of knowledge about theory, research, and clinical skills, and they are able to utilize these fairly well as they work with their clients. At the same time, though, we have seen that there are a host of other things pertaining to "real" world practice that the recent graduate has very limited knowledge about, and this makes the transition from trainee to practitioner significantly more difficult. Provocative as it may sound, we would suggest that the new graduate out of a typical training program is only about 70 percent of the way there, so to speak; significant gaps in their knowledge base still exist, which need filling for them to be fully prepared for the practice world.

That is the principle reason for this book; hence its title is *The Practical Practice of Marriage and Family Therapy*. We believe that the typical two-year master's program or even the three- or four-year doctoral program does not allow for a large amount of free time for the trainee; the average graduate student is rarely heard remarking about how much discretionary time (or income, for that matter) he or she has to do whatever he or she wants (perhaps it is a closely guarded secret, but we doubt it). Rather, graduate training programs are intensive and filled with activity, and they cover a great deal of essential material. Unfortunately, however, the mental health professional world is more complicated today than ever, and it is simply *impossible* for standard training regimens to cover everything that the trainee needs to know. This book is intended to facilitate the training process by addressing important areas that are rarely covered in typical marriage and family therapy training programs.

With that in mind, this book's intended audience is the population of persons who are in graduate school or who have recently entered the professional practice world. Trainees in marriage and family therapy programs and recent graduates from such programs are the most obvious audience, but we believe that trainees or recent graduates in social work, counseling, psychology, or in any other helping profession who have an interest in marriage and family therapy would benefit from reading this book. We also invite more experienced therapists to read this book as a refresher; if it has been a long while since you were in training or you have been wanting to learn more about the pragmatics of doing marriage and family therapy, this book might be helpful to you. The latter sections of the book in particular offer the more seasoned clinician some ideas that we have rarely seen addressed in the clinical literature, such as negotiating values conundrums, terminating clients, avoiding burn-out, and changing jobs.

As mentioned, this book's purpose is to address several issues that the typical training program simply does not have time to cover. We have divided the book into three sections that coincide roughly with the process of clinical development as it usually proceeds for most trainees. We open with a discussion of why the field of marriage and family therapy has been chosen as a profession; too often in our experience, trainees have not really evaluated what draws them to this area, and while anyone who has come so far to be reading a book like this one may not be excited about turning away from the field, we still think it is an important question to consider. We then move on to discuss how the real practice world is often different from the university training world.

In the second section, we discuss several ideas pertaining to actually commencing practice after graduation. These include finding a job and setting up good supervision, as well as several issues of normative practice, ranging from diagnosing and assessing clients to documenting treatment and dealing with money concerns. The emphasis for us here is mostly on the practical requirements of successful work, and less so on the theoretical considerations and in-session activities that are conducted, although to the degree that the latter are subject to the former, they are addressed.

Our third section deals with issues that are faced as the developing therapist continues to practice, such as handling philosophical and values differences, stuck cases, and termination; dealing with the legal system; avoiding burnout; and professional development, including changing jobs and career focus. These sorts of issues are the type to come back to from time to time as a means of reevaluating one's professional life. We end with a discussion of developing a specialization, something that many therapists investigate as their careers progress.

You will note as you read that we have adopted a rather conversational and informal style in our writing. We have kept citations and jargon to a minimum, reflecting our desire to make this a more lively and enjoyable read than the standard academic texts you may be familiar with (perhaps to the point of exhaustion). We also assume that you have some familiarity with the theoretical and clinical literature already, and so we spend little time on foundational material, focusing more on the utilitarian concerns that everyday professional work brings. We want this book to be a practical thought and idea stimulator for you, and the dry tone of more typical texts did not seem to be to us the best way to convey what we had in mind. We would like this book to be a "supportive supervisor/mentor over-the-shoulder" type of tool for you, and so the lighter tone and liberal use of humor (?) seemed a better way to accomplish that kind of feel. We hope you will agree.

Additionally, this book is not intended to replace more specific books dealing with theory, interventions with particular populations, or any other more focused issue. Plenty of excellent sources for those kinds of topics exist, and we have included a comparatively brief list of recommended readings after our reference list at the book's end. Thus, this book is intended to complement and supplement the graduate school preparation you have received or are receiving to help you become a more complete therapist at the outset of your career. We hope that reading this book will give you a slight edge as you get started in the marriage and family therapy field—an edge that you, your employer, and your clients may note and appreciate. Good luck and happy reading!

SECTION I:
BEFORE YOU GET STARTED . . .

The world of professional marriage and family therapy is quite an exciting one (otherwise you would have probably chosen something else, right?). Similarly, the road to becoming a competent and qualified marriage and family therapist is also exciting, albeit in different ways. We assume you are reading this because you have begun the journey, and we would like to welcome you. However, before we begin examining the practice of marriage and family therapy in the real world, we need to attend to some other things first. We want to explore what has brought about this career choice for you, and then we want to orient you to some of the differences between the training world and the world of professional practice.

Chapter 1

So You Want to Be a Marriage and Family Therapist . . .

Therapists are born, not made. That statement may strike you as surprising, curious, or perhaps even offensive, especially if you have spent several years and no small sum of money to earn the formal training and credentials needed to become a qualified clinical professional. Indeed, if therapists are not made, then why is it necessary to take all the classes, do the internships and externships, attend workshops and conferences ad nauseam, and participate in supervision and often personal therapy, all for the purpose of becoming a recognized and legitimate practitioner? Cynically, one might say it is all about money or control, or some other equally untoward reason, but that is not what we are talking about. The process of becoming professionally qualified is absolutely essential, but, in the final analysis, it is still true that therapists are not made primarily through formal training and education.

Certainly, this is not to be taken as a blanket endorsement of an organismic model of humanity, suggesting that our genetic makeup determines everything about us—a decidedly "biology is destiny" point of view. Frankly, we are not even sure we are smart enough to engage in an intelligent debate of something as philosophically and scientifically weighty as that. No, we will try to keep it simple and straightforward, both here and throughout this book. We are confident that you have already begun to address or addressed such heavy matters as part of your graduate training, anyway. So . . . where were we?

Therapists are born, not made. Or are they? In truth, such a statement is not completely accurate. Therapists, just as all humans, are born into a social environment, coming into the world with a com-

7

plete set of genes as well as preferences and predispositions. What is unique about therapists is that their training begins very early in their family environments (Titelman, 1987). So perhaps it would be better to say therapists are born into families in which they are trained unwittingly from childhood to be people-helpers. From then, their careers as helpers are launched. Thus, therapists start on the road to being therapists long before they go to graduate school, or even elementary school.

So, what is the point? It is a truism among mental health professionals that people go into these types of careers in an effort to figure themselves and their families out, or to save their parents' marriage, or deal with family-of-origin problems, etc. It has been said, half-humorously, that people from normal families tend not to go into mental health disciplines; rather, they are freed up to do the work of other professions—engineering, nuclear physics, teaching, medicine, driving heavy equipment, for instance—in which psychoemotional need-meeting is not at the forefront of what one does every day at the office. This in itself is not a problem.

The potential problem, however, is that in our experience, too many therapists do not give adequate attention to the whole motivational process that drives/draws them like moths to a flame into the mental health field. When this happens, a host of possible problems results. The purpose of this chapter is to challenge you to analyze and evaluate honestly your own reasons for becoming a mental health professional, specifically of the species *marriage and family therapist.* In short, why are you reading this book?

Because the tool you use as a therapist is your own self, i.e., your person (Aponte, 1992, 1994; McDaniel and Landau-Stanton, 1991; Nelson, Heilbrun, and Figley, 1993), it is essential that you know fairly explicitly what makes you tick. You can become a master of paradox, or exception finding, or sculpting, or externalizing, but all of these ways of working with people are mediated through you—your ideas, your values, your expectations, and your goals. And no matter how much you try to be a "neutral" person, your self gets in the way. This is not bad! This just is. Knowing what to do with this reality and how to do it is absolutely critical, in our view, in order to be an effective, ethical, and responsible therapist.

WHAT DO YOU TELL OTHERS?

When you tell others about your decision to be a marriage and family therapist (assuming you are still in training; if you are already a practicing professional, when you tell others what you do), what reactions do you get? Most people, in our experience, respond quite positively: "That's such an important profession, especially these days. Families and marriages need all the help they can get!" "Wow, you're really going to be dealing with some serious stuff, people's problems and all." "That's a tough career—I couldn't listen to people's junk all day every day." Less often, we hear responses such as the following: "Why in the world would you want to do that?" or "You?? How can you expect to help anybody when your own life is such a big mess?"

The former kinds of responses tend to be very gratifying. We very much like to be admired, if we are honest. Having family members, friends, and new acquaintances tell us what an important thing we are doing and how special we must be to do it is nice to hear. It is even sweeter when clients, either current or former, tell you what a good therapist you are or what a great difference you have made in their lives. Those can be most exhilarating and rewarding moments! And they should be.

The latter responses are ones we would rather not hear. Often, they come from people who are usually not very supportive of choices we have made in the past, are outright naysayers, or make a general habit of being discouraging. It seems that family members do this perhaps better than anyone! When this is the case, we can make an effort of discounting what we hear, chalking it up to ol' Uncle Fred's cantankerous nature. There are times, however, when we may need to heed such voices. More on this shortly.

When we receive validation for our decisions to be therapists and for the work we do, this is good. There is no doubt that, as society's complexity increases and stresses on families become greater, those who are specially trained and focused to work with families will become more important, and in large part, this is as it should be. Our profession is an admirable one, and our contribution to the well-being of individuals, families, and society at large is not insignificant. We should be proud of what we do and all that we have to offer.

I WANT TO BE A FAMILY THERAPIST BECAUSE: MY MOTIVES

The aforementioned aspects are all reasonable and respectable factors influencing us in the choice we make to be marriage and family therapists. They are worthwhile motives. But there is more to it than just that, and this is what is most salient for our purposes here. What do you tell others when they ask why you have chosen this profession?

In our view, the best answers to this type of question contain both the grand external factors—i.e., to address major problems in the lives of families and hence society—and more subtle, personal internal factors—i.e., to come to some understanding or closure with respect to growing up as a bruised human being in a less-than-perfect family. An overemphasis on either the external or the internal motivations can be taken as a sign of warning. It is essential to be able to balance honestly the two. Indeed, the internal and external factors ideally are complementary.

When answering questions of this nature from family members, friends, professors, mentors, acquaintances, and the like, therapists tend to emphasize the external factors. For clarity's sake, let us say these are the motives for the choice. They can be easily upheld. For example, the world needs relationship problem solvers, many parents need help raising children, couples need help making their relationships work, violence needs to be prevented or treated when it occurs, and the myriad other social problems that interface with families all deserve the attention of helping professionals. These answers are entirely valid reasons for choosing the career of marriage and family therapist. They are also safe ones with which very few people would argue. However, we believe that there is usually much more behind the career choice than only that. After all, if no one would disagree that marriages and families can benefit from some help, then it follows that there must be reasons why some people choose this career whereas others choose different careers.

We believe that internal motivations play the more important role in the choice to be a marriage and family therapist. Growing up in our families has pushed us in some way toward this career and not another (Dryden and Spurling, 1989; Sussman, 1992). Perhaps a parental divorce, or alcoholism, or some other difficulty character-ized the family system that spawned us, and the legacy stemming out of that situation has propelled us headlong into an attempt to "make things right" somehow. Whatever the situation may have been, we must eventually see it clearly and understand how it affects our clinical thinking and acting.

We are not intimating that it is necessary to share the most private or painful aspects of one's family life in a "warts and all" approach to whomever hazards to question what has led you to this career field. We *are* saying that credit must be given where it is due, and a major portion of that is drawn from the family in which you grew up. If you had grown up in the "typical, normal, significant-prob-lem-free" family (whatever that is), you very likely would not be particularly interested in spending the majority of your working life thinking about ego boundaries, alliances, overcontrolling parents, affairs, abuse, secrets, divorce, eating disorders, weird relatives, bed-wetting, and the like. It is even less that you would be drawn to a daily vocation of attempting to solve those problems in the lives of others (with the possible exception of talk show hosts—actually, it may be that hosting a talk show is one way of being a therapist).

The question is, then, "Where did this interest in family-related problems come from?"

WHAT DO YOU TELL YOURSELF?

Answering this question regarding the genesis of your interest in family-related problems requires an honest evaluation of what drives you to be a therapist. It may be that ol' Uncle Fred has a point that needs to be examined seriously. It also may be that you have already addressed personal issues that affect how you are as a therapist. In any event, the reasons we give ourselves for why we want to do therapy are what constitutes our *agenda*.

I WANT TO BE A FAMILY THERAPIST BECAUSE: MY AGENDA

Our agendas consist of our beliefs about what should and should not be—how families should be organized and how they should (and should not) function, how couples should make their marriages, etc. Our agenda is what tells us what we are supposed to work toward as the ultimate goal of therapy. It is the model we look to for our standards regarding health, strength, normalcy, deviance, and problem solution. It is the lens we use to see the practice world and the rest of life, too. It could be called a worldview, or one's philosophy of life. It could even be viewed as the god one serves.

Our agendas can serve us quite well when they themselves are clearly recognized because they can direct us very precisely about what to do. For example, if you grew up in a family in which your father physically abused your mother, you saw firsthand the pain and suffering that resulted. You knew long before your formal clinical training began that violence from men toward women is a bad thing, and your experience gave you a particularly keen appreciation for the problems inherent in wife beating. As a therapist, your training and familiarity with the violence literature has only served to reinforce your a priori convictions about violence; thus, you have no difficulty supporting and advocating strongly on behalf of a female client experiencing violence from her partner. So far, this is not likely a problem—it is an asset.

Let us take another example from a different perspective. Perhaps your parents divorced when you were ten years old, and it was a messy and chaotic situation. You and your siblings were often caught in nasty crossfires between your parents, and even other relatives and family friends. After a stressful court fight, you were put in your mother's custody and eventually lost consistent and meaningful contact with your father (not an atypical happenstance). This history indelibly affected your view of divorce as one of the worst nightmares a family can experience, and your reading of much of the divorce literature supports your personal experience. So when a couple with two school-age children comes in with some ambivalence as to whether to make a real go at turning their marriage around, you have no difficulty pointing out all of the considerations and issues they need to consider should they choose to divorce, and you are successful in increasing their motivation to work on the marriage. Again, your ability to do this is an asset.

Perhaps at this point, you are thinking to yourself that your experience growing up did not faintly resemble either of the above scenarios. Perhaps you grew up in a fairly "unexciting" family, in which your parents had an apparently functional marriage and you and your siblings all have turned out quite respectably. You have benefited greatly by observing numerous effective marital and family interactions and have a wealth of positive models from which to draw ideas and interventions that will be helpful to your clients. This, too, is a tremendous asset, one that will provide a most solid foundation for all of your clinical training.

Agendas, as the term often implies, are usually covert, and this is precisely why the agendas we serve can become problematic. Not only are our clients unaware of our agendas, but we too may be. When we are, we can find ourselves pursuing a goal or a course of action that is counterproductive for all parties. In the first scenario mentioned, let us say the client insists that in spite of the violence she does not wish to leave the relationship. You may say that you understand her point of view and believe that you do, but do you? Can you retract your own agenda far enough to truly hear what she is saying? If you automatically assume that she is too confused, too intimidated, lacking self-esteem, or just is uneducated, and that she would change her mind once her confusion was lifted, etc., then it may very well be that your agenda is reigning supreme, even above the explicit wishes of your client. Similarly, in the second example, if the couple decides after a few marital sessions that they just do not have it in them to work it out, how do you respond? If you say the decision is theirs to make, but then subtly or not-so-subtly apply pressure in the form of guilt or rejection, how well are you serving them? In the third description, if a client family's communication patterns and strategies do not closely approximate those you observed in your own well-functioning family, and you automatically assess them as nonoptimal, you may be guilty of forcing them into a mold that does not fit. There are many different ways of operating in families that may prove to be uniquely well-functioning, and this must be respected and evaluated on a family-by-family basis. We must be careful of the assumptions and judgments we make from our agendas.

Additionally, we recognize the potential volatility of the previous examples, and we wish to capitalize on it. Perhaps you have a very strong reaction to the idea that a woman being abused could truly want to remain in an abusive relationship, or that a couple could just "bail out" of a marriage without a great deal of effort (that you can see), or that families that use a lot of sarcasm may actually interact most effectively that way. The fact is, some women do choose to stay in violent relationships (as do some abused men), some couples appear to give up on their marriage without much effort to save it, and some families engage in patterns of interacting that we would reject outright for our own lives. If you have trouble accepting these as possible realities, then we suggest you may need to examine your agenda. You do not have to agree with or approve of a client's choices, but you do have to respect his or her right to make them. In any event, it is important to know why we have the responses we do and to be able to manage them. We also recognize that much of what we are discussing resides in the realm of values, a topic we will consider in more detail in Chapter 11.

It is when our agendas remain covert to ourselves that we run the greatest risks. Every person has "hot-button" issues, and developing a thorough awareness and understanding of them is absolutely essential if we wish to be the best therapists we can. In many instances, the mere awareness of a hot issue makes it more manageable, and most issues can be addressed and their effects minimized with some deliberate effort. This is what good supervision can accomplish. Sometimes, though, there are issues that we are never quite comfortable dealing with (at least at the time they are salient), and it is in these circumstances that we recommend you spend considerable time in self-evaluation and perhaps in therapy yourself.

It is important to note, however, that not every agenda which runs into problems with some clients needs to be changed. There are numerous legitimate disagreements about what a healthy marriage or family is like, and the breadth of perspectives on these topics needs to be respected and valued. The point we want you to glean is that you need to be thoroughly aware of why you choose the standards of health and functionality that you do, and also that sometimes the assumptions we make concerning standards are not good. Our agendas need to be overt and defensible so that anyone who asks receives a lucid and well-considered response.

SHOULD YOU BE A MARRIAGE AND FAMILY THERAPIST?

Unfortunately, there are individuals who are practicing or training to be therapists who, to be blunt, should not be. It is our sincere hope that you are not one of them, but the fact remains that not everyone is well-suited to be a marriage and family therapist. In our view, too many individuals in training and in practice are not there for the best of reasons. They either have not settled their own personal issues well enough to not become entangled in them in clinical situations, or worse, they have decided that their agendas are to be preeminent over all other concerns, including clients' wishes, supervisory suggestions or requirements, and professional codes of ethics. It is gravely disquieting that some research evidence has suggested that many clinicians routinely pay lip service to their ethics codes and then act according to their own values (Smith et al., 1991).

Integrating Your Motives with Your Agenda

An essential part of a clinician's development that ideally takes place—or at least begins—during graduate training is the integration of one's motives with one's agenda. This involves the development of keen awareness into the personal factors from our backgrounds that form the assumptions we use when doing therapy. The agenda becomes explicit and understood. It must stand the scrutiny of supervision, hopefully with several different supervisors. It may involve personal therapy or perhaps even family therapy. In the end, you must be able to point out the issues in your own family of origin and personal history that have influenced you to become a therapist, and you must understand the assumptions about normalcy and health that followed—either as what to do or what not to do. Furthermore, you must be able to identify the issues with which you are likely to struggle as a therapist when they are presented by clients and to recognize how you may be pulled to respond to them. Finally, you must develop a sense of confidence that you can manage those issues in the therapeutic context, even if managing means intensive ongoing supervision, cotherapy, or even possible referral. There need not be shame in admitting your clinical limitations and allowing for them. This is ethical practice.

As you become more aware of your agenda, we would encourage you at the same time to make use of the natural passion that agendas tend to elicit. Use the passion and conviction to become more expert in the areas that can pull you. If, for instance, a "hot button" agenda issue for you is family violence, become thoroughly familiar with the literature, including that which may be hard to accept or seems downright wrong to you. Opposing points of view, whether clinical, theoretical, or empirical, will sharpen your focus and help you develop a more fully integrated and effective clinical playbook. You will be both professionally and personally broadened. It also remains that you will likely be able to refine your passion and hone it to razor-sharp validity—your experience with personal violence will be complemented by the wisdom gleaned from the rest of the profession. It is a challenge that is ultimately worth both to you and to those with whom you work the significant discomfort that you will experience.

Issues You Need to Consider and Maybe Do Something About

There are several things to consider as you think about your motives, your agenda, and the implications they have on your clinical work. Obviously, the degree to which you are able to make choices and decisions instead of being guided by compulsions and emotionally driven directives will affect what you do in the therapy room. We are not saying that you should ignore or undervalue the emotional responses and "gut feelings" that are the stuff of the therapist's person and from which questions and interventions often flow. Rather, we suggest that the general frameworks undergirding your clinical work should be those that are freely chosen and that make the most sense to you.

There are times, however, when we may be less able to perform out of our well-thought-out convictions. Sometimes we get tired, both personally and professionally, and are unable to garner our resources in therapy to the degree we expect and desire. This is normal from time to time, and when we notice this, we owe it to our clients and ourselves to take a little space to renew our minds and refocus our perspectives. When these instances arise, it is absolutely essential that we pay serious attention to what we say and do with our clients so as to avoid doing them harm. Signs of trouble to watch for are trends that include losing patience easily with clients, losing interest in them, ridiculing them or pathologizing them (especially to colleagues), and hoping for no-shows or cancellations. These are signs of burnout, which we will address more thoroughly in Chapter 16.

Occasional feelings of burnout are to be expected in every clinician's life every now and again, but if you find yourself mired in them regularly, or avoiding them only by subtly booting out clients that are not "easy, likable, and motivated," it may be necessary to reevaluate your suitability for this career field. If you find that you are specializing in a particularly narrow set of client problems, and that other situations do not seem to remain in your caseload, you may be operating from a hidden agenda that ultimately could be your and your clients' undoing. Get help—some supervision concerning this is needed!

Beyond burnout remain the questions of goodness-of-fit from the outset. Most of us at some point early in our clinical training idealistically believe that we are going to make a major difference in the world by becoming a therapist. If your agenda includes the belief that you can save the world's marriages (and maybe even some in your own family), or that you alone have the necessary compassion or some other such gift, you are in need of a wake-up call. By the time your formal training is finished, you should have come to the realization that you will make a significant difference for some, thus affecting your corner of the world, but grandiose expectations that remain at this point smell of dangerous narcissism.

Other areas of concern are those in which therapists regularly cross the line from the normal call of duty over to being inappropriate, unwise, and/or unethical. There are myriad ways that this can happen. Danger signals include but are not limited to inviting clients to telephone you at home day or night at the drop of a tear, waiving their fees (or even paying them yourself—yes, it does happen), protecting them from the "prying" eyes and ears of supervisors and colleagues, and allowing the boundaries around your relationships with them to become blurry. Any therapist who feels that his clients must like him and think he is wonderful has a problem that needs immediate attention. Similarly, the therapist who believes that the client can benefit by working only with her is walking a dangerous line, as is the therapist who acts one way with a team behind the one-way mirror but is markedly different without the team.

Finally, there is controversy about when and/or if therapists should remove themselves from practice because of their own personal situations. Recently there was a dialogue on the internet LISTSERV for marriage and family therapists, MFTnet, in which the question was raised about whether a therapist who is having an affair should continue doing clinical work. It was interesting to see the various strains of thought that were presented, ranging from a firm "no" to logical follow-ups such as, "What about therapists who divorce? Should they also be encouraged to discontinue doing therapy?"

It seems to us that practical considerations and some rational judgment should be able to prevail. We suggest that therapists who are actively engaging in destructive behaviors should not practice. The questions inevitably raised, however, pertain to defining what destructive behaviors are. Few would argue that a therapist who is actively suicidal or homicidal is in a good position to work with others; thus, the therapist should not practice while in this crisis. The therapist's own "stuff" needs to be addressed in his or her own personal therapy, and we would encourage a gradual and deliberate approach to returning to clinical work. But what about the therapist who is having an affair? Should he or she continue to work with couples?

The American Association for Marriage and Family Therapy's (1991) professional code of ethics states that "[m]arriage and family therapists seek appropriate professional assistance for their personal problems or conflicts that may impair work performance or clinical judgment" (3.2). It seems to us that having an affair would be very likely to influence one's clinical judgment and performance, especially with couples. The whole issue of trust and the integrity of system boundaries is called into question for the therapist personally, and inevitably professionally as well. Does this mean that the therapist should discontinue conducting couples therapy? Most probably, but if not, then at the very least some intensive supervision is needed when working with couples to ensure that their interests are not jeopardized.

Regarding many other areas, the answers are even less obvious, and consensus is even harder to attain. Perhaps a good measuring rod against which to evaluate the validity or suspiciousness of a therapist's actions in a given situation is to present it to several colleagues of diverse opinions and approaches and get their input (Odell and Stewart, 1993). In therapy it is especially important that we embrace a multitude of perspectives to facilitate our work so as to avoid allowing our blind spots to negatively affect our clients. Our reactions to things may seem to us to be mild or "normal," but others who can evaluate us from an external position may be able to judge better whether we are suffering from an "agenda" delusion. This is valuable for us—and for our clients.

We hope that at this point you are more aware of your internal motivations for doing clinical work and that you have begun to engage some of the questions that every therapist needs to before they move out into the "real" world of clinical work. Perhaps you may be a little uncertain about what motivates you to work in this area, but we would encourage you to be bold with yourself and examine your motives and agenda closely. If you have several concerns related to your motives and agenda, now is the time to approach a trusted mentor, supervisor, or professional and get some answers. Become a marriage and family therapist out of as much confidence and honest conviction as you can muster, but not because you have come this far and it is too late to change. A poorly made choice now very likely will lead to much heartache for you and ultimately for those with whom you work. We expect, however, that most of you will continue on to productive and rewarding careers in this field. Before you start your career, however, we need to turn to some of the differences that often exist between the world of clinical training and the world of professional practice.

Chapter 2

It Ain't Like the University Clinic

Congratulations! You have just been hired by XYZ Agency as their new therapist/caseworker/case manager/intake coordinator, etc., whatever. You have a job, perhaps after several months of painstaking searching, sending out résumés and application letters, enduring unfruitful and anxiety-inducing interviews, and maybe even working a stint back at your Aunt Arlene's hardware store. Your laborious years of intensive graduate training and experience gathering have finally paid off as you now enter the "real world" of professional clinical practice. You get a salary (not a great one, probably, but one that is better than Aunt Arlene's); and most likely some paid vacation (maybe even two weeks), sick days, holidays, and personal days; benefits such as health insurance and continuing education support; ongoing supervision and training for licensure purposes; and even some retirement options. Plus, you finally get to do the work for which your dreams have aimed you. This is all very exciting! It is a reward worth savoring, and you should be pleased with yourself, having earned the true status of a professional. Enjoy the moment!

Perhaps you have already been employed in a professional position, and the previous paragraph brings back some warm memories (or not-so-warm ones, perhaps). It may be, too, that you will soon be actively seeking professional employment in the mental health field, and although you have been trained in marriage and family therapy, you may quickly find that the distinctions pertaining to particular species of clinician are less important to employers than to training programs. In any event, whether you are already out in the "real world" or will soon be, it is likely that at the start of your service career you are bustling with enthusiasm and zeal—and probably some trepidation as well.

Most marriage and family therapy training programs, regardless of their accreditation status with the American Association for Marriage and Family Therapy, have a clinical component that involves actual work with client families. These sites provide the student with the opportunity to begin to do clinical work under close supervision in an environment that is professionally supportive. This is an essential element in good training, but it does have some noteworthy drawbacks that tend to manifest when the former student, now a graduate, takes a professional position. This is especially true in programs that have their own campus-based clinics.

The truth of the matter is that practice in the real world is often very different from the training clinic world. There are numerous ways in which this is true, and in this chapter, we will focus on a few of the more common ones that we have seen. We will first turn our attention to philosophical and theoretical differences, and then we will discuss some of the pragmatic differences that are often apparent.

TRADITIONAL AND CONTEMPORARY PRACTICE ISSUES VERSUS SYSTEMS TRAINING

As a marriage and family therapist, your training has been founded upon the philosophical and theoretical tenets of systems theory. Regardless of whether you are a postmodernist, a constructivist, a modernist, a feminist, or whatnot, marriage and family therapy emphasizes the *systemic* contexts of the clients that you treat; in fact, it could be argued that your principal client is the relationship(s) between various individuals (Becvar and Becvar, 1996). This, as you are well aware, is a very valuable and useful way to think about human problems and their solutions. There is, unfortunately, one major problem: In the "real" world, systemic thinking does not mesh well with the reigning ideologies that govern mental health service delivery.

A brief and grandly oversimplified trip down history lane in the mental health field shows that the medical model has dominated and continues to dominate the way that people view psychological, emotional, and behavioral problems and their treatment (Doherty and Boss, 1991). Traditionally, mental health concerns in Western societies were viewed as stemming from individual pathologies, analogous to biological sicknesses. Treatment needed to be directed at the individual, uncovering his or her dysfunctional thinking and acting, working through the inevitable deleterious effects of bad parenting, reconstructing the personality, and "reparenting" him or her. Other members of the family were to be excluded from the "talking cure." At best, they were only distracting. At worst, they were toxic to the well-being of the individual patient, and their participation in treatment would only serve as a hindering contaminant. Therefore, including other family members was to be avoided under all but the most unusual circumstances.

More recently, the medical model has continued as the dominant ideology although more systemic approaches have shown up on the radar screen of applicable treatment models. For instance, the most recent edition of the American Psychiatric Association's (1994) *Diagnostic and Statistical Manual of Mental Disorders:* DSM-IV includes relational issues as an area of legitimate inquiry and treatment. That notwithstanding, the standard practice of diagnosing and treating the individual remains largely intact; the diagnostic categories (i.e., the codes used to indicate the precise nature of the treated problem) in the DSM-IV do not include relational issues as a primary concern. Many systemically trained marriage and family therapists find it very difficult at first to reconcile these apparently incompatible approaches to treatment. This is something for which you must be prepared and a topic we shall address more thoroughly in Chapter 4.

A second contemporary factor in the "real" world that often is not apparent in the university clinic is managed care. Although we will discuss managed care in all its glorious detail in Chapter 10, a brief overview and explanation is warranted herein. In short, managed care is a comparatively recent development in the way that insurance benefits are applied to medical treatment, including the delivery of mental health services. A managed care company evaluates the necessity of the services delivered and makes a determination as to their validity. Next, a decision is made regarding whether or not payment will be authorized. This, of course, often ends up as the final determining factor in whether services are obtained.

Managed care has had a profound effect on all forms of medical treatment, but it has the most impact in the area of mental health because of the difficulty of assessing both the precise nature and severity of a given problem and the specificity of how it is to be treated most effectively. It is often the case, for instance, that the need for therapeutic services must first be "proven" before a potential client's managed care company will provide a referral and also agree to provide coverage. Also, managed care companies usually require the individualistic lens provided by the traditional medical model; a systemic conceptualization of problems and their treatment is neither understood nor likely to be accepted as a valid therapeutic approach. Obviously, under such conditions, reimbursement is a near impossibility.

While managed care has had the desired effects of paring costs for services of questionable necessity and providing the impetus for mental health services to begin to examine their own efficacy, it has also made many aspects of standard treatment much more complicated. In addition, the specific criteria that managed care companies utilize in evaluating treatment often vary from company to company and state to state. This makes for an exceedingly complex and confusing environment in which to practice, even for veteran therapists. In our experience, most students in clinical programs have very little contact with managed care providers and are unprepared for the requirements concomitant with working with them.

DOING SYSTEMIC THERAPY WITH LINEAR CLIENTS, COLLEAGUES, AND SETTINGS

Given the previous discussion, the newly minted marriage and family therapist entering the practice world and discovering these realities is understandably going to be a bit uncertain about a great deal. However, there is more that needs to be taken into account. It is not just people somewhat external to the therapy world that are likely to be unfamiliar with and perhaps unappreciative and unimpressed by your systemic knowledge. Your clients, colleagues, supervisors, and even the institutions in which you are likely to work may have the same attitude, and this can be quite discouraging and disconcerting.

As has been mentioned, the dominant ideology remains the medical model, and marriage and family therapy—and to a lesser degree social work—are the only disciplines to reject it. Unfortunately, marriage and family therapists are only a fairly small minority, and we have to accommodate more to the world than it does to us. We must be able to talk their language competently as well as to maintain the integrity of our theoretical and philosophical positions.

It will often be the case, for example, that clients will approach you from the point of view that a particular individual has "the problem," and treatment must be directed at that individual. Given your systemic training, you will be particularly sensitive to the interpersonal, familial, and cultural contexts in which this person lives. You will also be more interested in the transactions and interactional patterns that characterize the individual's relationships than what is going on intrapsychically. Your instinct will be to try to broaden your therapeutic leverage by including other significant people in treatment.

At this point, your systemic orientation will run headlong into the rest of the world's linear mentality. Your clients may look at you suspiciously or be somewhat confused when you suggest including other family members in a session. They may also flatly refuse the idea. You may have seen this on occasion in your graduate training; thus, you may not be terribly surprised by some client responses.

What will probably surprise you is the response of almost everyone else. At the university clinic, your marriage and family therapy supervisor would be encouraging you to get other family members in; your colleagues would be offering systemic formulations and hypotheses about what may be helpful to the client, etc. In the agency, mental health clinic, or hospital, your supervisor and colleagues are just as likely to look at you as if you had several large holes in your head. You are likely to hear questions or comments such as, "What good is bringing this person's family in going to do?", "This person's family *causes* the problem; bringing them in is the worst thing you could do!", "That's not the way we operate here!", and "Including other people in treatment will not be reimbursable by the insurance company." The message may be quite jarring—the way you were trained no longer applies, or worse, it was simply wrong.

Along the same lines, if your clients typically go through a secretary or an intake person to make appointments, you can expect them to come in alone most of the time. Efforts you make to ask the intake person to consider encouraging clients to include other significant members of their social systems are likely to be met with some resistance. This is because the idea is a foreign one, but also because it puts the burden of engendering cooperation on the part of the clients on the intake person, who may not believe it to be a worthwhile treatment method anyway. The only likely exceptions to this will be those situations in which the client asks for a relational treatment specifically. Even then, once clients come in as a couple or family, your colleagues and supervisors may tend to break things down to the level of individual personality: "The whole problem here is this borderline woman," "This guy's so narcissistic, no wonder she's depressed," or "This poor child needs to have space away from these lousy parents, and therapy needs to provide that space." Precious little support may exist for systemic conceptualizations of problems or treatment approaches.

If so, and you are alone in your thinking where you work, it will not take long before you will begin to question what you have been taught, and you may find your thinking and working moving away from your training. This is not all bad, either, because the broader your ability to think about cases, the more effective and versatile you will be. We would encourage you to incorporate other ways of thinking into your repertoire, but we also believe that it is easier to move toward more linear thinking than it is to move toward systemic thinking. And you will *need* the latter to work effectively with couples and families.

Alternatively, you may find that some of your colleagues and supervisors may be quite open to systemic ideas, particularly if the work they see from you is solid. You may be able to educate your co-workers and help them to see the benefits of viewing problems from both the traditional medical model and also from the systemic lens. This is valuable, and it can be tremendously validating for you.

Unfortunately, at this point your enthusiasm may collide with the linear reality of the institutional world. Your professional setting may be governed by rules which state that seeing other members of a client's family is a violation of an individualistic treatment plan. The managed care company that reviews the case may reject the systemic approach outright. So, despite the support your immediate surroundings may offer, another roadblock may be in the way. This problem will require some creative thinking on your part to resolve. For instance, you may be able to see the individual client alone for part of the session and then include other members for the rest of the session, thus satisfying the agency's or managed care company's requirements. It is a sticky situation, though, that requires both integrity and innovation.

Pragmatic Differences

In addition to philosophical and theoretical differences, there are several other more practical concerns that many new clinicians find themselves somewhat unprepared for when starting professional practice. Among these are understanding and navigating the political situations in the professional setting and managing the many new realities and responsibilities that come with having an independent caseload. We will briefly discuss several such pragmatic issues.

Political Structure

All social groups have political structures and struggles, and the mental health agency is no different (nor is the university department). The major difference from the university that the purely professional setting has is in regard to its orientation toward its own members. At the university clinic, there are two major interests. The faculty and staff (ostensibly at least) are strongly interested in both the well-being and development of clinical students and the well-being of clients that the students see. The university is invested in its role as trainer as much as and probably more than its role as a service provider; thus, the priority on serving the needs of the student clinician is paramount. Toward this end, a great effort toward creating an environment conducive to the personal and professional growth of the students will be made. In effect, the university clinic will take care of its student employees as well as their clients. This reality should be largely unaffected by whatever research orientation the university maintains.

The professional setting, however, is much less likely to take such an approach because it assumes that the typical staff member requires much less in terms of support and/or supervision, and also because the needs of the clientele are most important. The new employee, fresh from graduate training, may find some initial support that tends to evaporate rather quickly as the mental health employer assumes the transition period is over. It is unlikely to place a high priority on the growth of the staff therapist because it has neither the time nor the sense of responsibility for it. Add to that the harsh reality that there are always others out there who could fill the position, and the new marriage and family therapist realizes that he or she is "not in Kansas anymore." This can be a jarring reality.

The political structure of the university department includes the element of producing a competent graduate; thus whatever coalitions, cliques, or other alliances may exist are all mitigated to an extent. The professional setting may have no such braking mechanisms in place; consequently the stakes can be much higher. The new therapist on the block may find herself being lobbied by various ideological groups within the organization and not know how to handle it. Our encouragement would be to tread lightly and avoid making overly hasty collegial friendships. Try to get to know as many staff members as possible before you start hanging out with a particular group. A good way to handle some of the pressure that may come from other personnel is to maintain some contact with your training mentors; they may be able to provide you with a balanced perspective or even just some words of encouragement that can be quite timely.

Another way to assess the degree to which you may be joining an organization experiencing political turbulence is to determine the annual staff turnover rate. The higher it is, the likelier it is that your new job may be more stressful than your interview may have led you to believe. Similarly, if no other person has been there for at least a year or more, it may be that this particular setting has an unusually high number of problems. While it may be that a high degree of staff turnover or a spate of new staff are not necessarily bad signs, and in fact may mean that a beneficial restructuring has taken place recently, it also may mean that the organization you are working for is highly unstable and tends to burn people out. We suggest keeping your eyes and ears open to note signs of potential trouble.

Supervision

On a related note, the kind of supervision you receive in your new position may be very different than what you had in training. Hopefully, your university supervision was both nurturing and challenging, with an emphasis on tailoring itself to your particular needs as the supervisee. You may find your professional supervision quite different. Instead of having a regular time for individual supervision like you probably had in training, for instance, much of it at the agency may be conducted "on the fly," or between appointments catch as catch can. Group supervision at the university hopefully was an environment in which all participants were fairly open to both suggestions and positive criticisms. At the professional setting, you may find cases presented more defensively, or with more "turfism" present. Colleagues who do not share your enthusiasm for systemic thinking, for example, may take particular pleasure in pointing out to you why they believe a given case may be giving you trouble.

Another aspect of supervision that you must consider as you enter the professional realm is the potential match or mismatch of degrees and training. Although your training has been systemic, and you probably are intending to qualify (if you have not already) for clinical membership in the American Association for Marriage and Family Therapy (AAMFT) and licensure as a marriage and family therapist, you may find that the supervisor you have in your first professional position is neither systemically oriented nor suitable to do supervision from either AAMFT's point of view or the state licensing board's. You may wish to see if there is another supervisor at the organization with whom you could work (do this carefully so as to avoid as much as possible hurting feelings, violating "turf," or making yourself look only self-interested), or you may petition the state board and AAMFT for an exclusionary ruling. We will examine this problem and some solutions more thoroughly in the next chapter.

If at this point you are finding yourself considering retail or are hyperventilating, please stop. We do not wish to create the impression that all mental health service organizations are clinical houses of horror in which ghoulish supervisors, stingy managed care companies, and petty, fiendish colleagues regularly reside and where political intrigue worthy of Tom Clancy occurs. Rather, we sincerely hope you will find your first professional position to be rewarding and fulfilling, populated by supportive colleagues and supervisors under an institutional structure that is facilitative of staff as well as client growth. There are many settings out there that do a pretty good job of this, but sadly there are also many that do not. By being aware of the potential problems, your adjustment to the real world should be a little easier.

Case Responsibility and Paperwork

Another practical difference related to supervision may be found in the degree of responsibility the new professional marriage and family therapist is expected to take for his or her cases. At the university, with its more consistent and deliberate supervision, cases that were of particular difficulty for the student clinician were watched closely, and guidance was fairly easily found. At the professional job, there may be the expectation that such supervision is unnecessary, even if adequate time for it exists. It is a very good idea to not be shy about getting input on cases from both colleagues and supervisors.

In the same vein, you probably will find that the amount of paperwork you are responsible to do will increase exponentially as compared to at the university training clinic. As you take on more responsibility for your own caseload, the care with which you must document all contacts and every other relevant piece of information must be meticulous. Your files may be reviewed periodically by supervisors or other administrators, and you must be able to justify any entry you made and any you did not. You will be expected to know all of the forms, policies, and procedures and to follow them carefully. We will discuss paperwork and documentation in Chapter 9.

Fees

At the university clinic, you may have had no problem collecting fees from clients. Most training clinics offer sliding scale fee structures in which even the highest rates pale against those in professional settings, and so it may have been no trouble at all collecting five, or twenty-five, or even forty dollars for a session. We have found, however, that many new professionals find themselves becoming rather awkward when they must collect sixty dollars or more for their work. In fact, the idea that they are charging fees in that range seems to bring about a strange reaction in itself.

In our experience, the reason that therapists struggle with this aspect of professional practice is because they have some lingering doubt about the worth of *their* work. They have no great difficulty explaining why the average fee for services around the country is approximately eighty dollars or more ("Fee, Practice, and Managed Care Survey," 1995; "Private Practice Fees, Incomes and Trends," 1996); when it comes to applying similar figures to themselves, however, their certainty seems to melt away. The fact is, folks, you have done the clinical training and educational preparation, and now you are the professional. You may not *feel* like your work is worth whatever fee is being charged, but it is. You will also find that most clients have much less difficulty with the fee than you do. We are not suggesting that you should just "pack 'em, stack 'em, and rack 'em" because you are worth it, but the competent professional is worthy of the wage he or she receives. We strongly suggest that you apply the following standard to your work vis-à-vis fees: Ask yourself if the session you just conducted is one you would willingly pay the fee for if you were the client. Most of the time, you should be able to say "Yes." If not, then maybe you have something in your agenda that needs more attention.

Client Type and Severity

We have often found it the case that university clinics and "real world" mental health agencies often have somewhat different clienteles. This is sometimes a function of location, but there is usually more to it than that alone. Most university clinics that are not located in metropolitan areas tend to be frequented more by clients who are in some way connected to the university, whether as staff, student, or faculty. Even if there is no direct connection, many people who are alumni or in some way consider themselves part of the university's community (e.g., they use the recreation center or library, or they attend sporting events regularly) are more likely to go there for treatment instead of a community agency, private practice, or other service provider. These types of clients usually have higher education and value it as an end itself, are more verbal, have a greater belief in the benefit of therapy, and often are higher functioning than clients who present to nonuniversity clinical settings.

What this means is that your training experience, while extremely valuable, may be incomplete in terms of acquainting you with a full range of clinical concerns. You may find that your new position's client pool is generally more severely impaired and chronic than that to which you are accustomed. You also may find that your clients are a more diverse lot of people ethnically, racially, socioeconomically, and in numerous other significant ways. Despite your "cultural diversity training," which most programs include, you may find yourself surprised at the ways you will need to stretch to work successfully in the real world. Do not look at this as unduly daunting, but be aware that your eyes may be opened rather abruptly.

Public and Nonclinical Staff Relations

Two final areas in which the university training clinic and the professional position may be quite different concern public relations, and the relationships you may have with nonclinical staff persons. Many professional settings require their clinical staff to perform some type of public relations work. This usually is for the purpose of increasing the organization's visibility and generating appropriate referrals from likely sources. The training clinic, on the other hand, usually does not have much of a need for such activities.

As an employee, you have the obligation to recognize that your behavior, on-site and off, has a bearing on your organization. This is particularly true in a field such as mental health. The world unrealistically expects mental health professionals to "have it together," and we need to—to a degree. Therefore, it behooves us to represent ourselves, our professions, and our employers well. For example, regularly becoming intoxicated on the weekends while working for an agency that emphasizes moderation for "regular" people and abstinence for abusers is neither smart nor healthy; it is also dishonest. Granted, an employer typically has no authority over how its employees choose to live their lives outside the agency, but sometimes seeing the entire forest is more important than seeing the individual trees. You never know who sees you doing what where.

When purposively serving as a representative of the employer, it is incumbent upon you to maintain your professional demeanor and represent yourself and your employer accurately. Cold-calling on potential referral sources is never a good idea. It makes you look disorganized and unprofessional, and it also raises questions about the quality of your services. "If they are so good, how can it be that they have the available time to just drop in on us whenever?" Rather, make deliberate appointments with the person(s) you need to see. This way, their time and yours is used efficiently. Describe your offerings, answer questions honestly, and do not be hesitant to delineate the parameters around your expertise and that of your organization's. When you receive a referral, acknowledge it with a telephone call or brief letter, and endeavor to maintain communication with the referral source within the limits of confidentiality. This common courtesy is amazingly uncommon in our experience.

Most professional mental health organizations, unlike university clinics, employ nonclinical staff: secretaries, accountants, bookkeepers, business managers, and the like. They are very important people in the organization's life, and you will find them to be of great consequence in yours as well, either positively or negatively. For example, in our experience, it is almost literally true that secretaries run the world. Treat them with respect and they will reward you; treat them poorly and you will regret it. They know where the forms are and often which to use when, what the policies are, who keeps what schedules, and other essential information. They run the copiers and the fax machine, create and maintain files, set up and log appointments, take messages and make phone calls; they are your connections to most of the outside world. They also may be the ones who direct clients your way versus someone else's, a function that can mean a difference in your pay. So, act accordingly.

It is also important to determine how much information about what needs to be shared with whom. A nonclinical staff person who scores a test for one of your clients, for example, does not need to know much about the case's particulars. You may find, though, that many nonclinical staff persons are more than willing to share their opinions of what a given client needs or some other clinical advice (do not be surprised when they are accurate!). This in no way obligates you to include them as regular consultants on this or any other case. There are more than enough leaks in the organizational grapevine as a matter of course, and the new professional needs to be careful to avoid adding to their number. At the same time, some of the more "notorious" clients of the organization will likely be known to almost everyone in surprising detail.

Finally, you most likely will have occasion from time to time to interact with nonclinical administrators. They can be among the most supportive and helpful of persons, or they can be among the most acrimonious and difficult. Either way, they are usually there, and usually they are comparatively powerful—i.e., they often are the ones who sign checks (and pink slips). Our advice: Accept them and deal with them professionally. They do not need or want to know every detail, in most instances, but they like to have a sense of what is going on. Become familiar with what they feel they need, and provide them with it as much as you can as personably as you can.

There are many other issues you will encounter as you move out of the training environment into and through your professional practice career. Having your eyes open and your expectations realistic will make you much more likely to thrive and much less likely to be thrown out of kilter. Our hope is that as you continue through this book, you will find many questions that you had not thought to ask and answers you never expected, as well as useful information you have known you need. We hope you are now ready to proceed into the real world of professional practice.

SECTION II:
BEGINNINGS

Now that we have examined you and the "why" behind your decision to become a marriage and family therapist, as well as some of the more obvious differences that exist between training and professional settings, it is time to move on to the so-called nuts and bolts. Your career in the service delivery field is about to begin, if it has not already, and the task in this section is to address in some detail several pragmatic elements of the real world that we have mentioned previously and a few we have not. We will commence with you getting started in your first clinical job; proceed to engaging the linear world while retaining a systemic mind-set, including intakes, diagnoses, and other realities; and then move on to aspects of case formulation and intervention strategies that can help you maintain a systemic clinical approach. We will then move on to address the use of nonsystemic tools, treatments, and referrals, as well as the practical realities of documentation and case management. We will finish with an examination of some of the issues related to finances, insurance, and managed care. By the end of this section, you should have a good understanding of many of the realities of the mental health practice world and be able to function effectively in it.

Chapter 3

Securing a Place to Practice

Beginning in the field of marriage and family therapy is not quite as simple as just getting a job. In fact, it can be dauntingly complicated. For example, the rules and regulations pertaining to licensure and credentialing in all clinical mental health disciplines including marriage and family therapy vary from state to state and profession to profession. As of this writing, forty states have some form of licensure law or certification governing the practice of marriage and family therapy specifically; these laws and certifications may or may not have anything to do with clinical membership in AAMFT. In the remaining states, marriage and family therapy practice could be subsumed under such fields as counseling, clinical counseling, social work, or a subspecialty of psychology or psychiatry. In a few states, marriage and family therapy is not a recognized form of practice at all. Even in the states with specific licensing guidelines, marriage and family therapy may be dealt with by a composite board that regulates several mental health disciplines in addition to marriage and family therapy. Trying to determine whom to talk with about what can get confusing in a hurry.

Regardless of the particulars, obtaining your own independent license should be a primary goal at the forefront of your mind as you go about selecting your first real world position. This credential will legitimize you to your colleagues and the public while providing a wider range of career choices to you. It will allow you to be released from supervision as an institutional ongoing reality (remember, it ain't like the university clinic); nonetheless, we certainly would encourage you to make use of regular collegial supervision. A license will also likely make you eligible to receive third-party reimbursements (i.e., insurance), and you may apply to managed care companies, preferred provider organizations, and health maintenance organizations as a provider of services to whom they may refer their members. A license is a key to success, so get one.

Parenthetically, you should be aware that if you decide to practice somewhere other than the state in which you were trained, you may not qualify for a license (and you may have to take additional courses, or worse, such as having to complete another graduate degree program) even if you have a license in your current state. A word of warning: Do not assume that reciprocity—having a license in one state will ensure the receipt of a commensurate license in another state—will be available until you receive a judgment to that effect in *writing* from the correct licensing organization. Also, do not assume that professionals in either state know what they are talking about regarding licensure requirements—they are not the ones who award licenses. If you are contemplating relocation, do your homework and contact the necessary licensing groups ahead of time. The connection between professional credentialing (e.g., AAMFT membership) and state licensure is often murky at best, depending on the state. It would be prudent to pursue both, but as totally separate objectives.

But first things first. The first order of business for you is to obtain a license in your state. Typically, you must meet both academic and supervised experience requirements to obtain any type of license or certification to practice independently. Hopefully, your graduate training will take care of the academic end of things. On the experience side, however, you will almost certainly have to work under a licensed professional (in marriage and family therapy, clinical counseling, social work, psychology, or psychiatry) for a period of time until you meet the supervised experience criteria for an independent license in your state.

This chapter will focus on several areas related to beginning your clinical career. The first area pertains to obtaining the appropriate supervision for licensure and credentialing. The second area is the annual or biannual continuing education requirements you will usually have to meet to retain your license or certification. Third, we will discuss the importance of malpractice insurance and the reasons that you must have it in place before you begin clinical practice. Finally, we will discuss how to make the most of your supervisory relationships when you first begin to practice, and we will provide you with some guidelines in terms of competencies that you may wish to pursue as you develop professionally

SUPERVISION FOR LICENSING AND CREDENTIALING

It is essential to know the laws of both the state you are trained in and the state you plan to practice in regarding the various types of clinical mental health services. This should have been a part of your investigation of various programs before entering graduate school. If not (or, equally likely, if the laws have changed), you should become very familiar with the various standards and criteria. Again, remember that the final arbiter of truth in matters of licensing is the state board, not your major professor in graduate school or your potential employer. Get the answers from the state, as frustrating and time-consuming as that may be.

Although many employers are quite specific in their requirements when they hire to fill a position, others are not. For the latter, just about any clinically trained person may suffice. It usually depends on the type of agency or practice and the funding sources that support it. Knowing the law and knowing what you need to continue progressing toward independent licensure is your responsibility. In interviewing for a job, you should always ask the following questions:

- "Who would be my clinical supervisor?"
- "What are this supervisor's academic credentials and licensure?"
- "Does this person provide the type and scope of supervision required by the board of the license that I am working toward?"

Asking these questions will ensure that you do not accept a position that, while giving you a paycheck, will delay your achievement of independent licensure. Employers are primarily focused on meeting the needs of their own agencies and thus may not view your specific goals for licensure as a marriage and family therapist as a top priority. The attainment of your career goals, both short-term and long-term, require that you focus on obtaining the licensure necessary to achieve them.

Still, you may find yourself in an employment situation in which you are not going to be receiving the supervision that you need for licensure, professional credentialing, or both. It is certainly not unheard of for an individual to take a job because he or she needs the money, and concerns pertaining to licensure take a back seat when it comes to paying bills in the present. If this turns out to be your situation, you have a few options. It may be possible to petition the state board and/or the professional organization for an exclusionary ruling, which basically is a request by you that the state or organization accept "alternative" supervision because of your special circumstances. For instance, AAMFT will make allowances for alternative supervision if there are no AAMFT-approved supervisors within a certain distance or if agency policy prohibits the discussion of case material off-site. It may also be possible for your employment supervisor to become an acceptable supervisor just by applying to the appropriate board or organization with a relatively minimal amount of paperwork and documentation. It probably will not hurt to ask, at the very least. In the end, however, if no acceptable alternatives can be arranged, you may be stuck for a while. If so, keep your eyes and ears open to ensure that you will be aware of any changes that may take place, either in your employer, the law, or the availability of other positions either within or outside the agency. Be patient and persevering—it will be well worth it.

CONTINUING EDUCATION

You will most likely be updating your education for either maintaining a license, qualifying for a license, or fulfilling your own interests for professional development. You absolutely must know the rules that apply to your license. Conferences and workshops usually obtain some type of sanction from licensing/credentialing boards for continuing education credits. This makes their program more attractive to potential participants and allows you to pick topics of interest that also meet your continuing education needs. While continuing education units (CEUs) are usually only given to programs deemed relevant to your license, it is important to both research the conferences you are interested in and to devise your own professional development "game plan." Questions to consider would be the following:

- "What conference or training will help me to be more successful in my present position (and hence be likely to be approved and paid for by the agency)?"
- "What specific skills, theoretical orientations, and client populations do I need to work at developing further to attain an acceptable level of competence as a well-rounded therapist?"
- "What specialty area of practice do I feel I might like to develop as I mature as a therapist?"
- "Will this conference/training complement the post-graduate study I am planning or pursuing?"

Your continuing education is also pursued informally through the professional reading you do in your spare time. (Surprise! Professional reading should not stop with the end of graduate school.) The sheer number of books and professional journals that are available is staggering. As soon as you join some organizations, you will immediately begin receiving brochures and catalogues of all kinds, sizes, and shapes. They all generally have one thing in common—the subtle (or not-so-subtle) message: "You cannot afford to pass on buying our various publications or attending our workshops if you truly want to be a competent therapist who has a genuine interest in your clients' welfare." Your fears, doubts, and insecurities can wreak havoc on both your ego and your checkbook if you are not careful. Obtain the counsel of supervisors, senior clinicians at your agency, and/or your former training faculty to assist you in determining your choices and direction regarding professional reading and conferences.

PROFESSIONAL MALPRACTICE INSURANCE

Unfortunately, we live in a litigious society in which the focus is often on how a person can make money from the mere perception of possible error by another person, especially a health care professional. However, this is the world we currently live in and hence must prepare for in order to protect ourselves. You may be lucky and never face a lawsuit against you, but that is not the kind of risk we would encourage you to take. For this obvious reason, malpractice insurance is not a luxury; it is an absolute necessity.

Generally, a therapist's first job is in some type of agency or health care facility. These types of institutions will have their own comprehensive malpractice insurance that covers all their services and the various staff providing them. So, this means that if you work in this type of facility, you do not have to worry about malpractice insurance, right? Wrong! Absolutely not! Although your work will be covered under such a policy, you are not out of the woods far enough yet. Most any lawsuit will have multiple defendants—your agency, your supervisor, and you. Even though a malpractice insurance policy for an agency will have a standard type of coverage, you must remember that insurance companies do not make money by paying out claims and, in fact, make substantial profits from finding ways to not pay claims.

Therefore, in addition to the coverage of your agency, you should obtain your own malpractice insurance. This could be very helpful in cases in which the agency's insurance has specific clauses or "loopholes" that allow them to give you, the therapist, less-than-adequate coverage. Your own insurance would also be helpful if the agency decided to "turn on you" in an effort to absolve themselves of any responsibility that they, in fact, have but wish to avoid through keeping the focus on you and your portion of the responsibility (we hope that you are not too disillusioned with the "real world" as you read this, but we would prefer you be prepared and wary than unprepared and naive). It is best if all parties—the agency, your supervisor, and you—have their own malpractice insurance that attends to the individual interests of each entity. Rather than waiting until you begin contract or private practice work outside an agency setting to obtain your own coverage, it is best to be proactive (i.e., "better safe than sorry") and obtain coverage when you first begin clinical practice.

Most all professional organizations in the mental health field will have a particular policy and/or carrier that they recommend to their members. Often there are reduced rates for members that are much more affordable than if you obtain a policy independently. Some organizations, like AAMFT, have an additional program (for a fee) in which members can obtain general legal consultation through a service of experts on issues concerning mental health/marriage and family therapy. Consult membership brochures for specific details, or call the national headquarters directly. If you are considering several organizations before making your choice regarding a professional affiliation, you should investigate the malpractice and legal assistance programs that each organization offers.

SETTING UP A GOOD SUPERVISORY RELATIONSHIP

As you begin your professional career journey, you will have to navigate your way through professional challenges and personal confusion and doubt. The relationship with your clinical supervisor is a crucial factor in how well you weather the various storms and progress in your professional development. Although it is impossible for every supervisee/supervisor relationship to be a match made in heaven, as a supervisee, you must communicate well with your supervisor in order to make the relationship as beneficial as possible. Despite what you may think, competent supervisors do not want passive and dependent supervisees who wait, defer, and hang on the supervisor's every word and glance (White and Russell, 1995). Also, competent supervisors do not want supervisees who believe and/or act like they have all the answers and hence feel they do not need any supervision. It is your responsibility to enter the supervisory relationship ready to both actively contribute and be open to constructive criticism. To make supervision a successful experience, your responsibilities as a supervisee include a continuation of the self-examination we hope began in your graduate training, the assessment of various supervisory styles with your positive and negative responses to each of them, and a collaborative assessment with your supervisor of the goals identified as most important to your development at that point in time.

Self-Assessment

Your graduate school education should include both formal academic and clinical training as well as the beginning of a critical examination of your self. This type of examination and assessment is vital to your understanding of how your "personal self" impacts your "professional self." In entering a supervisory relationship, it is necessary that you make a current assessment of your various strengths and weaknesses, both personal and professional (Aponte, 1994). A supervisee who sees none of her strengths and tries to hide her weaknesses is a therapist whose insecurity will be felt and easily misinterpreted by clients as a reflection upon them as a person/client. A therapist who runs from his confusion and doubt will usually leave clients feeling the same way. A supervisee who exaggerates his strengths and denies or evades his weaknesses is a therapist whose grandiosity will also be easily misinterpreted by clients and presents significant danger to both them and himself. A therapist who distorts her view of self and feels her work is beyond question is an accident waiting to happen.

Supervisory Styles

It might be said that there are as many different styles of supervision as there are supervisors. While this may be somewhat of an exaggeration, it is nonetheless true that each of us (supervisors and supervisees) has a personality with which others must contend. There are, however, some identifiable styles or systems of supervision that are common to clinical supervisors in the field of marriage and family therapy. Although you may think that you do not need to understand the theories behind supervision until you become a supervisor yourself, it is in fact very important to understand them as a beginning therapist/supervisee. To ensure maximum benefit from your supervision experiences, you need to know something about how supervision works and how your personality will respond to different styles of supervision. This is not to say that a negative response on your part to a particular style of supervision means that this style is wrong for you. On the contrary, each different style of supervision (like different styles of doing therapy) has something important to offer the supervisee. Your warning to clients that therapy will be difficult and sometimes painful for change to occur is equally applicable to you in the process of your supervision. It is very valuable to examine both your positive and negative reactions to a supervisor or supervisory style because it forces you to be more conscious of yourself and what you bring into the therapy room with your clients. Your openness to the confusion and discomfort you experience in supervision is vital to your becoming a more mature and competent therapist.

Supervisory styles may reflect the theoretical foundation that a particular supervisor feels is (1) the best overall approach for clinical supervision in general, (2) the best approach for supervising clinical practice with a particular client population, (3) the best approach for the supervision and learning of a particular type of counseling or psychotherapy, (4) the best approach to supervision with the personality of a specific supervisee, or (5) any combination of the above. Different supervision models emphasize different perspectives on the supervision process (Liddle, 1991). A developmental approach focuses on the therapist's overall strengths and weaknesses as a clinician and creates a mutually determined plan for the therapist's growth and improvement. A skills or task approach focuses on specific skill acquisition and learning to accomplish specific tasks within the therapeutic process. A psychodynamic approach incorporates the need to examine the various dynamics of the therapist-client relationship. An approach focused on the "person of the therapist" emphasizes the therapist's understanding of one's own self and personal history as it impacts the use of self as the primary instrument in the therapy process. A systems approach focuses on the therapist-client system as a whole, analyzes the therapeutic situation, and determines the elements and interrelationships that govern the functioning of the system. A structural model has a supervisory focus on the therapist's tracking of the organizational structure of the family as the primary source of emotional and behavioral problems. A strategic model is a brief and transactionally focused supervision with specific emphasis on the therapist's tracking of the strategies, functions, and meanings evident in the family.

One final note that you should be aware of with regard to supervision has to do with the notion of isomorphism, also called "parallel process" by some (Liddle, 1988). To be brief, the major thrust of isomorphism rests in the belief that dynamics in place in the client family will be replicated with the therapist, who will then replicate the same patterns with the supervisor. The way a client family system is organized will transfer to the way the client-therapist system is organized, which will in turn organize the supervisor-supervisee system. To break this tendency, the supervisor and supervisee will need to take a meta position to the process and be able to talk about it, which will then affect the therapist-client system, etc., in reverse order. Watch for it, because it will assuredly show up. When it does, do not be surprised at how pervasive it is. In time, you will find yourself seeing it without needing the supervisor's immediate input. And you will also discover creative ways to make use of it as a mechanism for change.

SUPERVISORY GOALS IN BUILDING THERAPEUTIC COMPETENCIES

The area of *supervisory goals* is sometimes overlooked in the fast-paced work of an agency setting. The financial challenges experienced by most mental health care facilities create a high demand on productivity where supervision can be easily relegated to the backseat in favor of activities that generate revenue. In this atmosphere, a regularly scheduled supervision session can often be canceled and rescheduled or can simply digress into "How's it going?", "Any problems I need to know about?", and "Is that all you have for me today?" This pattern is not in your best interests, although you initially may be pleased to not be in the "hot seat" of supervision so much.

To develop as a therapist, you not only need substantial amounts of clinical experience but also a sense of the specific areas and skills in which you need to concentrate your efforts. The supervisory experience is much more than a required formality; rather, it is a necessary continuation of your training as a therapist. The growth necessary to mature as a therapist comes both from substantial clinical experience and the important focus and feedback a supervisor can provide. With the help of your supervisor, you can create goals to be tracked, redesigned, and/or expanded in your supervision sessions to reflect your development as a therapist. Without a good supervisory relationship, you can easily misjudge your work and overlook your blind spots. Supervision can provide attention to key areas that can form an outline for creating, assessing, and tracking your goals, and hence, your progress as a therapist. Specific developmental areas for these supervision goals could include the following:

- *Theoretical Integration:* Supervisees demonstrate understanding of various theoretical orientations and the ability to integrate theories into case formulation and intervention.
- *Specific Skill Competencies:* Supervisees demonstrate specific counseling skills in marriage and family counseling.
- *Case Formulation:* Supervisees demonstrate ability to gather information in opening sessions to construct a working understanding of the individual/marriage/family system. Supervisees also demonstrate the ability to present case formulations in a professional manner during individual and group supervision sessions.
- *Treatment Direction/Intervention-Assessment Cycle:* Supervisees show ability to determine a plan for treatment and ability to expand and alter this plan through the cycle of intervening and reassessing.
- *Autonomy and Self-Direction:* Supervisees exhibit the ability to think independently and pursue directions in treatment without the availability of supervisory feedback.
- *Self-Examination and Use of Self in Therapy:* Supervisees show capability and use of self-examination in assessing and expanding awareness of one's own issues activated in the therapy process. Supervisees also show appropriate use of one's personality and life experiences in a therapeutic manner as well as the ability to successfully utilize individual and group supervision feedback.
- *Personal Values and Motivation:* Supervisees demonstrate values consistent with the therapeutic helping profession and the field of marriage and family therapy; they demonstrate self-starting qualities to achieve skills improvement and expand knowledge of the field.
- *Professional Ethics:* Supervisees demonstrate awareness of professional ethics, especially those concerned directly with client welfare.

The use of a *competency checklist* approach can assist you in recognizing and identifying specific skill competencies. The list presented here includes a wide variety of theoretical orientations, client populations and settings, treatment phases, interventions, impasses, and presenting problems and/or diagnoses that a marriage and family therapist would most likely encounter in clinical practice. The list is thorough, but not exhaustive. As a trainee, you can use this list to track experiences during internship and subsequent clinical experiences when first entering the field. Our intent is not to intimidate you, but to help you recognize the scope of practice in the field and the need to generate competency in the various areas. This allows the supervisee and supervisor to assess accurately progress, strengths, weaknesses, areas of special interest, and overall exposure to clinical experiences in the practice of mental health counseling and marriage and family therapy.

Theoretical Orientations

- Structural/Strategic
- Communications/Brief/Solution-Focused
- Experiential/Humanistic
- Transgenerational/Bowenian
- Psychodynamic/Objects Relations
- Cognitive-Behavioral
- Constructivist/Narrative

Client Practice Settings

- Outpatient
- Inpatient
- Day Treatment/Partial Hospitalization
- Home-Based
- Residential/Institutional

Client Populations

- Family with Young Child
- Family with Preadolescent
- Family with Adolescent
- Family with Young Adult

- Family with Adult Child
- Single-Parent Family
- Stepfamily (his)
- Stepfamily (hers)
- Stepfamily (theirs)
- Stepfamily (his, hers, theirs)
- Dating/Premarital
- Cohabiting Couple
- Newly Married (seven years or less)
- Married (seven to seventeen years)
- Married (eighteen years or more)
- Individual Child (preschool, grade school)
- Individual Adolescent (junior high, high school)
- Individual Adult (college-aged and older)
- Alternative Family Forms

Treatment Phases

- Initial: Alliance and Initial Assessment
- Middle: Interventions and Changes, Reformulating Goals
- Ending: Generalizing Changes and Termination

Specific Interventive Skills

- Building Therapeutic Alliance
- Genograms/Exploration of Family of Origin
- Reframing
- Symptoms and Metaphors
- Motivating Client Initiative
- Tracking
- Creating/Directing Enactments
- Paradoxical Interventions
- Confrontation
- Role-Playing/Sculpting
- Coaching/Modeling
- Use of Humor
- Homework

Specific Impasses (Inevitable Challenges/Headaches)

- Family member reluctant to attend therapy
- Child/adolescent reluctant/refusing to respond to questions
- Child/adolescent reluctant/refusing to talk in front of parents and/or siblings
- Parent/spouse confronting therapist's position/motives
- Family member trying to administrate therapy sessions
- Family stays intellectual and avoids behavioral focus
- Family attempts to terminate on verge of significant step or breakthrough
- Family member attempts to undermine progress/change via regressive acting out
- Family stays stuck—does not follow through with homework or other commitments made in treatment

Specific Presenting Problems/Diagnoses

Note: These are diagnoses most typical to marriage and family therapy-oriented clinical services.

- Child and Adolescent Problems
- Child Behavior-Related Learning Problems
- Attention Deficit Disorder/Attention Deficit Hyperactivity Disorder
- Oppositional-Defiant Disorder
- Conduct Disorder
- Disruptive Behavior Disorder
- Encopresis/Enuresis
- Separation Anxiety Disorder/School Refusal
- Substance Abuse/Dependence

Mood Disorders

- Dysthymic Disorder
- Major Depression

Anxiety Disorders

- Panic Disorder (with/without agoraphobia)
- Phobias

- Obsessive-Compulsive Disorder
- Post-Traumatic Stress Disorder
- Generalized Anxiety Disorder
- Sexual Dysfunctions

Eating Disorders

- Anorexia
- Bulimia

Impulse Control Disorders

- Intermittent Explosive Disorder
- Stealing
- Firesetting
- Gambling

Adjustment Disorders

- Depressed Mood
- Anxiety
- Mixed Mood
- Disturbance of Conduct
- Mixed Disturbance of Emotions and Conduct

Personality Disorder–Related Behavior Problems

- Antisocial
- Borderline
- Histrionic
- Narcissistic
- Avoidant
- Dependent
- Obsessive-Compulsive

Other Diagnoses

- Relational Problems
- Problems Related to Abuse or Neglect
- Bereavement

- Academic Problem
- Occupational Problem
- Identity Problem
- Religious/Spiritual Problem
- Phase-of-Life Problem

As you can see, there is a lot out there to become familiar with, and you should expect it to be a process that occurs over the course of no small amount of time. No therapist ever "arrives," and is so good that he or she is successful with almost every client that happens into the office. Rather, the process of becoming an accomplished clinician is a career-long endeavor. It starts now, though, when you begin your professional work. This is why it is so important to make the most of your time in supervision. We have found that many clinicians who are no longer required to be supervised miss it a great deal, and they will go to impressive lengths to obtain some ongoing input from other clinicians. Use supervision well while it is readily available. Never become so smart that you cannot learn anything more.

Chapter 4

Integrating Systemic Assessment and Traditional Clinic Intake Protocols, or How to Diagnose Clients Who Have Families, Part I

Once you have managed to find a place to practice and have done all of the necessary things associated with getting started in an employment setting (e.g., finding your office space, becoming familiar with policies and procedures, filling out tax forms, and learning where the bathrooms are located), it is time to start seeing clients. You probably are quite excited and maybe a bit nervous about it, and that is as it should be. The excitement and the little bit of anxiety associated with starting in a new position is present for most clinicians all through their careers. However, it is a possibility that during the interview process, your enthusiasm may have contributed to a little cloudiness in your understanding of what will actually be required of you in your new job, especially if this is your first clinical position. Not to worry, reality will descend upon you soon enough.

Hopefully, as part of your clinical training, you have learned the importance of conceptualizing therapeutic work from a systemic perspective. As you will recall from Chapter 2, however, among most mental health professionals, as well as among the managed-care companies and insurance underwriters that usually pay for the majority of treatment, the dominant ideology regarding therapy remains staunchly individualistic. But it is not just the professionals out there that maintain this perspective. The rest of the world—i.e., clients and referral sources—tends not to believe in family treatment either. In short, it seems that the real world's inhabitants, our clients, do not tend to value the systemically oriented clinician's view any more than the traditionally trained therapists do. Therefore, if you are a systems-trained therapist, you quickly will find it necessary in most clinical settings to be able to converse somewhat fluently in the language of the more traditional psychotherapeutic world—while simultaneously maintaining your systemic perspective.

If you have selected this book for the very reason that you have not been trained from a family systems model, then we hope to offer you at least a taste of a way of thinking about client problems that will make an important difference in how you view clients and conduct therapy. We hope that as a result, you will notice a significant positive change in your effectiveness and in the amount of enjoyment you have in conducting therapy.

THE TRADITIONAL INDIVIDUAL APPROACH TO AN INTAKE SESSION

If you have not been convinced yet of the importance of being able to work from an individual point of view, we will run through it one more time. So, why is individual thinking important? Because it is the way that most of the rest of the world still thinks about psychological and behavioral problems and their treatment. This includes the majority of groups out there that pay for therapy services in most settings. Because of the medical orientation of practitioners, theorists, state licensing boards, and utilization review experts in disciplines such as psychiatry, counseling, social work, and psychology, providing services tends to be conceptualized from the perspective of having an individual patient with a specifically diagnosed problem (or problems), and then using a step-by-step treatment plan designed to remedy that person's problem.

Generally speaking, doing an intake the old-fashioned way involves assessing the individual identified patient (IP) in terms of a particular disorder. You will note immediately that the terminology used in this approach takes on a medical flavor from the outset, hence, the use of the term "patient". Included in this determination is an appraisal of the patient's current mental status, symptoms, history, medical condition, and psychosocial context (usually emphasizing stressors and other service provider relationships, among other social descriptors).

A major part of this process involves determining what it is that is causing the patient to require services. Specifically, what *clinical disorder* is requiring professional attention?

This information is gathered in the intake session and organized around arriving at a diagnosis, or perhaps diagnoses, usually along five dimensions, or to use DSM-IV terms, axes. Each axis represents a particular domain of assessment. Axis I refers to primary psychological or clinical disorders (e.g., major depression, adjustment disorder, schizophrenia and psychoses, eating disorders, etc.). These diagnostic criteria are the ones that many insurance programs and managed care companies insist on in order to authorize payment. If you can not arrive at a legitimate Axis I diagnosis, you may find that the client's insurance will not pay; then you have a problem, and so does the client. One positive addition in the DSM-IV, which was not part of the DSM-III-R (American Psychiatric Association, 1987), is the inclusion of relationship problems as acceptable Axis I diagnoses. Whether clinicians use these diagnoses and insurance companies reimburse for them remains to be seen.

Axis II refers to personality disorders and, when necessary, developmental disability. We find that most of the characteristics about people that are distasteful, irritating, or eccentric are usually available for use in assessing criteria for a personality disorder. Axis II deals with how a person more or less functions in his or her typical way of being. Rather than viewing them as symptoms that are present in response to some particular stressor, these characteristics develop steadily over time to a point where they may become pervasive (i.e., they affect significantly all aspects of a person's perspective and functioning). Axis III refers to the patient's medical condition, focusing in on physiological concerns mostly. Axis IV is concerned with psychosocial and environmental issues that may affect the individual's functioning or treatment, and Axis V is for the clinician's evaluation of the patient's general functioning, on a numerical 1-100, low-to-high scale.

In addition to the foregoing, you will need to become competent at conducting a mental status exam in that first interview. Mental status questions are for the purpose of determining how well the patient is connected to reality and how appropriate he or she is for therapy. Does the patient know his or her own name and history, today's date, why he or she in this office, etc.? Numerical ability (counting by threes, for example), general knowledge (who was the first president of the United States?), memory, and attitude toward therapy and the interviewer are also usually evaluated. The clinician's job through this is to be able to ascertain whether this patient has the mental capabilities to engage in traditional talk therapy; if the patient is convinced that he or she is a Twinkie, or that all therapists work for the CIA, regular psychotherapy alone is probably not going to be the treatment of choice.

Your last major objective in the traditional individual intake session is to develop a tentative treatment plan. This involves mapping out the treatment steps you believe are necessary to engender change adequate to remedy, or at least significantly alleviate the severity of, the diagnosed problem. Included in the typical treatment plan are statements about ruling out suspected disorders or conditions; referrals for appropriate tests, medical exams, etc.; the anticipated length of treatment; the expected outcome (i.e., prognosis) of the case; and how and when the case will be evaluated.

THE SYSTEMIC APPROACH TO AN INTAKE SESSION

Why is systemic thinking important? Basically, it offers the most complete picture of the client. Systems thinking sees the individual first and foremost within their immediate relational context (Becvar and Becvar, 1996). From there, patterns of communication and relating with others (whether others are individuals, groups, or even institutions) are evaluated and noted. Individuals do not exist in a vacuum, and a systemic perspective directs our attention to the contexts in which the person lives and the patterns of relating that create meaning in their lives. Systems thinking suggests that, rather than a static disorder that is to be treated like a medical disease, most problems can be treated through attention to relational transactions and their constructed meanings.

A systemic approach also allows us to avoid attaching labels (very rarely positive ones) to individuals. You will find in short order that many clients will come into an intake session and give you a very clean DSM-style description of their problems. These are therapy veterans who sometimes know the lingo better than most beginning therapists! Although that may be helpful in terms of making paperwork, diagnosing, and history taking easier, it shows that many clients take the labels applied to them into their personal identities. Labeling can reduce clients' abilities to solve their own problems in their own ways because they think they *are* something, and once a label is taken in as a part of one's identity, it can be hard to uproot. For example, no longer do I suffer from depression, but I *am* depressed. These may seem to be subtle semantic differences, but they can mean a huge difference in both how the person participates in his or her own treatment and how the professional proceeds in conducting it.

Notice as well with a systemic lens that the terminology has shifted from "patient" to "client." A "patient" is someone to whom something is done (i.e., passive) whereas a "client" is someone with whom something is done (i.e., collaborative). Some in the family therapy field would go on to say that the best term is consumer or customer as they are people for whom a service is provided (Weakland and Fisch, 1992). In any case, the position of a client or consumer is very different from that of a patient, both in terms of how the professional views them and how they view themselves. The systems approach places the recipient of therapy services in a position of strength and responsibility, and it concurrently reduces the importance of the professional. Instead of being experts on patients and their problems, therapists using a systems lens more closely resemble collaborative guides that help clients develop their own unique solutions (Guttman, 1991).

Related to this is the strong probability that if you do not try to include a systemic point of view, you will likely find that you keep seeing some of the same clients with the same problems over and over again in a course of several treatment sequences. Just as likely, you will get therapy veterans who have seen many therapists over many years and are still dealing with the same concerns. Without a systemic approach, you will see some clients improving or interacting in symptom-free or symptom-reduced ways when they are with you, only to have their previous difficulties recur once they are returned to their a priori contexts, including and most powerfully their families (Whitaker and Ryan, 1989). When this happens, it is not very surprising that therapists become frustrated and tend to burn out as do clients who decide they cannot be helped. Everyone loses in this situation.

There are other problematic outcomes, as well. Therapists who regularly see apparently infinitely repeating clients sometimes view families, spouses, etc., as toxic influences that need to be cut out of the client's life in order for them to get better. The negative consequences of such an adversarial attitude for society notwithstanding (and they should not be underestimated), it also remains that clients are much more likely to fire their therapists than their families. Again, nobody wins.

Another equally pernicious result of this is that it contributes to a negative cycle. The client is viewed as chronic and increasingly pathological, as evidenced by the intensified use of Axis II terms— "she is such a borderline," "he is a narcissist," etc. This serves to dehumanize clients and crystallize them into their problems while at the same time distancing us from the hope of change, our responsibility to pursue it, and even our own humanity (Doherty, 1994). This, of course, is likely to reduce the effectiveness of therapy (people often live up or down to the expectations of others whom they view as significant in their lives). As therapy becomes less useful as a place where they are viewed as increasingly pathological, clients may become even worse and more stuck, and the whole process goes on. Nobody wins, and everybody loses.

INTEGRATING SYSTEMIC AND INDIVIDUAL APPROACHES

Aside from the difficulties among the various mental health professions when it comes to deciding whether to work primarily from an individual or family systems model, another challenge just as daunting is posed by clients. Simply put, the real world often does not believe in families when it comes to clinical work. Instead, people tend to think that problems exist and reside within the psyches of individuals. You will see ample evidence of this mindset easily within your first month of clinical work.

Examples to watch for include clients who say: "Fix my child who is ADD, ADHD, suffering from low self-esteem, wetting the bed, beating up kids, being sexually abused, failing at school, unmanageable, etc." Similarly, you will hear, "Fix my adolescent who is rebellious, smoking and drinking, using drugs, staying out, having sex, running away, failing at school, etc." Beyond the child/adolescent target, though, you will get adults saying, "Fix my spouse/partner/girlfriend/boyfriend who is depressed, angry, absent, unfaithful, complaining, confused, controlling, drinking, etc." Or you will hear, "Fix me—I'm depressed, codependent, anxious, lonely, addicted, a survivor of abuse, wanting to understand myself, etc." In each case, the idea is that there is *one* person with a problem that needs to be taken care of by the friendly, neighborhood professional therapist. Oftentimes, any intimations by the therapist (intentional, serendipitous, or not-really-even-there-but-heard-anyway) that someone other than the IP might need to participate in therapy are met with some version of the classic "it is not my problem" reply.

So, what do you do? Integrate the individual intake protocol into an overarching systemic lens. The traditional, individual approach to client intakes actually can be adapted fairly easily to include systemic questions. Doing an intake from a systemic vantage point does not preclude making appropriate use of the language of individual treatment. Being able to do this is especially important when clients present the problem in relational terms, as in "we need marriage counseling," or "we need family counseling." Unfortunately, the majority of the clients you see most likely will not come to you for explicitly relational problems, even if that may be the most accurate description of their situation (Doherty and Simmons, 1996).

Let us say an individual wants therapy for herself. Obviously, this person is considering herself as the IP. She most likely expects you to simply set up an appointment for her alone, and you will be off and running. But, you may not want to go that way quite so automatically. You may choose a different, more systemic way to work, assuming you have some latitude from your employer to work in the way that seems best to you. Also, it is probably easier to conduct an intake session from an individual perspective while still including other family members than it is to conduct a systemic intake session while having to develop an individually oriented approach to treatment that meets the requirements of the real world.

So, who do you include in the intake when you have an individual requesting services? Ideally, you want to include at least one other person in the intake with the IP. There are many ways to do this. You can simply request that members of the client's significant social system accompany her to the initial interview. You can make that into a standard operating procedure for yourself, and if you present that to the client as normative and expected ("I would like for you to bring in your spouse, and/or your sister, etc."), she may not have a problem with it. Treat it as a matter of course. If she asks you for a reason, you can give a quick and simple answer, such as, "It's important to get as much information about the situation as possible, and another person who knows you will be able to provide a perspective about things that will be valuable." If she balks or says that no one else can or will come, then you have just received your first significant systemic information. We will discuss ways to get other members of the system in more fully in Chapter 7. You can even ask people who really cannot bring another family member in (e.g., all their relatives live hundreds of miles away, or they are no longer living) to bring in a friend, or perhaps the person who referred them to you. In the end, if there is no other person that can be brought in, there are still ways to work with an individual from a systemic perspective. We will delve more into that shortly.

When the IP is a child, it is often much easier to get the parent or parents in for the intake although you may still have to ask. For the first session, anyway, parents usually have little problem participating in what they consider their child's therapy. Sometimes parents have the expectation that their child will not talk in front of them, or perhaps needs an "advocate" (that would be you, by the way), and they do not wish to spoil that for the child. The problem with this is that the child in all likelihood is going to go on living with the rest of the family and the therapist is not coming home with them; thus subtly derailing the expectation that therapy is done exclusively with the child is a good idea early on in treatment. Most of the time, you will probably want parental involvement to some degree whenever you are working with children.

In any event, when everyone is on the same page, or at least they think they are, in terms of expecting an individualized approach to treatment, including other family members may not be so difficult. This is because most people are still comfortable participating in treatment as long as the focus of "therapeutic attention" is "the person with the problem." Besides, the IP is usually somebody's loved one, and most people will at least want to make a token effort at being a help to their loved one.

What happens when a relationship is the patient? This is where the situation becomes a little bit tricky. Traditional intake protocols, as discussed earlier, include in some form the same key features—mental status, psychosocial history, tentative diagnosis, and some sort of preliminary treatment plan typically targeted at an individual—all of which you can address while still maintaining a systemic frame of reference regarding a relational problem. Even with the newly included relational diagnoses in the DSM-IV, it is highly likely that your approach will need to focus more on one person than on a dyad, triad, or larger group of people for either or both insurance purposes or agency policy.

So, one of the first orders of business will be to decide whom to call the IP. You can approach this a couple of ways. You can be direct and tell the clients that one of them needs to accept the IP position for policy or payment reasons (when it comes to money, a lot of people become quite cooperative), and you can leave it up to them to decide. This is a very collaborative way of addressing this issue, and many in the MFT field would probably say this is the most ethical (Tomm, 1992), but doing it this way may be unnecessary or even undesirable. You can often determine the IP more subtly by asking clients which of them is most distressed about the situation, by observing which of them seems to be most distressed, or perhaps by noticing who is more invested in treatment. You then can assign that individual the IP position when you begin your documentation. Many clients presenting relationship problems will not care much about any of this; therefore, your decision-making process can remain between you and your supervisor.

Situations will occur, however, in which the clients' input in choosing the IP has significant relational and treatment implications. A good example of this would be a couple's situation wherein a wife is upset with a husband who sees no need for changes in himself, but rather that "she has the problem." Even if it is apparent that, from an individual perspective, the wife easily qualifies for a diagnosis of a major depressive episode, for instance, explicitly giving her the IP position may actually serve to validate the husband's point of view and further entrench a stuck system. In this situation, downplaying the significance of the diagnosis is important, and highlighting the interdependence of the two would be a good idea. Or a valid diagnosis also could be applied to the husband. In this case, an Axis II label (e.g., narcissistic) probably would be effective in maintaining some stability in the system—uncomfortable though it may be. Such a situation is sort of an "I have a label, and so do you" scenario, a marital version of the international détente of Mutual Assured Destruction. The clients then may be dissuaded from using the labels against each other. Then again, such diagnostic labels may turn out to be just another type of ammunition in an ongoing war. This is certainly important systemic information that you will want to use in treatment.

Sometimes, only one family member is covered by a third-party payer, and when this is the case, that person is the IP if insurance is to be billed. It is unethical to lie about who the IP is so that insurance can be billed (AAMFT [1991] Code of Ethics, Principle 7.4). It is not unethical, however, to focus treatment on one of the individuals in the case file—even if the relationship is the primary issue being addressed. In most clinical settings, however, your intake and subsequent case file ultimately must be developed in such a way that you can show that you have an individual IP; a diagnosis; an assessment of the individual's mental and emotional functioning; the client's sources of support, strengths and weaknesses, psychosocial history; and a treatment plan to remediate the client's problem. You can develop all of these from the intake while still working from a primarily systemic framework, as well as when working on a relationship problem.

After you have chosen an IP, forming an initial tentative diagnosis and the assessing mental status is next. Asking how the problem has affected everyone will get you some pertinent information pertaining to individuals' memory, affect, insight into the problem, and severity of the problem, among other things. Observing how each person presents also will provide valuable information pertaining to these issues. You will find that standard systemic interviewing will usually provide the answers to many of the specific questions on a typical mental status exam. Most likely, you will have more than adequate information to address the level of individuals' mental and emotional functioning, and the few blanks remaining may not need to be answered (unless required by your employer or a third-party payer).

Asking other family members their perceptions of the problem situation may produce some strikingly different answers, while also giving you an initial view of the individual's psychosocial history and some possible treatment approaches. It may be that the IP's suicidal ideation in the past, for example, produced a marked increase in the family's cohesiveness; while this information may or may not appear on the psychosocial history, it certainly offers suggestions for how to defuse the IP's danger to him or herself.

The standard psychosocial history questions can be asked to the family as a group. Again, how they are answered will give you a great deal of important systemic information. Most traditional intake protocols include a concern about whether symptomatic behaviors have appeared in other members of the family, and this can be addressed by asking the family in a general manner their beliefs about how the problem started, when it got worse (or better), why it happened and continues to happen, etc.

Identifying sources of support, strengths, and weaknesses is also an important traditional intake issue. Asking the IP directly who their support persons are can begin to address that question, and a good way to validate that question is to ask more circular questions (Selvini Palazzoli et al., 1978) to the other family members. For example, you can ask a given individual who in the family he or she thinks is most disturbed by the problem, who would be most upset if it got worse, how each other person in the family would respond if the problem got worse or better, etc. It may be that the persons the IP identifies as most significant are not the same persons the rest of the family identifies, in which case you know more about how the family and the IP operate.

After you have gathered enough information to choose an IP and have developed a tentative diagnosis and an assessment of the person's functioning and history, you will need to begin developing a treatment plan. This may be the most difficult aspect for the clinician trained in a systemic way because of the need to think in a linear fashion about an individual problem. Even if your approach to treatment is going to be systemic, you still need to be able to document how your interventions will specifically address the diagnosed problem. You may want to bone up on some of the literature detailing the treatment of traditionally individual problems using systemic methods, such as the treatment of individual depression using behavioral marital therapy (Prince and Jacobson, 1995). (The October 1995 issue of the *Journal of Marital and Family Therapy* edited by Sprenkle, was devoted to treatment efficacy and is a gold mine of useful references.) In addition, you may wish to highlight the elements of your systemic thinking that pertain to the IP and the diagnosed problem, e.g., punctuating the circular patterns in such a way as to emphasize the individual's place in the system.

If you have not had much systemic training or experience, you may have a hard time seeing how to make maximum use of any additional participants. You should consider many factors. Asking open-ended questions about the nature of the problem is one strategy that will give you a great deal of valuable information, regardless if you have one person in the room or six. When there is more than one, it is often a good idea to ask the IP the question first, and see what response you get. If the answer includes some popular self-help jargon ("I'm codependent") or other more clinical terms ("I'm depressed"), it can tell you how the client, and possibly their family, thinks about the problem, and how they may think about solutions. It also can help you get a sense of how they think about therapy, i.e., whether they view the problem as being within an individual or perhaps has something to do with more contextual issues.

The client you see in your office individually very likely does not behave in the same way as when he is with his family; thus, including the client's family actually may help you to formulate a more accurate diagnosis. In addition to listening to the content of what is said, you can observe how information is revealed, again regardless of how many people you have. Complexity is increased with more participants so you must develop the ability to pay attention to multiple levels of information simultaneously. Making a brief note, for example, of whether people speak for each other, or if there is hesitation to say things that might make other people in the family look bad, or who is on whose side can provide extremely useful information.

Regardless of your training, spending a few moments at the end of the intake to ask some of the "drier" questions (regarding memory, mathematical functioning, orientation) to the IP alone, assuming one can be identified comparatively readily, can be beneficial. If your client is not presenting a relationship as the problem, seeing the IP alone for a few minutes may also serve to reduce the family's anxiety about being included in therapy in an ongoing manner. It is important to not be too provocative or discomforting too soon.

WRITING UP THE INTAKE

After you have shuttled your clients out the door of your office, you may want to take a few minutes to reflect on the intake session before you actually begin to document it. The actual write-up that you do will be heavily dependent on the setting in which you are working. If your agency is one that works primarily from a systemic perspective and that poses no problems in terms of policy or payment, then you can write up your intake in a systemic way, emphasizing the communication patterns, genograms (i.e., family trees that include quality of relationships, coalitions, significant individual and family traits, and the like), interventions you used, your hypotheses about the system's functioning and the symptom within it, and your plans for your next session with them.

On the other hand, if your employment situation requires a more traditional individual approach, you will have to abide with that policy and write up the intake emphasizing one individual and his or her symptoms, tentative diagnosis, mental status, psychosocial history, and the treatment plan you recommend. You can add systemically oriented notes in a separate part of the write-up, or you can include them more subtly in the notes themselves. Either way, it will be important to be conversant in both languages, systemic and individualistic, both in therapy and in your notes. In the next chapter, we demonstrate how this might look in actuality.

Chapter 5

Integrating Systemic Assessment and Traditional Clinic Intake Protocols, or How to Diagnose Clients Who Have Families, Part II: Case Examples

In this chapter, we will flesh out more fully the pragmatic realities associated with learning to be bilingual in the mental health field, that is, speaking both in systemic terms and individualistic terms. We will present two "typical" cases that you as a therapist may expect to work with in many clinical settings. In each case, we will demonstrate how you can operate from both models. The first case appears to be suited quite naturally for the traditional individual treatment model, whereas the second presents as a relational problem. With the first case, which seems a straightforward individual problem, we will show how a traditional clinic intake assessment can be translated into a systemic assessment for an expanded perspective on the case. With the second case, which is a relationship issue, we will show how a systemic assessment can be translated into a traditional intake protocol for consistency with an individually oriented clinic philosophy.

CASE #1: AN "INDIVIDUAL" PROBLEM

In this case, a ten-year-old boy is presented as the identified patient for the intake assessment. The information that you have on paper in front of you is scant, detailing only that the boy is getting poor grades and is in trouble at school, and that he also is wetting his bed. The referral was made by the boy's mother. In addition to the boy, it would not be unusual at all for the parents to expect to be involved in the intake, and you can take advantage of this expectation to ask them to include his siblings as well. If there is any question about their involvement at this point in treatment, you can make it clear you want them to be present.

Your initial interview with them takes the traditional fifty to sixty minutes, during which time you ask questions pertaining to the problem's onset and specifics, family responses and stressors, and the boy's medical and developmental history. You ask questions of not only the boy, but the parents and sister (perhaps to a noticeably lesser degree) as well. At the end of the interview, you have a fairly voluminous amount of data, from which you now must draw up your case file. Depending on your clinic's policies and requirements (and/or that of the third-party payer underwriting services), your case notes will take on a particular format. Below, we show how your intake write-up might look from the traditional individual model, and then we show what it might look like from a systemic lens.

Traditional Clinic Intake Assessment

Identifying Data: Jimmy Smith is a ten-year-old Caucasian male who resides with his biological parents, Rob, age thirty-six, a sales manager for a manufacturing company, and Laura, age thirty-five, a schoolteacher, and his younger sister, Cindy, age six.

Presenting Problem: Jimmy's parents report that he has demonstrated a sudden decline over the last three months in his school performance. They also report outbursts of rebellious and argumentative behavior at home and at school with his teachers and peers. The teacher reports that Jimmy sometimes refuses to do his assignments or only partially completes them because he is in a hurry to move on to more fun-filled activities. They also report that he has begun wetting the bed, which he has not done since he was five years old. The parents report that they have attempted to deal with his behavior by restricting television, Nintendo, and other play activities to get Jimmy to work harder at school and be more cooperative at home and school. They have also cut back fluid intake and encourage trips to the bathroom each evening in an effort to control the bed-wetting, so far without success. Jimmy was generally quiet and minimally responsive to questions during the intake interview and chose instead to draw pictures and then throw them away.

Previous Mental Health Treatment: None

Family Psychiatric/Psychological History: Jimmy's parents have been married for twelve years and report no significant traumas or tragedies in the immediate or extended family. Both parents report no history of psychiatric or psychological disorders in their respective families of origin. Both parents deny any alcohol or substance abuse problems with themselves or in their families. Both parents indicate that they did not have any significant emotional problems while growing up nor did they exhibit any of the symptoms demonstrated by Jimmy.

Medical Problems: Parents report no history or current difficulties with medical problems for Jimmy. They did indicate that they have not taken Jimmy to his pediatrician regarding the bed-wetting, but they had planned to very soon.

Mental Status Examination: Jimmy was oriented to person, place, and time. He was nicely dressed and well groomed, had appropriate weight and height for his age, and demonstrated no overt signs of psychomotor retardation or agitation. His affect was somewhat blunted and his mood was quiet. Jimmy made little eye contact with the examiner. His speech was hesitant and somewhat soft at times, indicating discomfort and/or embarrassment. There were no indications of hallucinations, delusions, or disturbances in thought processes. He did not verbalize any suicidal or homicidal ideation, nor any death wishes. Parents report no such verbalizations at home. Jimmy appears to be of average to above-average intelligence with no indications of deficits in skills regarding insight or judgment.

Diagnosis:

Axis I   309.4 Adjustment Disorder with Mixed Disturbance of Emotions and Conduct
Rule out 313.81 Oppositional Defiant Disorder
Rule out 307.6 Enuresis

Axis II   V71.09 No Diagnosis
Axis III   None (medical exam with pediatrician scheduled shortly)
Axis IV   Moderate: Problems with Primary Support Group (i.e.,
           rebellious toward parental directives)
           Educational Problems (i.e., not completing schoolwork
           and uncooperative attitude with teachers and peers)
Axis V   Current GAF (Global Assessment of Functioning) 75,
           Past Year 90

Treatment Plan: Individual and family therapy intervention

Treatment Goals:

1. Decrease rebellious behavior and increase compliance with directives of parents and other authority figures
2. Increase appropriate and productive expression of emotions
3. Eliminate bed-wetting problem via behavioral intervention and/or medication from pediatrician

Summary

The foregoing is a fairly typical write-up of a case from the traditional individual psychotherapy model. Some additional features that are sometimes included but were not in the present case may concern the amount of time intervention is expected to require, the precise manner in which problems will be met with specific interventions, and how the case's progress will be evaluated. Other components can include the referral of the client to other professionals for specific purposes (in the above case, a referral to a pediatrician to check for bladder infections or the like has been suggested, but additional referrals may be recommended), a greater degree of depth with regard to psychosocial history, or a collateral family assessment. The particulars will vary with clinic policy, and we would encourage you to be attentive to the requirements that prevail upon you. Overall, however, the basic elements have been addressed adequately.

One other obvious thing to note about the above write-up is that despite the inclusion of other family members, the focus is on

Jimmy. This attention to one individual is the cornerstone of the traditional model, and if the patient were a single adult coming in alone, such attention would remain the same. The advantage the previous case presents immediately is that other system members can be part of the case from the outset; unfortunately, this will not always be a possibility.

Now we will look at the same case from a systemic perspective. Notice first how the format of the actual write-up is different—it has a more fluid narrative form. It is no less precise, however, and the "objectiveness" of the voice remains. Also notice how the complexion of the case changes as we attend to and describe what is happening with both children rather than just Jimmy, and what has been "brewing" with the parents that may have something to do with their current situation. All told, the focus of the write-up is quite different, even though we use much, but not necessarily all, of the same information.

Systemic Assessment

The Smiths are Rob, age thirty-six, a sales manager for a moderate-sized corporation, and Laura, age thirty-five, a schoolteacher. They have been married for twelve years and have two children, Jimmy, age ten, and Cindy, age six. The family is seeking therapy for behavioral problems with Jimmy. They report that his academic performance has shown a sudden decline and that he has been exhibiting anger at home and school by defying the directions of adults. The parents report that he will sometimes refuse to do his school assignments or only partially complete them because he rushes through them. He seems not only uncooperative with his teachers, but also is in frequent conflict with his peers. He has also begun wetting the bed, which he has not done since he was age five. The parents report denying him television, Nintendo, and other play activities to try to elicit better behavior. They have also attempted limiting his fluid intake in the evenings and taking him to the bathroom several times before going to bed. They report little success thus far.

When the parents were asked about his interactions with other family members, Laura reported that Jimmy has become very argumentative, particularly with her. She indicates that Rob is frequently out of town on business; thus, the parenting responsibilities most often fall to her. When asked to further explain the stress of handling these responsibilities and how it affects the rest of the family, Laura reported concerns about their daughter, Cindy. These concerns focused on Cindy's reluctance to go to school each morning and her tendency to report headaches and stomach aches in an effort to stay at home. This has been troubling to both parents, but more so to Laura as she is a first grade teacher. Laura reports that Cindy did well in kindergarten but began having these difficulties when she started first grade. Laura reports that she has tried all types of reassurances, including phone conversations with her while she is at school and including a small stuffed animal in her book bag. Neither effort has been effective, and Cindy often becomes upset and is unable to function in the classroom. The situation typically results in her either being picked up by Laura and taken to the maternal grandmother's home or her being allowed to spend the day quietly working in the school clinic with the school nurse.

At this point a simple genogram was constructed to elucidate family history and relationships. Rob is the oldest of three and has two younger sisters. He describes his parents' marriage as quite traditional. His father is a factory worker and his mother a clerical worker, and both are employed by rather small companies. Rob states he is the first person in his family to go to college, and that this is a source of pride, particularly for his mother. Rob reports his relationship with his parents seems adequate to him. He reports that he enjoys spending time with his father but does not feel particularly close to him. Rob reports that he feels closer to his mother, but that she does not often express her prideful feelings openly for fear of hurting Rob's father's feelings. She is said to believe that Rob's father would feel that she was criticizing him and comparing him unfavorably to Rob.

Laura is the youngest of three daughters, with her father being a physician (surgeon) and her mother a rather traditional homemaker who is involved additionally in several social clubs and community volunteer activities. Laura attended an exclusive private college where she excelled and considered a career in medicine. She eventually chose elementary education, and she completed both a bachelor's and master's degree prior to beginning her teaching career. Laura reports she has always been very close to her father, and that this has created tension between her and her mother. Laura also reports that her father had always hoped Laura would be the child who would follow in his footsteps as a physician and that he had great difficulty in accepting her decision to pursue a career in education.

Rob and Laura state that they met during college as their schools were in close geographical proximity. Laura states that she married Rob because he was very comfortable, down to earth, and easy to talk to. He was very much like a "regular person," i.e., significantly different from the types of men she met at her school. Rob reports that he found himself attracted to Laura because she was very pretty, and comfortable to be with—despite the fact that she came from a wealthy family. Rob was pleasantly surprised that Laura (and her family) liked him and were interested in having him around. He states that he often felt that he had been adopted as their "only son," as both of Laura's older sisters had yet to marry.

The couple was then asked how well they believed they were doing as a "team," both in parenting the children during these current difficulties and as being spouses to each other at this point in the marriage. After initial hesitation, the couple indicated some conflict about small issues regarding the children (types of friends, social activities, behavioral expectations) prior to the onset of both Jimmy and Cindy having these current problems. This discussion led to comments by both Rob and Laura about how they have begun to disagree about many things they were trying to decide on jointly. One key example they were asked to provide had to do with conflict about purchasing a different house. From here, their conversation became increasingly animated, and they began to engage in an escalating sequence of complaints about each other, revealing hurt feelings, resentment, and anger, and frequently talking "past each other." During this time, Jimmy moved toward a corner of the room and became more absorbed in his drawing while talking to himself rather loudly, and Cindy became fearful and ended up interrupting the discussion by telling Laura she did not feel good and wanted to use the restroom.

Major themes brought out in the conversation consisted of the following: (1) Rob's belief that Laura does not parent the children firmly enough and Laura's belief that Rob is unsupportive and not involved adequately in parenting; (2) Rob also expressed, apparently for the first time, considerable resentment regarding Laura recently informing him that she and her parents were having frequent conversations about concerns relative to Rob and Laura's family, including concerns about the children's behavior; Laura reported much surprise and confusion as to why this would bother Rob because "they are only concerned because they want what is best for us"; (3) Laura expressed her fears that Rob would insist they buy a new house that was close to his parents and friends, and she would be further isolated from her sources of support (even though they all live in the same town). It appears that closeness/distance with each of their families of origin is a source of potential tension that has recently surfaced.

The couple was asked specifically about how they viewed the interactions going on between them and how these might be affecting their children. They reluctantly admitted to a lot of "sniping"— being irritated with each other and not talking as much, nor were they doing things much as a couple. Two recent incidents seemed to highlight their current difficulties: Rob had forgotten for the first time a ritual of giving Laura a bouquet of flowers on the anniversary of their engagement, and Laura had failed to inform Rob of a weekend trip she had planned for herself and the children with her parents while he was away on a business trip. Both reported feeling a little taken for granted while firmly stating that their first concern and desired focus of the treatment should be their children's current "adjustment problems."

Systemic Treatment Issues Assessed for Consideration at This Time:

1. Simultaneous presentation by both children of behavioral and physical symptoms that generate increased need for parental interaction
2. Symbolic function of children's symptoms in questioning the strength of the teaming and leadership of the parents and the potential consequence of some type of loss/abandonment due to marital instability
3. Each spouse as "the chosen special child" by the opposite sex parent in their family of origin and its impact on separation/individuation issues and unrecognized agendas in spousal choices

4. Spousal, couple, and family life expectations related to differences in family-of-origin experiences of education and socioeconomic status
5. Overall quality and productivity of marital communication at the twelve-year marker in the marriage

Treatment Recommendations:

1. Increase parental education, exploration of, and agreement about parenting strategies, ideally without children present, including a decision tree about how to handle both children's behavioral symptoms.
2. Increase spousal involvement with each other as partners; suggest some form of dyadic activity designed to help them focus more on each other.
3. Recommend pediatric exams for both children.
4. Negotiate and develop appropriate boundary between spousal/parental subsystem and both families of origin.

Summary

This case has been viewed from a systemic lens and written up accordingly. Interactional patterns and family-of-origin connections were noted, and, as can be seen, a much more thorough picture of the family's current status has been gleaned. Depending upon the particular systemic approach to which you are partial, your write-up may contain some additions or deletions. For example, in the above description, a fair amount of attention was paid to family-of-origin issues, which is consistent with several family therapy approaches (e.g., Boszormenyi-Nagy, Grunebaum, and Ulrich, 1991; Framo, 1992; Freeman, 1992; Kerr and Bowen, 1988), but a strategic therapist may have spent considerably more time outlining the attempted solutions and the specifics associated with them and much less time on family-of-origin connections (e.g., Fisch, Weakland, and Segal, 1983; Haley, 1987; Madanes, 1981). A structural therapist may have spent more time exploring the various boundaries and subsystems (e.g., Minuchin and Fishman, 1982), or a narrative therapist would have concentrated more on the story they told and the meaning they attributed to Jimmy's and Cindy's behaviors, as well as the significance these events played in their lives (White and Epston, 1990). A genogram (McGoldrick and Gerson, 1985) was constructed herein, but that is not always included. Additionally, a homework assignment may have been given, or perhaps an in-session task might have been assigned. In any event, the case's presentation and the focus of treatment according to the write-up is markedly different.

CASE #2: A "RELATIONAL" PROBLEM

Our second case comes from a different starting point. A woman has called the clinic requesting marital therapy because an affair has been revealed by her husband. Again, all you have on paper are a few items pertaining to names, ages, and the fact that the husband has had an affair and is willing to come in for therapy. In contrast to the first case, however, there is no question that more than one person, i.e., both spouses, will be present for the initial interview. You may already know that there are specific insurance or reimbursement requirements, and so you may begin to think about them now. The question in this case may become, "How do you handle a relationship problem if your intake protocol requires you to deal with individuals?" We will present here first a systemic assessment of this couple, and then present the write-up of a more traditional individual protocol.

Systemic Assessment

The Johnsons, Chad, age forty-four, and Ellen, age forty-one, have been married seventeen years, and they have requested marital therapy as a result of Chad's revelation several weeks ago that he had fallen in love with another woman and was considering filing for a divorce. Immediately after sharing this revelation, Chad reports that he became acutely depressed. He states he felt confused about himself and very guilty about hurting Ellen and potentially disrupting their children's lives. The couple reports that they have three children, Dana, fifteen years old, Bud, thirteen years old, and Nicki, eight years old.

Ellen reports that she feels betrayed, confused, and "a little" frustrated as if they have been on hold while Chad decides what he wants to do. She also states she has not known how to respond to questions asked by the children, who have apparently noticed their parents' overt changes.

Both spouses report a willingness to participate in therapy, but each appears to have individual goals and concerns. In their initial responses to questions of why they called for an appointment and what they felt they needed to address in therapy, both spouses seemed cautious and expressed restrained resentment. Ellen indicated that she very much wants the marriage to be "put back together," no matter how long it may take. In contrast, Chad stated that he was unsure of what he wanted, but that he did consider divorce an appropriate course of action when someone is unhappy in a marriage. They appeared unwilling to be directly angry with each other, but rather were unusually reasonable given the severity of what seems to have transpired. While each acknowledges pain—Chad feels depressed, confused about himself, uncertain of what to do, and guilty, and Ellen feels hurt, confused, and betrayed by his other relationship—they were very calm and somewhat matter-of-fact about the whole situation.

While the therapist gathered the perceptions of the couple about their marriage prior to this crisis, Chad and Ellen reported that their friends and relatives often state to them that their marriage appears ideal. Both spouses are professionals, Chad as a junior executive in a local corporation and Ellen as a college professor. In addition, they stated that their children are viewed very favorably by family, friends, and teachers. They agreed with each other that they have much to be proud of. Ellen describes Chad as an energetic individual who enjoys working around their home, in addition to his many hobbies (golf, racquetball, jogging, and photography). Chad describes Ellen as intelligent, attractive, outgoing, an excellent cook, and a good housekeeper for him and the children. Their descriptions yielded an impression that, despite being a dual-career couple who appear to admire each other, Chad seems to be the more central figure at home and that Ellen enjoys doing "special things" for him.

The couple were asked questions to obtain a history of their marriage and their families of origin. Ellen began by stating that their marriage has always been very good and that she was happy to be there for Chad and to attend to his various needs. She stated that she always thought he was happy and was amazed to find that he had become involved with another woman. Although Chad did not indicate previous feelings of unhappiness about the marriage, he had difficulty sharing his feelings about Ellen or his perceptions of the relationship. His comments were limited to apparently ambivalent statements about Ellen's love for him and his commitment to the family.

Ellen states she was the oldest of three children from a lower-middle-class background where her parents worked long hours running a small and struggling neighborhood business. She had much praise for both her parents; nonetheless, upon further questioning, she described her father as quite dominating in a very quiet, withholding manner and her mother as someone who always thought about others first and mostly did things to please others (especially her husband). She stated that her father was preoccupied with the financial survival of the family and that she and her sisters looked exclusively to their mother for emotional reassurance and a sense of order and purpose.

Chad stated that his parents divorced shortly after he was born and that his "family" consisted of his mother and a stepfather whom he "really knew little about as a person." He did indicate that he has a brother six years older than he who lived with their father until adulthood. When questioned about the dynamics of "his" family, Chad indicated that his mother was the dominant personality and that his stepfather was very passive and emotionally absent or depressed. He stated that he never discussed his parents' divorce with either parent or his brother, and that many other pieces of information commonly shared between family members were understood to be "off limits." He stated also that he has never felt much curiosity about the whole situation.

At this point Chad was reminded by Ellen to address the fact that his mother had died quite suddenly a little over two years ago. Chad acknowledged this fact but was reluctant to provide more details, limiting his description to his mother's medical problems. After several interruptions by Ellen during which time it became obvious that she was determined to "tell the story and spill the beans," Chad became less communicative. Ellen indicated that neither Chad nor his stepfather cried at any time during the funeral arrangements or the funeral itself. She felt their stoic manner was unhealthy and related that she has been concerned about Chad ever since his mother's death. Chad reluctantly agreed and added that his stepfather had gradually slipped into a very serious depression in the six months following the funeral. He stated that he has little contact with his stepfather who becomes too overwrought with emotion whenever he and Chad speak. When pressed about his father and brother, Chad indicated that neither attended the funeral and that this was consistent with the pattern of "two families" that were divorced from each other.

At this point Chad stated that the session should focus on the "real matter at hand"—his relationship with Sheila and his confusion about his marriage. During the questions that followed, Chad indicated that he had dates with several women over the last year and a half, which he described as brief affairs. When asked about his feelings during this time, Chad stated that he thought he had begun to lose his bearings and was in some indescribable sort of turmoil about what he wanted out of life. Ellen's response to Chad's story was curiously disaffected.

Systemic Treatment Issues Assessed for Consideration at This Time:

1. A dual-career marriage with many attributes of a traditionally structured marriage, under stress from an extramarital relationship as well as normative developmental events (e.g., children in adolescence)
2. Guarded and/or constricted expression of emotions by both spouses during a stressful time for the marriage, with the notable exception of Ellen speaking for Chad in exposing events in his emotional life
3. Same-sex parent/stepparent role identification, with Ellen's mother overtly codependent, and Chad's absent father and emotionally absent stepfather
4. Impact of Chad's mother's death on the marital relationship and the timing of the beginning of extramarital affairs
5. Examining the issue of "betrayal" in the lives of both spouses and the implications for the marriage and ultimately the family

Treatment Recommendations

1. Come to agreement about the purpose of this therapy—is it to put the marriage back together or for the purpose of exploring

that as one possibility—and explore the implications of either/both positions.

2. If there is agreement on exploring the marriage's viability, initiate a moratorium on Chad's extramarital relationship for a period of time sufficient to allow reasonable chance of success. If there is not agreement, individual therapy may be needed.

3. Refer both partners for HIV tests.

Summary

This marital therapy intake write-up takes a fairly standard intergenerational Object Relations systemic approach (e.g., Scharff and Scharff, 1987). The systemic therapist could have taken just as easily a more behavioral approach, investigating how things have (or have not) changed since the affair came to light, for example, which would be characteristic of some brief family therapy approaches (e.g., Budman and Gurman, 1988). Approaching the case from a more psychoeducational skills training model (e.g., L'Abate, 1981), or an experiential one in which the emotional states of both spouses are explored would also be consistent with a systemic point of view (e.g., Whitaker and Keith, 1981). In any event, the focus is on the relationship and the consequent issues associated with handling infidelity; neither spouse's individual concerns take immediate precedence.

Furthermore, the treatment recommendations in this case are quite short-term in their focus. It may take several sessions to determine whether they want to work on the marriage, and if so, then the treatment goals would change accordingly. However in this case, we are not sure what the clients want to accomplish so we cannot set off in any direction until we know where they wish to go. It is not unusual for cases in which affairs have happened for the first order of business in therapy to be determining what the couple wants to do (and this can take quite some time). A significant amount of time may be spent exploring the possible scenarios that may result if a given course of action is chosen, and simultaneously, the systemic therapist can utilize that time to further observe and understand the way the couple's marital system functions. Does Ellen always talk for Chad when it comes to emotional matters, and is she blocking him or does he "move over" and expect her to fill the vacuum, or both? What are the implications for their children and themselves should Chad (or Ellen) decide to divorce? In the period of deciding to decide, much may still be done.

Now we will look at the same case from the perspective of a traditional, individual-oriented clinic intake assessment. Because it is not unusual for individual therapy to be pursued by either one or both spouses in this type of situation (and in fact it may be recommended), either Chad or Ellen could be an identified patient in this case example. To account for this possibility, we will present both assessments. Notice how the assessment reflects the traditional clinic orientation of working with individuals and meets the requirements of documenting a numerically coded diagnosis and specific individually oriented treatment goals that insurers and managed care companies maintain. Again, the content of the actual interview is the same, but the way it is dissected and particular parts highlighted is markedly different.

Traditional Clinic Intake Assessment: Ellen Johnson

Identifying Data: Ellen Johnson is a forty-one-year-old Caucasian female married seventeen years to Chad, age forty-four. There are three children from this marriage, Dana, fifteen years old, Bud, thirteen years old, and Nicki, eight years old. It is the first marriage for both. Ellen is a college professor.

Presenting Problem: Ellen presented a somewhat emotionless story of her husband informing her of his involvement in an extramarital affair and his uncertainty as to whether or not he wants to remain in their marriage. She stated that despite this announcement, her husband has appeared depressed and confused much of the time. She states that she feels confused because she has always viewed their marriage as a very good one with almost no overt conflict. She reported feeling somewhat anxious and depressed as she is unsure of what she should do in response to her husband's announcement. She also reported some feelings of anger, but that they are "not very strong." She is certain that she does not wish to be divorced from him and is worried that his friends and/or a mental health professional might encourage him to seek divorce as a resolution to his situation.

Previous Mental Health Treatment: None

Family Psychiatric/Psychological History: Ellen reported no history of psychiatric or psychological disorders in her family and denied any alcohol or substance abuse problems with herself or in her family. She indicated that she did not have any significant emotional problems during childhood, adolescence, or young adulthood.

Medical Problems: None reported

Mental Status Examination: Ellen was oriented to person, place, and time. She was attractively dressed and groomed, and is observed to be a physically fit individual. She demonstrated mild psychomotor retardation as evidenced by rather deliberate and constricted speech. Her affect was constricted, her mood was quiet, and she displayed expressions of uncertainty and confusion. Her speech was appropriate but somewhat constricted. There were no indications of disturbances in thought processes. She did not verbalize any suicidal or homicidal ideation, nor any death wishes. Ellen appears to be of above-average intelligence with commensurate insight and judgment.

Diagnosis:

Axis I	309.28 Adjustment Disorder with Mixed Anxiety and Depressed Mood
Axis II	V71.09 No Diagnosis
Axis III	None
Axis IV	Severe: Problems with Primary Support Group (i.e., husband's infidelity and possibly seeking a divorce)
Axis V	Current GAF 70, Past Year 90

Treatment Plan: Marital and individual therapy

Treatment Goals:

1. Increase productive emotional expression with self and spouse.
2. Reduce overall frequency and intensity of anxiety so that daily functioning is not impaired by resolving the core conflict (marital discord).

3. Verbalize an understanding of the relationship between constricted affect, repressed resentments, and depressed mood.
4. Develop additional coping skills and sources of emotional support as needed.

Traditional Clinic Intake Assessment: Chad Johnson

Identifying Data: Chad Johnson is a forty-four-year-old Caucasian male married seventeen years to Ellen, age forty-one. There are three children from this marriage, Dana, fifteen years old, Bud, thirteen years old, and Nicki, eight years old. It is the first marriage for both. Chad is a junior executive for a local corporation.

Presenting Problem: Chad stated that he is involved in an extra-marital relationship with a woman named Sheila and is uncertain at this time whether he wishes to remain married to Ellen. He also states that he has been suffering from severe depression, confusion, and guilt feelings since telling his wife about his affair and his desire to leave the marriage. He reported problems such as lacking sound sleep, fatigue, lack of appetite, poor attention and concentration, low self-esteem, and feelings of confusion and hopelessness at times.

Previous Mental Health Treatment: None

Family Psychiatric/Psychological History: Chad reported only two significant traumas or tragedies in his immediate or extended family. He stated that his parents were divorced when he was an infant, resulting in little contact with his father. He also stated that his mother died approximately two years ago, which resulted in decreased contact with his stepfather with whom he was raised. He reported no history of psychiatric or psychological disorders in his family of origin and denied any alcohol or substance abuse problems for himself or his family of origin.

Medical Problems: None reported

Mental Status Examination: Chad was oriented to person, place, and time. He was attractively dressed and groomed, and he has an athletic physique. He demonstrated some psychomotor retardation in his gait and speech, indicative of depression. His affect was constricted, his mood was quiet, and he displayed expressions of uncertainty. His speech was appropriate but somewhat constricted. There were no indications of disturbances in thought processes. He did not verbalize any suicidal or homicidal ideation, nor any death wishes. Chad appeared to be of above-average intelligence with commensurate insight and judgment.

Diagnosis:

Axis I   300.4 Dysthymia (Neurotic Depression)
            Rule out Major Depression
Axis II   V71.09 No Diagnosis
Axis III   None
Axis IV   Severe: Problems with Primary Support Group (i.e., extra-
            marital affair and resulting uncertainty about marriage)
Axis V   Current GAF 60, Past Year 80

Treatment Plan: Marital therapy, with possible concurrent individual therapy

Treatment Goals:

1. Decrease depression symptoms via increased emotional expression in identifying crucial aspects of his depressed mood.
2. Identify, describe, and increase daily awareness of relationship issues that led to dissatisfaction and extramarital affairs.
3. Decrease the level of conflict and dissatisfaction in the marriage by identifying and resolving long-standing resentments/ issues.

Summary: In both of the individual write-ups, the focus is again on the individual in question and her or his particular symptoms and concerns. The clinician's major goal concerns alleviating each individual's problems even though in both cases, relationship therapy may be the recommended treatment. In this way, a relational issue that is at the heart of therapy can be viewed from a traditional individual lens.

Arguably, however, the individual approach is not as satisfying or complete as the systemic lens, which examines both people in the context of each other. At the same time, it is obvious that the systemic perspective does not have a codified manual of "relational" diagnoses that can quickly and easily be attached to a case assessment (The recently released *Handbook of Relational Diagnoses and Dysfunctional Family Patterns* [Kaslow, 1996] is an impressive stab in that direction). Most often you will identify terminology utilized that is sometimes generic to systemic thinking or sometimes linked to a specific systemic theoretical orientation or model. For this reason, the systemic approach does not lend itself to quick and easily understood universals that professionals across the board can recognize.

At this point, we hope that you have become convinced of the benefit of incorporating systemic thinking into your standard operating procedures in therapy even though it may not always be welcomed by your associates or easy to do in practice at first. But it can and, in our opinion, should be done. Being able to converse fluently in both the language of the traditional individual model and the systemic model will make you all the more effective to colleagues, supervisors, and clients alike. In the next chapter, we will show you some additional ways to accomplish this.

Chapter 6

Case Formulation:
So What Do I Do After the Intake?

The initial stage of treatment is obviously a crucial part of the process of successful clinical work. After all, therapy that does not go beyond the intake is not going to go very far. Despite those theorists and scholars, and there are several, who believe that single-session therapy is a treatment of choice (e.g., Talmon, 1990), most therapists and clients tend to expect things to proceed through a course of treatment that includes several sessions. Some in the single-session school argue that under the increasing influence of managed care, single-session approaches may eventually dominate the therapeutic landscape (e.g., Rosenbaum, 1994; Talmon, 1993). Perhaps they are correct, but in our experience, making accurate predictions of this nature is akin to predicting the weather—a lot of impressive theoretical and statistical models presented with plenty of confidence usually end up containing only a degree of validity. We are not disparaging single-session therapy, but rather we are saying that it is not very likely that it will be *the* treatment modality of the future.

If we are right, it is going to be important for you to develop the ability to formulate treatment over several sessions from intake to termination. To use an aviation metaphor, getting off the ground is important, to be sure, but staying in the air after takeoff is nothing to take lightly either. The results of a failed takeoff can range from being annoying to being messy to being tragic. However, aircraft that get off the ground successfully have to return to it somehow, and if the return is not done correctly, tragedy will be hard to *avoid*. The range of outcomes is quite limited. Therapy is often the same; a client who drops out after the first session or two *may* not be up in the air far enough to be severely damaged, but a client who is mishandled in midflight is a likely disaster. So, just as it is important to be competent at conducting intakes and initial interviews, it is at least as important to be competent at conducting a full course of treatment.

In our experience, clinical training programs do a very good job of preparing trainees to do initial interviews and perhaps the first two or three sessions. There are several reasons for this. First, the initial phase of therapy has received a great deal of theoretical attention, in which writers of therapy books and articles have spent no small amount of time detailing what needs to take place (e.g., Brock and Bernard, 1992; Haley, 1987; Worden, 1994). Also, research into the process of therapy, although certainly not exhaustive, has focused more on the first few sessions than later ones (can you recall ever seeing an article or book with a title such as *The Ninth Session of Therapy*?) (Bischoff and Sprenkle, 1993). Second, therapy starts quite definitively when clients come in; accordingly, the normative goal of getting under way is easiest to focus on in training. It can be more formulaic. Third, people usually present for therapy with a particular problem they want help with, and so the initial phase of treatment is focused mostly on ascertaining what needs to be done to resolve the problem and beginning to make changes. Finally, later sessions in therapy tend to be more nebulous in terms of their focus. Often this occurs because clinicians may lose sight of the goals for therapy or because what they are trying to accomplish—e.g., personal growth—is itself more nebulous. Thus, research into later sessions is harder to do and rare to find (hence the paucity of articles and books like the above; anyone looking for a good thesis or dissertation topic?).

Therapy may get started definitively, but it tends not to continue that way for many clients. A very large percentage of clients (maybe most of them) in the majority of practice settings do not terminate in an organized way (Phillips, 1987). Rather than discussing with their therapists that they feel they have received what they came for and planning a termination session or sessions, they just stop coming. The last contact you may have is the phone call canceling a scheduled appointment, or not infrequently, a no-show. This can be annoying for the therapist as it is lost time, and it is also a lost opportunity to discuss what about the therapy was valuable and what was not. This kind of feedback is very important to be able to access, both for clinicians and for clients, who may benefit from a reminder of their positive changes.

Unfortunately, it is the rare training experience wherein the student is trained well to do eighth sessions, twelfth sessions, or terminations, and we believe this contributes to the apparently haphazard conducting of later stages of treatment. Possibly, terminations in therapy tend to be disorganized and unexpected precisely because clinicians are not well trained in formulating a full course of treatment. Therefore, they do not do a good job of educating their clients about the process of therapy itself. Many clients may not realize that it is generally in their best interest to make decisions about termination in consultation with their therapists.

This chapter's purpose is to help you to begin to think in terms of mapping out the course of therapy with clients as a normal part of clinical work. Once you have developed this skill, you can pass it on in turn to your clients and even your own supervisees (it is not too early to think in terms of yourself as a possible supervisor/trainer of therapists, too, you know!). One obvious caveat to bear in mind, however, is that there are no magic procedures, interventions, or persons in therapy that result in happy endings all the time. Even so, being able to conduct all stages of therapy well is a key to increasing your success rate with your clients.

IDEAL VERSUS PRACTICAL TREATMENT GOALS: DOABLE THERAPY

Practicing marriage and family therapy under ideal conditions would be both fun and reasonably predictable, resulting in problems solved, people functioning at their best, and relationships fine-tuned to a point of almost digital precision. The typical client would present for therapy with a fairly clear and attainable set of goals, realistic expectations for reaching them, a high degree of internally driven motivation to make changes and be responsible for them, and a personal and social context supportive of doing so. If the problem was thought to be individual in nature, the client would be very open to the idea of including other people in therapy and learning to function better within his or her context. If the problem was a relational one, the clients would all be equally motivated, honest, and cooperative, both with the therapist and with each other. For the therapist's part, interventions would be derived straight from a comprehensive and integrated theory of human psychosocial functioning with the precision of a surgical procedure, and the impact would be exquisitely effective. Changes would be welcomed and integrated into the system, which in turn would shift to accommodate them, thus maintaining positive gains. Then, at the agreed-upon end (which would be at most several months), the clients would thank you for your invaluable help. This sounds good, right? Well, in the real world, as you undoubtedly know, it just does not happen this way.

Typical clinical training usually revolves around the mastery of theory and the development of several specific clinical skills derived from theory, both of which are absolutely essential to becoming a competent professional therapist. To accomplish this, most programs immerse the student in the theoretical clinical literature and the research literature that has grown up to support (or occasionally refute) it. Of equal or perhaps even greater significance for our purposes here is the fact that this literature also contains a large amount of case study as well, detailing the numerous different ways that therapists work in actual practice with real clients. With few exceptions, the case studies that make it into print tend to present success stories, wherein the writer discusses the particulars about the client(s) and the theory behind the problem(s) and solution(s), and then describes why what was done worked. For the student of therapy, this is often a very useful way to learn.

Unfortunately, there are several assumptions inherent in such an approach to training that we believe may actually cause problems for the learner. First, trainees may develop a skewed vision about the way clinical work actually proceeds. Few therapists are so organized in their work that at any point they can fully elucidate their theoretical and clinical rationale for everything that they do. The truth is that many therapists operate from a template that is both scientific and artistic at the same time; this fact seems to remain overlooked at the heart of the debate about the pragmatics versus the aesthetics of therapy (e.g., Goldenberg and Goldenberg, 1996). Experienced therapists make good use of virtually all of the data they receive, whether verbal and "rational," or nonverbal and intuitive. Reading case studies, one may find that the latter part is underemphasized; this is to be expected, however, given the nature of "clinical instinct."

Second, most case studies written by experts are ones that show that therapy *was successful*. This leads trainees to expect positive outcomes perhaps more readily than they should. If therapy were baseball, case studies would be press accounts of clutch hits, tremendous defensive plays, and shrewdly calculated managerial strategizing that made the win happen. The only problem is that we know a lot more about how to win baseball games than we do about helping people make long-lasting changes in their lives, despite there being no shortage of theory. When trainees expect their work to look like what they read about or watch on videotape, they are setting themselves up for disappointment and, quite possibly, trouble.

One useful way that we suggest to think about clinical work that helps control unrealistic expectations is to divide up your cases into approximate thirds. About one-third of your cases you can expect to do reasonably well, making noticeable progress with the clients working quite cooperatively/collaboratively with you. These clients are the closest to the ones previously described as being ideal—although we would not go so far as to say they will be easy. They may be quite challenging, but the overall theme of this group is that they will make therapy work for them. You will probably feel like a successful therapist, too, after finishing up one of these cases.

Another third of your cases will work with you more or less consistently, but will be more difficult and will likely present you with more twists and turns in the therapeutic road. They may view therapy as helpful at the end, but you may be hard-pressed to be able to offer an explanation as to *why*, and you may be likely to characterize your work with them as disjointed, atheoretical, and a lot of just plain "winging it." You may be very surprised in some instances to discover that you were perceived as very helpful. Some of these cases, however, can provide you with some of your most rewarding challenges and some excellent opportunities to learn and grow as a therapist.

The final third of your cases you can expect therapy to fail. This may mean that they do not return after the initial interview, they cancel and do not reschedule, or they may come back but just never seem to make any movement in treatment. For any variety of reasons, your work with them will probably not produce anything positive, especially from your point of view, in terms of therapeutic change. It would be unwise, however, to write these cases off like bad debts, because then you would miss valuable learning opportunities. After some time, for example, you may find yourself wishing you had another chance with them, or you may find there were issues for you that got in the way of your work with them. You may also find yourself learning to deal with professional frustrations in a better way. Therapeutic failures, too, can help you stay humble.

Another problem with the exclusive use of case studies in training is that it tends to result in imitation, a sincere form of flattery that is a major dud as a treatment modality. The potential hazard with watching "Master Therapists" is that part of what makes them so impressive and effective is unteachable. Nobody does strategic therapy à la Haley like Haley (e.g., Haley, 1987), or solution-focused therapy à la Weiner-Davis like Weiner-Davis (e.g., Weiner-Davis, 1992). Each therapist must make the model that is chosen fit with his or her individual personality and therapeutic style, not simply (or not so simply) an imitation of the master demonstrating it. Our trainees are often amazed and incredulous at how Carl Whitaker could get away with falling asleep while treating his clients (Goldenberg and Goldenberg, 1996), which is something that most therapists should *never* try. Nonetheless, this does not preclude trainees from developing their own brands of absurdity or provocativeness; in fact, effectiveness demands that trainees develop their own creativity.

Another reason that the expert therapists students are exposed to on tape, at conferences, and in case studies are not always wise choices to emulate is because the treatment approaches they are known for often are not ideally suited for all kinds of clients in all situations. An astute example of this occurred several years ago at the national convention of AAMFT. A famous "Master Therapist" conducted a live interview with a client family as part of the "Master's Series" that the conventions have included regularly for many years, and to be blunt, it flopped miserably. To the therapist's immense credit, she did not stay with her model to the point of ramming it down the clients' throats (no small feat in front of hundreds of enthusiastic clinicians eager to jump on her therapeutic bandwagon), but rather she adjusted to meet the clients where they needed her. In the postsession discussion, the therapist stated that what had been seen was a clear demonstration of the limitations of her model, and she made an all-too-rare but entirely appropriate concession that the model is not for every client in every situation.

The point of all this is that therapists just getting into the practice world need to concentrate on doing good, solid, "doable" therapy. This translates into developing realistic treatment goals and an appropriate plan to meet them. Both your clients and you will suffer if you are unable to do this well. Therapy needs to be practical first and foremost. It is not magic; it will not be effective with every problem or person, and sometimes it may even be contraindicated (more on that later). Being a competent therapist requires that you be able to construct a practical, feasible, and complete course of treatment for clients on a consistent basis. It also requires that you never place your theoretical beliefs above your clients' reality; if one of the two has to be wrong, it is your theory.

ASSESSMENT NEVER ENDS: CONSTRUCTING AND RECONSTRUCTING STRATEGIES

After the intake has been completed, you should have a fairly large amount of information with which to begin working. However, in our experience more than one trainee has anxiously stated, "Now what do I do with all this information? I'm not sure where to begin." Obviously, although it is better to have more than less, it is not enough just to gather lots of information in the intake/initial treatment phase. The value of this information is in how you use it to construct a plan that guides you in moving therapy forward.

Although the term "assessment" is usually thought of as an activity that begins the therapy process, we want to expand assessment to suggest that (1) it is a broad-based examination of several facets of individual and systemic functioning, and (2) it is an ongoing activity that keeps the therapy process proceeding in a meaningful fashion. This means that assessment is a broader inquiry than most therapists typically think about, and that it is something that does not end after just a session or three. Throughout this book, we have emphasized the need to be "bilingual" in the profession, and in the area of assessment and planning therapy, it is of particular import.

In order to increase a therapist's overall effectiveness, we believe it is imperative that the ability to assess using the specifications of many approaches is developed. The earlier this is done in one's professional career, the better, and the earlier in treatment, the better. At the beginning of therapy, the typical clinician can afford to hedge his or her bets a little bit about exactly how to proceed until enough data have been gathered to formulate a plan. The wisdom herein is to take this time to map out the approach to therapy that a number of models would suggest, rather than the more common approach, which is to "search for and include all information that is compatible with my template and discard the rest." In this way, you can evaluate the problems and possible solutions from a number of otherwise competing perspectives. You will also have a diversity of treatment options from which to choose.

Most beginning therapists tend to be particularly anxious about their work, and so they tend to stick pretty close to the models and approaches they know best. What is important to recognize, however, is that this is also true of experienced veterans. When presented with a new case, for example, the strategically oriented therapist is going to begin assessing things with an eye for attempted solutions and paradoxical interventions (Haley, 1987), whereas the Bowenian therapist will be looking for family-of-origin themes pertaining to differentiation and triangles (Kerr and Bowen, 1988). All of this is to say that we each have our preferred templates with which we organize our clinical work, and this is a good thing. What is problematic is that first, we can become overreliant on our preferred approach to the point of being ineffective with cases that do not readily match up with our model's assumptions, and second, we also routinely overlook valuable information that we could and should be using according to other approaches.

In constructing and reconstructing strategies over the course of the initial, middle, and later phases of therapy, it is often useful to think in terms of *game plans*, i.e., the overall approach to achieving the goals that are the purpose of therapy, and *interventions*, i.e., the various specific techniques we will utilize to accomplish these goals. This process will allow you to maintain an underlying integrative theoretical structure while at the same time provide you with enough flexibility for your clinical instinct to be a useful resource in conducting actual sessions. Devising a theoretically sound and collegially tested game plan will be invaluable in guiding you on this complex and sometimes convoluted journey called psychotherapy.

Let us develop the game plan metaphor further. In many sports, a coach and his or her staff develop a tactical blueprint that outlines precisely (as much as possible) how they plan to approach the game. The game plan is based largely on the scouting reports of the other team, as well as on an evaluation of their own strengths they bring to the field. The plan also may include situational factors, such as playing at home or on the road, and weather or field conditions, and how these may affect the contest. The game plan outlines the goals that are to be accomplished and how they will be achieved, with the obvious desired end being a victory.

In the same way, therapists need to develop game plans as they approach their clients. The notable breakdown of the metaphor is that most therapists are not out to defeat their clients (at least we hope this is so!). The coaching staff for therapy is the therapist and his or her supervisor and colleagues; the scouting report is the initial diagnostic systemic assessment that was done at the intake (or perhaps over the telephone, or both); the evaluation of what we bring is seen in case assignment and matters of supervision, cotherapy, and/or consultation; and situational factors may include anything from insurance coverage to family support to church membership and the like. The desired end result is a victory over a problem or set of problems.

In sports and in therapy, it is important to remember that there is always more than one way to get where you want to go (keeping in mind that you have to know where it is you want to go in the first place or you may end up somewhere else). An athlete or team that develops a tremendously effective strength runs the risk of that strength becoming the single greatest liability in the event that there is nothing else to fall back on when the strength does not work. Similarly, as we have mentioned, extensive training in a particular theoretical approach is certainly valuable, but it can also be the single biggest cause of dysfunctional tunnel vision for a therapist.

In this instance, a therapist becomes overly attached to a single course of action in treating a case, and if it does not work, therapy gets stuck. (You may note the systemic parallel here with how clients can get stuck in trying to solve a particular problem. This is no accident, and this is what makes supervision so valuable.)

Obviously (perhaps to the point of redundancy, but it is worth repeating!), the strategies you construct should not be carved in granite from the moment you complete the initial assessment phase nor from any particular theoretical perspective. Like a good coach, good therapists (with supervisors and colleagues) always have a game plan that is multifaceted. If their best or first plan fails, they must have other avenues to try to accomplish their goal. They watch how the game unfolds and how their initial plan is working. If it is successful, they stay with the plan until it reaches completion or is no longer effective. If it is not, they quickly adjust by shifting to the next alternative they have devised that now appears to have the best chance for success. If they do not develop a comprehensive, dynamic and flexible plan, then they are very likely to be at a loss at the first sign of trouble. When this happens, the risks run high.

One other thing to consider when you construct your game plans is the difficulty involved sometimes in deciding when to switch tactics. It is not necessarily wise to jump ship at the first sign of a loss in therapeutic momentum. Indeed, it is often the case that systemic change follows temporary retrenchment—things often get worse before they get better. However, if you get stuck and remain there for a while, then the wisdom of having the backup plan on hand to turn to is plainly evident. We will discuss being stuck in therapy more fully in Chapter 13.

Let us consider an example. You may see a family for several sessions during which time you assess the systemic dynamics. The adolescent children are acting out in oppositional-defiant ways at school and in the community. The father is very detached and peripheral to the family members and their activities. The mother struggles like a battle-fatigued single parent, and the children resent that she sometimes vents her frustration with their father toward them. How might you begin to approach a case like this one? What would be your game plan? What might your second and third options be if your initial plan is unsuccessful? The point is to begin exercising your mind to develop a variety of ways to work with them; brainstorming like this is common in group supervision, and it seems to us that we should make it a part of our own normative way of thinking about our work. In the following, we present some possibilities that one might think of to use in the previous scenario.

Your first choice might be to use the father as the entry point into the family. If so, how will you do this specifically? Do you approach and support him as the wise, observing consultant while assuming he feels unneeded and/or unwanted by the rest of the family? Do you emphasize his importance by stressing that the children need two active parents to balance and complement each other (i.e., "the kids can't make it successfully without you")? Do you get father to talk about his family of origin (especially his father) to understand what supports his detachment? Or perhaps you assume he is in the position he desires and proceed to underscore his peripheralness to the family in hopes he objects to being ignored more formally.

Conversely, or as a backup strategy, you may choose to focus on the mother as a more accessible entry point into the family. If so, do you explore how she and the children may have pushed the father out in reaction to their fear that he may abandon them? Do you focus on how the mother may receive much comfort through the power her husband's detachment provides her? Do you focus on the marital and family-of-origin histories to determine how the pattern of distancing both began and is currently maintained? For each possibility, how intensely do you want to address the issue and for how long? When will you need to switch methods if that becomes necessary?

As you can see, there are many possible options for the goals you might set in approaching this case—and those mentioned may or may not be good places to begin with this family. Part of determining how to proceed also involves deciding how *you* are most comfortable going into therapy; what is important to keep in mind is that your reaction may indicate precisely which way to start (either because of comfort or a lack thereof). In any event, establishing a game plan means outlining the various goal options you have to choose from while maintaining ample flexibility to switch and/or revise the plan based on the response and results you get in the sessions. It pays to be both persistent and flexible.

There is a wealth of information about specific interventions and ideas for constructing strategies in the literature (e.g., Trepper and Nelson, 1993). We heartily recommend that you read as much as possible to gain maximum exposure to them. We also recommend that you work on taking risks in trying new things as part of your training and supervision experiences. What you devise and utilize, though, must in some fashion fit or connect with your current game plan, your clients, and your person in the role of therapist. To blindly imitate another therapist is to assume that their personality (which hopefully is congruent and comfortable with what they are doing) and yours are identical. Your strategies for accomplishing your goals must not only relate well to the case you are treating but also to who you are.

However, you must recognize that no matter how brilliant an intervention or technique may seem to be, limitations always exist. The most important limitation to remember is that a technique simply imitated or an intervention randomly utilized, without being theoretically and/or intuitively connected to the case you are treating, is potentially useless at best and disastrous at worst. To imitate what you observe someone else doing as a therapist has no value if it is not relevant and appropriate to the dynamics of the case and the goals you have established for the case. The work of other therapists (from the master therapists on videotape to your supervisors, cotherapists, and colleagues) is most valuable when it is used to help you think more creatively about your own cases. Again, there is always more than one way to get to where you want to go.

To return to our previous example with the family we discussed, what specific strategies might you utilize to get them activated and working in therapy? Do you begin with homework assignments, and if so, are they educational and tutorial about overt communication patterns, for instance, or are they of a more paradoxical nature? Do you talk to the parents directly or through conversation with the children about the wisdom of their misbehavior that results in pressing the parents to get together on something/anything? Do you stay focused on the presenting symptoms to gain the trust of the family (particularly the father) before overtly expanding the frame to highlight marital, parental, and other systemic issues, and if so, how long do you focus only on the presenting symptoms? Do you depathologize the children by working from an historical perspective with focus on family-of-origin dynamics? Consulting different writings can be helpful if you look for insight and inspiration in constructing strategies rather than simply imitating those you read about. Look for principles more than particulars. The unique dynamics of the case you are treating and your personal style of presenting and interacting with clients are the key ingredients in formulating useful strategies.

A good game plan is useful as long as you do not expect to move forward without any complications. We suggest you remember that there are many interventions and techniques used in the strategizing of therapy. It is more important, in the end, to be successful rather than to be preoccupied with any particular theoretical approach. It would be nice if we could simply pull out a map and know exactly where to go, but therapy is not that simple. For us, some of the real rewards in being therapists are the surprises we experience. Constructing strategies means having ideas of how you will proceed while paying close attention to what emerges along the way and how it influences the reconstruction of your strategies within and between sessions.

As you develop as a clinician, you will find yourself more comfortable doing more thinking and less worrying about most of your cases. Your strategizing on the whole will become more mature and creative, and you will probably be able to relax a bit more. At the same time, you will develop an ever greater appreciation for the complexity and wonder of human problems and solutions. One final word of advice as you construct your strategies: Stay humble, even while your confidence grows.

We now turn to a discussion of how to practice in a consistently systemic fashion that includes on a more-or-less regular basis other members of clients' systems. Learning to at the very least consider including them is part of developing good game plans. After all, knowing what players you have available is essential if you want to increase the likelihood of a desired outcome.

Chapter 7

Ways to Engage the Family in Therapy ("Why Do You Want Me to Bring Her/Him/Them In?")

As a marriage and family therapist, the job you have been trained to do is to work with people who need professional psychotherapeutic help to solve problems. Your training focus, again as a marriage and family therapist, has most likely been on working with couples and families—i.e., the systems, or relationships, of people. As a mental health professional, however, and certainly after reading this far into this book, you should realize that what you are trained to do and what your job requires of you are not necessarily the same. In real world clinical work, you will see couples and families, but you will see plenty of individuals, whether they are adults, adolescents, or children, with whom you will be expected to work *individually*.

This chapter's purpose is to help you to see ways in which to work systemically by including other members of the individual client's family or social environment. First, we will examine some of the potential obstacles you should expect to encounter when attempting to increase the number of participants and why these obstacles are in place. Second, we will present some strategies for use in overcoming the obstacles. You will notice, too, our assumption that the problems under consideration here are typically thought of as individual ones and that problems of a relational nature are less troublesome in terms of including additional persons in therapy. This is partially true and partially untrue. It is not uncommon for one spouse, for example, to present for therapy for a marital problem and the other spouse refuses to participate. At the end of the chapter, we will discuss this issue in greater detail and include some ways to engender reluctant participants' cooperation in therapy for problems that obviously are relational.

OBSTACLES TO OTHER FAMILY MEMBERS' INCLUSION

After the intake session, the challenge for the systemically oriented therapist often becomes how to get other family members to participate in therapy with the identified patient. This can be difficult even if they were present for the intake, have met you, and also feel comfortable with you. Continuing in what they consider an individual's therapy is not appropriate or desirable from their point of view, and so they can often become rather reluctant to attend subsequent sessions. If family members have never come in for a therapy session, it can be even more difficult to elicit their cooperation and involvement.

Resistance to the idea comes from several places, several of which should not be a surprise to you. The first and often most powerful source of resistance can often be the individual client. Among the reasons for this reluctance is the medically oriented nature of psychotherapy in the mind of the typical layperson; the thought is, "This is my problem and not anyone else's so nobody else needs to be here." This thought can be particularly pervasive when the client has been in therapy before, and it can be deeply entrenched if they now have returned with the same complaint(s). The client is probably accustomed to being the sole recipient of therapeutic attention and expects that to continue. In fact, we have found that in many instances, clients can seem rather possessive of their therapists, and are very reluctant to share them, even with their own families and at the therapist's request. Further, having another person or person(s) involved only serves to underscore the sense of invaded privacy that some people feel already going into therapy on their own. This combination of factors can make clients very leery about bringing in other members of their families or significant social systems to participate in what they view as their own personal therapy.

Another variation on the same theme concerns some individual clients' embarrassment or shame about having a problem that requires professional help. Including other family members or significant others in treatment seems to be quite the opposite of what is desired—i.e., a solution to an individual problem that does not even need to be divulged to the client's family or anyone else. The individual may believe that if the family found out, reprimands, ridicule, and even the possibility of being disowned may ensue. Add to that the situation some clients have wherein the family has always given the role of symptom bearer to one particular person, and the desire to avoid being so-labeled again is quite understandable. In some circumstances, you may be well-advised to keep other family members' participation minimal—or even excluded altogether. However, in our view, that happenstance as a therapeutic necessity is much rarer than most clinicians expect and in fact create.

Related to shame and embarrassment is the idea some clients have that the family itself needs to be protected from shaming. In some instances, the client feels this way alone, and in others, the family may make it very clear that they, too, hold that point of view. Most family secrets fall into this realm, wherein individuals have true stories about the family that the family knows about but pretends to remain ignorant of or believes that things are best left unsaid or in the past. Either way, the individual is often willing to shoulder a tremendous amount of personal pain and suffering for the sake of protecting the family secret. Suggestions about including other family members in therapy are almost certain to be met with a cool reception by the individual and perhaps by the family as well.

This leads us to the second common source of reluctance to include other members of the individual client's social system in treatment: the family itself. The family often shares the medical model expectation of psychotherapy that the individual client holds, namely, that there is one person with the problem and thus only one person needs to be treated. The thought here is that "it is not our problem." The family expects that you will work with the troubled family member, and when you have brought about a solution, the family will be appreciative and the client fixed. These families often have a kind of benevolent detachment that allows them to remain superficially connected but largely unable and/or unwilling to see their systemic involvement in the development, maintenance, and solution of the problem.

Sometimes the family's attitude is one of genuine concern but puzzlement over why they may be useful in treatment, and so with some explanations, they may be open to participating. Other families will be concerned, but perhaps will have given up on trying to help and will not be very willing to take part, even if invited. Then there are those families who refuse to be involved, taking an attitude that "this particular family member—your client—always has had difficulties in life, always has been depressed, etc." There may be a thinly disguised (or not-so-thinly disguised) attitude of blaming toward the symptomatic client, such that the person deserves the symptoms they endure, or that they are evil, etc. Again, the issue of family secrets surfaces, and it is the families that refuse to be involved, staunchly maintaining an individual focus, that can be among the most difficult to elicit cooperation from in therapy.

When the individual client and family collude to maintain the belief that an individual focus is necessary, your job can be doubly difficult. The client will attempt to convince you that the family does not need to participate, or does not want to, and the family will attempt to defer to the needs of their symptomatic member (in sometimes amazingly compassionate-sounding ways). However, this kind of uniformity of perspective can actually be useful to you, both in thinking about treatment approaches and in approaching the family to participate. You need to be aware of the traps, though, and plan carefully how you will work. We will turn to suggestions for engendering family participation in a moment, but first we wish to discuss the final two common sources of resistance.

Surprisingly, many times the thought of including other family members in treatment meets instant rejection by the therapist him or herself. Therapists are sometimes co-opted quite innocently into feeling a strong need to protect symptomatic individuals from their families (and everyone else, too). After having heard some of the messy stories that clients have to share about their experiences with their families, a desire to keep them from further damage at the hands of an apparently highly dysfunctional system is only natural. Unfortunately, it is also very limiting, and often serves to reinforce the implicit assumption that only individuals have problems that therapy can address, or that it is the individual that always should be the focus of treatment. It is a good idea to check yourself when you find yourself automatically ruling out including other family members in a given client's therapy.

A second reason that therapists often decide not to bring in additional system members has to do with simple fear. Perhaps it would be better to broaden that from fear to an understandable desire to avoid having to contend with sometimes "crazy" families. You never know what will happen when you bring in family members, and that uncertainty adds a degree of potential volatility to the equation that can make even seasoned veterans very nervous. If that is the reason you find yourself balking at bringing in other family members, you need to grit your teeth, get some supervision, and maybe bring in a cotherapist to bring your anxiety levels down enough to make it possible. Whitaker's (Whitaker and Ryan, 1989) belief that good therapy involves having fun and being a little out of control is a useful one to remember in this instance.

By the way, we are not advocating a "get 'em in at all costs under any circumstances" mentality; under some conditions, bringing in other family members may be a huge clinical error (e.g., in cases of incest or abuse, it may be terribly counterproductive to try to bring in other members of the family). We are saying, however, that bringing in other family members is often a good idea, and therapists often do not try hard enough to accomplish it, either because they get out of the habit of doing it or are unable to think of ways to make it happen. This can and should be changed.

Finally, some resistance to getting other family members in comes from pragmatic sources such as agency policies, managed care or insurance company reimbursement requirements, or supervisors who determine ultimately what you can and cannot do. Your supervisor, for example, may not be qualified to supervise systemic therapy (although we doubt that many supervisors would say that, regardless of their training), and thus you cannot see more than individuals. Some reimbursement requirements are so strict that anything other than individual treatment is not billable, thus creating a limitation. It may be, too, that your actual job description does not lend itself well to doing couples or family therapy, and so it may be best to not rock the employer's boat much. If this is true for you, we encourage you to not forget systemic practice!

STRATEGIES FOR GETTING RELUCTANT FAMILY MEMBERS TO PARTICIPATE

Now that we have discussed the typical obstacles to systemic practicing, we shall turn to some strategies you can employ to attempt to get other family members into therapy, at least for a session or two. At first, it may seem rather pointless to try to change the minds of people who do not wish to be a part of someone's therapy. After all, if they were willing to come, getting them in would not be a problem at all from the start. We have found that it is rather unusual for most nonsymptomatic persons to be very enthused about being in therapy, and in many cases, they just do not want to be involved much. This is due in part to ignorance about systemic therapy (i.e., medical model thinking) and in part to a desire to not need therapy. Other reasons as well may play a part.

Let us first assume that the reluctance of other family members to participate is the result of a lack of education about how they can be helpful. In such scenarios, getting their involvement may require only a brief statement or two detailing how they can be valuable. Such comments as "I need a consultation with the family for a broader perspective" or "More heads means more information and more solutions so having multiple perspectives in here is very important" may serve to engender family members' cooperation. Once family members become involved in treatment, it is often not too difficult to keep including them or to be able to call on them with some predictability at any given point in therapy, especially if the focus of treatment ostensibly is the identified patient.

Unfortunately, systemic treatment does not always handle nonsymptomatic family members in ways that maintain their comfort. It will happen at some point in most cases that the focus of attention will be on someone other than the IP, and in these situations, you will need to be ready to help reluctant family members to participate or to continue participating. There are many ways to do this, ranging from playful and gentle to rather heavy-handed to quite strategic. You must be able to operate in any of these areas as necessary if you wish to keep more people in treatment than just symptomatic individuals.

The key is determining when to challenge and when to seduce. Some families do very well when they are confronted with a rational and logical explanation for why their participation is crucial to successful treatment. Explanations of this nature tend to be challenges that many families are willing to meet. Other families that view treatment of more than the IP as a threat will not respond well to this type of approach; thus, you may need to seduce them in some way. We have developed a list of strategies that can be used to challenge, seduce, or both. We call them, only partially tongue-in-cheek, the List of Appeals. A caveat or two: If you are uncomfortable with any of the following strategies, by all means do not attempt to use them. It should also be noted that there are no magic bullets that will work every time to get other family members in, just as there are no foolproof interventions, therapy models, or therapists. Also, we assume that confidentiality requirements have been addressed properly before you make contact with outside persons.

Appeal to Future Reality

One implicit misconception about therapy that some families (and individual clients) have is that therapy is de facto an ongoing, regular, and permanent part of life, like eating, celebrating holidays, and paying taxes. The expectation of having a therapist sometimes is that "you are my therapist . . . forever." Most clinicians, in contrast, tend to think in terms of one day, sooner or later, working themselves out of a job with each case. In instances in which clients and their families hold the expectation of permanent therapy, reminding them that therapy (at least from a systemic point of view) is not supposed to be a regular part of the rest of one's life can be useful. The future reality is one in which the IP ideally is functioning well enough to not need regular and ongoing treatment.

The assumption for many families is that there will always be a therapist for the IP; hence, the family's involvement or participation is irrelevant and unnecessary. Challenge that assumption directly by stating that (1) you are not forever, (2) your care and concern for the IP, genuine as it is, can never replace that of the IP's own family, (3) the family and IP will likely have to deal with each other for many years to come, and (4) you are not coming home with them. You can underscore your point by stating that because of the foregoing, it obviously is not in anyone's best interests for you to be the IP's permanent surrogate family.

This manner of challenge can provide potent impetus for change. The family may change therapists to find one that will accept the role they expect (which unfortunately may not be very hard to do, but at least you will be freed from the potential frustrations, and the family may remember you if and when they come to a point where they really want to do something differently). Conversely, the family may be jolted into becoming more willing to be involved in treatment. There needs to be the understanding that changes are not genuine until they occur in contexts outside of therapy, and the most important context is usually the family.

Appeal to Logic

Many families that have had little involvement in a member's therapy in the past, or little contact with mental health services at all, may not recognize that systemic therapy is a viable, perhaps highly recommended, approach. They may not understand very well how their roles may affect the person with the problem; in fact, they may reject the idea that they have anything to do with it. For your part, attempting to explain the various intrafamilial connections and patterns may prove to be frustrating and time-consuming, only to yield minimal results in getting others into therapy. You may be able to bypass all of this by appealing to the following logical thought: "You may not have the problem, but you may have the solution."

This places the family in the perhaps unfamiliar position of being helpful in the eyes of the professional. For the many families that have been vilified by their symptomatic members' therapists in times past, this reversal could be quite refreshing, and it may open up a host of new behavioral and interactional possibilities, which eventually lead to significant change. It may also serve to empower those families that never realized the degree to which they can influence situations typically thought of as pertaining only to a given individual.

Appeal to Caretaking

A similar strategy to appealing to logic is the idea that the therapist needs help to accomplish the job—help that only the family can provide. Oftentimes, families view mental health professionals in terms similar to medical personnel. Specifically, the professional is the expert and knows all that is needed to be able to succeed. Family involvement is not necessary, and certainly the professional would not need assistance from laypersons. To be asked directly for assistance via inclusion in treatment might be an intriguing and flattering change for family members.

Alternatively, some families feel so stuck with their difficulties related to the IP that they feel a sense of commiseration or sympathy for the clinician. After all, the family understands the frustrations that occur in dealing with the IP, and now they may empathize with the therapist that "has to work with their dysfunctional family member." They may have a strong desire to take care of the clinician, to keep him or her from giving up or feeling hopeless with their member.

Being a new therapist in these circumstances can be very useful. You can appeal to the family's desire to be helpful to *you* as the professional, irrespective of the IP. As a new therapist, the family will be likely to feel your need to succeed and that may resonate with them to the degree that they will go out of their way to help you if asked. Saying "I need your help" may open the door for the involvement from other family members that makes a big difference.

Appeal to Protection

Another strategy that can be utilized to engage other family members in therapy is to appeal to their need to protect the IP, themselves, or both from the threat a well-meaning but largely incompetent therapist may present. Peter Sellers' unforgettable detective Inspector Clousseau from *The Pink Panther* movie series comes to mind here, as does Peter Falk's feigned dull-witted character in *Columbo*, wherein an apparently bumbling incompetent gets the job done well. Appealing to protection from incompetence requires the clinician to take a step beyond needing help, but it must be done carefully. You will need to look almost a bit loony, or very frustrated, or give the appearance of being at your wit's end, while at the same time not pushing it so hard that the family or IP just drops out. One way to do this is to send the IP home with rather strange homework assignments of a strategic nature. An example of this might sound like the following: "When you feel really depressed and hopeless, it is important to not send your family mixed signals by telling them you are okay. Therefore, go to your room and turn off all the lights, sit in the middle of the floor in the dark, and moan and sigh until you feel a little better, or until they come and talk to you." The family's response to these sorts of maneuvers may be intense and negative, but their willingness to come in and see what is going on is likely to be increased. Once this happens, you can capitalize on their presence to make sure you are getting things right, all the while introducing new ideas and information into the system.

Appeal to Correct Representation

A variation on the appeal to protection is the appeal to correct representation. People do not like to be thought poorly of in most cases, and here is where you may take advantage of family members' desires to look like wonderful people, or at least normal, decent human beings. The basic idea here is to give unusual or provocative feedback about other family members that will eventually have the effect of making somebody come in to straighten you out. You may find that the IP will vigorously defend his or her family members, even if this causes personal hurt (after all, that may be the reason the IP is in therapy in the first place). You must not appear to accept unquestioningly his or her story in its entirety, but rather reserve the right explicitly to wonder about the accuracy of what you hear. This is where the Freudian notions of the unconscious, etc., can be so useful, even if you do not subscribe to object relations ideas. You can use these terms and others to offer persistently unpalatable interpretations and explanations that will ultimately get back to the family and make them feel that they are not being viewed accurately.

Once they come in, if they do, you may have to deal with their ire, but you will certainly have their attention. This is when you can take a friendly yet skeptical position: "I know you would never do or say anything to deliberately hurt so-and-so [or something to that effect], but I wonder if you can do this and that . . . to prove it." The family members may make changes less for the IP and more so that they will look better in your eyes, or so that they can escape from the trap you have set for them.

Appeal to Pride

Sometimes engendering cooperation on the part of reluctant family members requires direct provocation. If you have found the family unwilling to participate after several attempts to include them, you may have to raise the intensity by interpreting their refusal as fear, specifically as fear of change. This may *feel* manipulative, but in all likelihood, you are merely calling a spade a spade. Many families get stuck, as you will recall from your theory courses, when they are unable to manage a transition, whether "normative" or unexpected (Hoffman, 1981). Thus, symptoms develop, and treatment may be sought. Interestingly, most families do not want to admit being afraid of change, or at least some members of families will not want to admit it.

When you bring their hidden fears to light by saying that you can understand their reluctance to participate because they are afraid, they are placed in the position of either accepting your statement that they are afraid or proving you wrong. This is an appeal to pride. Many men in our culture especially do not like to be called "chickens," especially when they are being told that their fear of something as innocuous-appearing as talking to somebody at some clinic about another person's problems is understandable. This can be a very good way to get otherwise emotionally closed persons into therapy.

Appeal to Guilt

Most of the time, family members feel bad about the IP's problems, even if they do not believe they have anything to do with them. You can attempt to get their participation without ever directly addressing their contribution to the system by appealing to the guilt they would feel if they did not do everything they could to be a help to their suffering member. Utilizing a "you should keep up with the Joneses" attitude, wherein you state that you usually have little trouble getting other family members in because they care for their IPs and that it is a typical procedure for you, can be a powerful motivating force. It may be, too, that many family members understand at some level that the IP does not live in a vacuum and that there must be some connection for them to examine in therapy somewhere. By appealing to their latent guilt, you may provide the impetus for them to come in and make something happen.

Appeal to Duty

When you are working with children, one way to make it easier to keep parents involved is to appeal to their sense of duty. Parents, even parents whose children are well into adulthood, will do for their children things that they would never do for themselves, and one of those things is going to therapy. An adult may simply refuse to acknowledge a problem in him or herself, but when it comes to a problem manifested in a child, the rules change. You can make good use of this. As you know, many child-focused problems have systemic underpinnings that need to be addressed to alleviate the presenting symptoms, and it is much easier to make systemic interventions when more of the system is in your office. Even if your focus is ostensibly the child, it should be comparatively easy to include the parents regularly by appealing as necessary to their sense of duty.

Appeal to Frustration

Many times, a family with an IP will be very frustrated with the stuckness they experience. This is especially true if the problem is a chronic one. If they have been to therapy before and have yet to see significant progress in the IP, their frustration may make them more willing to participate. Then again, they may staunchly refuse because to do so would be to accept the possibility that the problem includes them. Either way, their frustration is useful leverage, and you can appeal to it as needed.

Among the ways to do this is to adopt Haley's stance about making a pact with the devil (Haley, 1984). You can do this by telling the family that you have some ideas that may make a difference for the IP and for the family, but that you have some concerns that they may not be really ready to hear them and act on them. In fact, tell them it may be precisely the worst thing they can do, and that they are not yet frustrated enough to warrant change. It will be likely that the family will be amazed at you and then they may go to significant lengths to tell you that you are misreading them. They may be willing to do almost anything to relieve themselves of the albatross of stuckness, at which point you have them ready to cooperate.

Appeal to Fear

The next step up from appealing to frustration is appealing to fear. Chances are that if the family is frustrated enough, the only thing they would admit to being worse than change would be no change (even if they are highly ambivalent). At this point, you can threaten to fire them and/or the IP because they will not cooperate with your treatment plan. If you are viewed as the last hope and they believe that if therapy with you does not make a difference, they are going to receive back their symptomatic member unchanged, their underlying systemic commitment to no change may be put in jeopardy. You need to be careful that this particular appeal makes sense. Your supervisor or agency director may not be enthused about this strategy at all.

Appeal to Cynicism

Finally, some families resign themselves to the belief that their IPs will never change and therapy is not going to be effective. They usually stop short of advocating discontinuing treatment, though, if for no other reason than it does not reflect well on them. The appeal to cynicism is an attractive escape for the family that believes things are hopeless, because it comes from a professional who is saying that things may be better left alone and that it is possible nothing more can be done. Before this position is ratified, however, you need to advocate that it may be a good idea to get together with the family and the IP to see for certain if this is true. In a way, the family is being challenged to test the mettle of the IP's stuckness in ways they may have not done before.

Remember, the goal of all these strategies is getting others in—what happens once they arrive is another story, which we will address later. You should not expect that you will be successful more than you are not. When it comes down to it, some family members just will not attend therapy for any reason or any person. You need to recognize this and try working around such limitations when they are placed on you. All you can do is make the effort to get other family members in. When you are successful, you will probably find therapy often goes a bit better, but you are certainly not doomed to failure if you cannot engage reluctant family members in treatment. Their absence just makes treatment a little harder.

COUPLES THERAPY WITH RELUCTANT PARTNERS

Commonly, you will find yourself in an initial interview with an individual who is half of a couple and who states that marital or couple therapy is desired, but that the partner will not attend. In our experience, more often it will be the woman in your office and the man who is portrayed as reluctant—but not always. In any case, this is a special problem because the object of therapeutic attention is supposed to be a relationship, but you do not get to see it firsthand.

How can you get the other person in? First, you should ask the partner who is present if he or she in fact asked the other partner to come. Surprisingly, the person you are seeing often is *assuming* the other person is reluctant, and has not actually asked him or her specifically to come to see a particular therapist (you) at a particular time on a particular day because the expectation is that the answer will be no. This is useful systemic information. Sometimes, all it takes is encouraging your individual client to actually invite the partner.

Sometimes, however, the invitation is refused. At that point, determining the *why* can be beneficial. It may be that the reluctant partner has been blasted by a therapist before—we find that some people are leery of therapists who are the same gender as the spouse. If there is no reason given (assuming the partner you are seeing is telling you the truth—sometimes a large assumption!), or if you have no reason to believe that anything the presenting partner can say will do the trick, you can ask the client for permission (get the consent forms signed) to call the partner and ask him or her yourself. In that conversation, you may make use of any of the appeals already discussed in this chapter. The appeals to correct representation, pride, and duty have shown in our experience to be particularly useful in engaging reluctant spouses. To a lesser degree, the appeals to protection and cynicism can also be useful with reluctant pertners.

The difficult reality, though, is again that some people will not participate in therapy under any conditions. In those instances, you must work with what you have access to, and you must do the best you can with that. Sometimes that will be enough to bring about change; other times, it will not. All you can do is put forth your best effort.

Chapter 8

Referrals and the Use
of Nonsystemic Tools

In this chapter we will discuss the types of referrals that a marriage and family therapist typically will have to consider in clinical practice. In our experience, beginning therapists have a limited amount of contact with and knowledge of other sources of help, and this is unfortunate. Although the referral sources we will discuss often themselves depart from the systemic thinking that characterizes marriage and family therapy, they can add a degree of thoroughness at a level meta to the client system, which will complement the therapy you provide for them. As we have previously discussed, there are distinct advantages to considering the systemic perspective for the valuable expanded view of a case it can offer; however, it is also important to consider the value in the type of expanded view offered by nonsystemic referral sources. In short, from a systemic point of view, including nonsystemic referral sources in treatment is a very smart and systemically valid way to practice! Those nonsystemic tools we will examine are psychological testing; psychiatric evaluations regarding psychotropic medication and psychiatric hospitalization, referral, and consultation with other physicians and referral and consultation with nonmedical service providers.

PSYCHOLOGICAL TESTING

It is important to remember that human beings are very complex and complicated systems themselves. The information gathered from questions to and observations of clients and family members is the heart of a systemic approach to therapy. However, it would be foolish to assume that this approach we find so valuable to understanding human problems is the one-and-only way to proceed, or that it is alone always complete. Puristic assumptions aside, organic and emotional complications exist that are not readily identified in the therapy process and that may have serious implications for the treatment of a client/couple/family. In addition, intrapsychic phenomena in individuals may have a profound impact on the relationships they create and participate in and the behaviors in which they engage. Psychological tests allow for the possibility of accessing and interpreting (and perhaps making very logical sense of otherwise hard to understand) data that therapists routinely encounter.

Although psychological testing is sometimes viewed with the skepticism associated with an exercise in "looking into a crystal ball," there is very useful information available when a referral with very specific questions and/or concerns is made to a competent clinical psychologist or school psychologist. A number of important issues can be explored through psychological testing that may have a crucial bearing on the treatment of a case. For example, in instances in which the level of a person's intellectual ability may be uncertain, their ability to understand and participate adequately in therapy is in doubt. The same can be said for the issue of academic ability in a child with learning and behavior problems or an adult whose avoidance tendencies may be due to embarrassment or shame regarding poor reading, writing, or math skills. Problems with extreme or bizarre behavior can raise the concerns of neurological dysfunction due to trauma, substance abuse, or disease (delirium, dementia, and amnesic disorders); communication and pervasive developmental disorders in children and adolescents; and the disturbed thought processes involved in schizophrenia and other psychotic disorders. Personality factors can also be identified that affect or organize the ways in which individuals routinely operate, and knowing something about these can make a great difference in how you go about working with clients.

An issue pertaining to testing of unquestionable popularity in recent years is the area of attention deficit/hyperactivity disorder (ADD/ADHD). Many parents are concerned (or convinced) that their children's learning and/or behavioral problems may be better treated (and accepted by the parents' ego) as biochemically based problems with attention, concentration, memory, impulsivity, and hyperactivity, which require a formal diagnosis with medication and special educational programming. There is also an increased interest on the part of adults who, with this issue's recent popularity, feel the need for diagnosis and treatment of a now-identified "legitimate" problem that they feel they have experienced beginning in childhood on into the present. Implications for therapy are important when considering whether these concerns are legitimate problems needing special services or convenient "scapegoats" to avoid confronting more challenging issues with regards to the child, adult, couple, or family.

A final area is the topic of repressed memories or partially acknowledged traumatic events from the past. While there has been some real concern expressed about the overzealous pursuit and diagnosis of these conditions by narrowly focused "symptom specialist" professionals, there are times when behavioral patterns and verbal reports of a client raise a question regarding the presence of disturbing but unconscious experiences. The carefully considered, cautious, and patient approach to evaluating suspected unconscious issues through psychological testing can be useful to a marriage and family therapist with serious concerns about a client's emotional functioning.

Some of the tests and measures that the competent marriage and family therapist should be familiar with at the fundamental level include intelligence tests, with two very popular ones today being the Wechsler Adult Intelligence Scale (WAIS) (Wechsler, 1981) and the Wechsler Intelligence Scale for Children (WISC) (Wechsler, 1991); various tests of continual attention/performance; projective tests such as the House-Tree-Person Drawing Technique (Buck, 1970) and the Rorschach (Exner, 1978); and personality/symptomatology inventories such as the Minnesota Multiphasic Personality Inventory (MMPI) (Hathaway and McKinley, 1989). Each of the named instruments enjoys a wide acceptance among the various mental health disciplines, and each can provide some extremely valuable information about a given person's functioning. The MMPI, for instance, can help a therapist understand the way a client attempts to be perceived and the degree to which they experience some of the symptoms they have, as well as provide data pertaining to alcohol and substance abuse, responses to authority, and somatization. If you are unfamiliar with these measures, we encourage you to develop a basic understanding of them so at the very least you may utilize them in cases where they have been administered, if not suggest their usage on your own initiative.

Two caveats to bear in mind with regard to nonsystemic tests and assessments such as those mentioned previously: First, marriage and family therapists are not usually trained to administer or interpret these instruments; thus if you have not received formal training on them, you may not present yourself as an expert on them, nor can you use them on your own without a formally trained clinician (usually a psychologist). Second, these instruments offer windows of information concerning the clients to whom they are applied, but they are not necessarily any more or less valid than simple in-session observation. Yogi Berra's humorous contention that "you can observe a lot just by watching" is very true; therefore, avoid the trap of assigning undue weight to written tests and measures. (We are confident that most systemically trained therapists will not have any problem staying away from this mistake, but it is worth mentioning anyway.)

PSYCHIATRIC EVALUATIONS
FOR PSYCHOTROPIC MEDICATION

The use of medication for emotional or psychological difficulties has been practiced and condoned for over half a century, and in recent years, medicine has developed some rather impressive means through which to reduce people's suffering. Our understanding of the biological components of psychopathology has grown significantly in the last few decades, and while by no means is our education complete, we are now able to help effect changes in thought, attitude, and behavior via medical means, in addition to psychotherapy. Consequently, an area of major focus in the delivery of mental health services today, in the era of managed care, is the usage of psychiatric evaluation for prescription of psychotropic medications. With a very real premium being placed on time and resource efficiency, the use of medication to alleviate symptoms (or decrease their severity to allow "regular" psychotherapy to be more effective) is more readily sought.

The use of medication is not without its controversy. There are some professionals who are concerned that managed care companies emphasize this approach to treatment for fiscal efficiency at the expense of quality. There are other professionals concerned that we are promoting an overreliance on drugs to simply mask or alleviate symptoms without any real attention to helping people change how they think, feel, and behave. While both points are well-taken, situations do exist in which the overwhelming physiological and psychological qualities of a symptom make functional daily living a near impossibility. In these situations a client can experience difficulties ranging from decreased benefit of psychotherapy to feeling so overwhelmed as to consider or attempt suicide to escape their "emotional torture." Under these kinds of circumstances, medication can make a huge difference.

Referral to a psychiatrist for a medication evaluation is best considered when the symptoms present either severely disrupt daily functioning or severely disrupt the client's ability to participate in therapy. Symptoms considered here would include depression, anxiety, manic episodes, seizures, hallucinations, delusions, obsessions/compulsions, psychotic thought processes, severe disruption of memory and attention, and serious impulsivity with a potential result of injurious behavior to self or others—suicidal and/or homicidal ideation. The mere presence of one of these symptoms is not a sufficient cause for instant medicating, of course, as it is always a matter of the degree of severity.

This continuum of severity contributes to medication's controversial status. Some clients are nearly totally disabled by a symptom, whereas other clients cope with their difficulties fairly successfully sans medication. What is even more confusing is that some clients cope well at some times and then not at all well at others. A very general rule of thumb to follow in our experience is that if clients can manage reasonably well without medicine and if they do not desire it, it may be that they can stay away from it and still remain functional. The key is to be able to determine where "functional" ends and "disability" begins, which of course varies from client to client and episode to episode.

It is a good idea to be open to both the client's wishes and what benefits may be reaped with medication. Sometimes, it is merely a matter of persuading the client to give medicine a try, while at other times clients' experiences of medicine (and/or psychiatrists) lead them to avoid it like the plague; therefore, creative alternatives need to be considered. Another possibility is the fact that some clients do not always judge themselves very well when it comes to what they need regarding medication, and this is where having input from other family members, physicians, and other sources of information regarding the client's severity can be most helpful.

As a nonmedical provider of mental health services, you must have a solid general understanding of the usage of psychotropic medications. The current medications being utilized and the background of classes of medications can best be obtained through a course or workshop and accompanying textbook on psychopharmacology for counselors and therapists; the *Physician's Desk Reference* (1997), which is updated annually, comes to mind as a user-friendly (insofar as that is possible) manual that is quite popular. We recommend periodically purchasing a pocket reference manual on psychotropic medications that specifically details types of medications by symptom or problem, medication names (brand name and generic), dosage ranges, and the potential and frequency of specific side effects.

In addition to these written sources, it is important to have a human source to consult for information when discussing medication with clients or other professionals. You must always remember that, unless you have had the proper *medical* training, it is unethical for you to provide advice regarding medications. However, it would be equally unethical for you to be uninformed about the medications your clients may already be taking or may be prescribed during the course of treatment with you. You are in the best position when you can acknowledge that you have a familiarity with medications while clearly referring questions concerning specific advice about medications to a physician.

A marriage and family therapist (or other mental health professionals) may encounter specific problems regarding medications.

There are situations in which a client can become over-focused or overinvested in what medications can do for him or her. The hard work of psychotherapy is a relatively unattractive choice when a client is infatuated with the "magic bullet" fantasy that a medication can make their whole life different in a matter of a few short days or weeks. In this instance, a client's investment in "normal" therapy often heads south rather dramatically, and the stage becomes set for major disappointment for the client. There is not much you can do to prevent this usually, but you can otherwise provide a cautiously optimistic and supportive voice that remains there for the client when the medical miracle fails to materialize.

At the other end of the spectrum is the client who is rigidly resistant to even considering a medication consultation despite experiencing debilitating symptoms. It is often a fear of the unknown, media stories or gossip about bad experiences of others, or a belief that the use of medication is an indication of weakness of character that sets the stage for this rigidity. It can be helpful to use analogies of someone taking an antibiotic for the flu (short-term use) or insulin for a diabetic condition (long-term use) to help explain the logic and potential value of a psychotropic medication.

Another potential problem is the client who "doctor hops," that is, someone who gathers prescriptions from numerous physicians (while not telling any one physician about the others) in an effort to stock a "home pharmacy" for instant access to the "quick fix." These clients can be particularly dangerous because of the availability of these very potent weapons (especially when mixed with alcohol) that are a much less messy and unattractive means of committing suicide than are using guns, knives, or automobile crashes. The other danger is that very few clients have any idea that some types of drugs are lethal when mixed together; thus, committing suicide by accident is a greater likelihood. (These more serious types of situations regarding medications will be addressed in the next section.)

As a therapist, it is not your job to unduly push or decide that a client should seek or avoid medication. It is your ethical responsibility to give a client your best judgment. You are advising the client to do no more than consider the suggestion or recommendation that medication may or may not be helpful to his or her task of relieving symptoms. You also have the ethical responsibility to be aware of what your client is taking so that you can factor that into your treatment approach. Ultimately, however, the client's medications are the client's responsibility.

PSYCHIATRIC EVALUATIONS FOR PSYCHIATRIC HOSPITALIZATIONS

There are times, either as part of an intake session or at some point during treatment, when clients will demonstrate a severity of symptoms and quality of mental status that requires psychiatric hospitalization. Mental health agencies will have either a psychiatrist on staff and available either in person or by phone, or they will have a relationship with a psychiatric unit of a local hospital when they need to have a client referred for emergency evaluation and hospitalization. Most often the concern is that the client would be harmful to themselves by either self-mutilation, suicidal gesture, or suicide attempt, but a fair percentage will be more at risk for doing harm to another person or persons. The predominating emotions for most clients in these situations could include the following: anxiety, fear of feeling unsafe or fear of dying as a result of either a specific or unspecified cause; anger, feelings of rage toward and a desire to hurt oneself or others; depression, overwhelming hopelessness with a desire to be dead or to kill oneself; and psychotic thought processes resulting in cognitive impairment auditory and/or visual hallucinations, delusions, strong internal messages to hurt oneself or others. The underlying theme here is that the client is judged as posing a *serious* threat of harm to someone, either self or others—or both.

Your role as a therapist is to identify and assess these characteristics in a client and consult with the appropriate supervisors and/or qualified personnel regarding the appropriate course of action to take. In some situations a client might agree that he or she needs to be hospitalized, and in fact, those clients who have been hospitalized before may have a better sense of their own situation and needs than you. Alternatively, you may be able to enlist the help of a family member who is either present or available who can persuade the individual in question that psychiatric hospitalization is the safest course of action at this point in time. In any event, most hospitalizations that you will have a hand in will be in all likelihood voluntary admissions, where the client makes the decision to be admitted and signs himself or herself in (even though it might be done grudgingly).

In other (fortunately less frequent) situations, clients might strongly resist any suggestion of hospitalization despite verbalizing their intention to hurt themselves or others. In these situations a procedure for involuntary hospitalization may be warranted, and this can become quite uncomfortable for everyone involved. Many licensed nonmedical mental health professionals are certified as public health officers. These individuals, as well as physicians, psychiatrists, and police officers, can generate documentation that allows the client to be forcibly taken to a locked psychiatric inpatient facility for a period of time (often seventy-two hours) for observation and evaluation for his or her own safety and that of others. As a beginning therapist, you will almost never be in a position of making a decision regarding hospitalization by yourself. However, you may very well be the first professional who will interact with the client and/or family when such a crisis occurs.

One thing that we believe is quite rare in most marriage and family therapists' formal training is discussion about what to do when you have a client hospitalized. Obviously, the specific rules and regulations concerning nonhospital professionals' involvement in an inpatient's treatment vary from institution to institution, but in our experience many new professionals seem to "forget" about their hospitalized clients while they are inpatients. This is unfortunate, and is often a large missed opportunity.

Consider for a moment how your average clients are likely to feel upon a hospital admission. They may feel a deep sense of shame and failure that they now cannot seem to even function independently at all, and in fact are on a suicide watch where someone checks on them every fifteen minutes day and night. They may be truly embarrassed in front of family, friends, and colleagues, especially if they attempted "something stupid." There may be a fear that you, the therapist, will be disappointed or angry at them because they are apparently worse and not better. Add to that the varying degrees of compassion and attention they will receive in this strange place from these unfamiliar professionals (that they may have no trust in), as well as the unpredictable nature of interactions with peers dealing with a cornucopia of issues ("I'm not crazy, but some of these people here are!"). Finally, factor in the sudden awareness that the doors are locked and the belief that patients cannot just leave when they want to, and you can imagine that the supportive and concerned face you provide can really add a boost to the power of your therapeutic relationship. (Unless an admission is ordered by a certified public officer, adult inpatients can sign themselves out whenever they want, although most people do not realize this, especially when they are in such a turbulent emotional state. When clients hospitalize themselves as a precaution against suicidal or homicidal threat, they can leave at their own choosing if they cannot be judged as at serious risk and thus be involuntarily admitted. In these situations, a self-initiated discharge is considered AMA, against medical advice.)

Our advice is to continue your involvement as much as possible with hospitalized clients insofar as you can. At the very least, visit or call your client, and try to have release of information forms signed so you can talk with the psychiatrist in charge of the case, as well as other hospital staff. We have often found that inpatient clinicians welcome the input of outpatient professionals who are involved in patients' treatment. If you can have a hand in treatment planning or in consultation, or even have a session or two during your client's stay, so much the better, but regardless of the degree of your hands-on involvement, we suggest you encourage your clients to avail themselves of the various therapeutic opportunities an inpatient setting can afford them.

REFERRAL AND CONSULTATION WITH OTHER PHYSICIANS

Regardless of your contact with hospitals, psychiatric and otherwise, it will not be unusual for clients to want to discuss either current or past medical problems that affect their emotional functioning. They may relay this information in the initial diagnostic assessment when specifically asked about medical concerns, or in subsequent sessions when they feel more comfortable about sharing this information. It may also occur that a medical problem develops during therapy and would be a concern the client wishes to discuss at that time.

It will be important, as it was with psychotropic medications, that you have a familiarity with medical conditions and treatments. A comprehensive medical dictionary or encyclopedia, such as *Stedman's Medical Dictionary,* at your disposal will allow quick access to information about medical problems a client may report in therapy. As there will also be times when you are asked to consult with a client's physician regarding his or her psychotherapy and the treatment of concurrent medical problems, your familiarity with the client's medical condition will be especially important. Your consultation with the client's physician can be vital in generating a sense of trust for your client as well as in the physician who would potentially refer other clients to your agency, and to you specifically.

Again, it is critical that you remember that you cannot offer or give "medical advice" regarding a client's medical concerns. Even if you have personal knowledge of the specific problem, you must direct a client to a physician for advice and recommendations. The last place you would want to be is in a courtroom hearing your client state, "My therapist told me that I shouldn't worry about XYZ medical condition." It is appropriate to be able to demonstrate that you have some understanding of your client's medical condition. However, conveying this understanding to your client should never be presented as competency in medical matters or any specific advice or recommendations. The only recommendation appropriate for you as a marriage and family therapist to make to a client is for him or her to consult a family physician or a specialist regarding the condition in question.

For this reason, it is important to have available a list of physicians about whom you have some knowledge personally, or through colleagues or other clients, that you can utilize when a client needs a referral but does not have a regular physician he or she can consult. Examples of other medical (or medically related) professionals that would be included in this category include dentists, chiropractors, physical therapists, occupational therapists, and massage therapists. Offering to contact the physician or other professional personally on the client's behalf is not a bad idea, either. This way you can initiate contact with the other persons as well as make the referral process smoother for your clients.

It may be a client's wish to discuss medical conditions that cause him or her anxiety and concern, but about which he or she has not yet discussed with a physician. It is both appropriate and ethical for you to advise a client to seek a medical consultation to resolve his or her questions and concerns. Clients may be frightened to discuss the condition with family members and hence deprive themselves of the valuable support they need to face their fear and consult a physician. In this particular situation, your value may be as a trusted but "neutral" party who can provide the encouragement to them to have the problem addressed by a physician, i.e., the "better safe than sorry" strategy.

REFERRAL AND CONSULTATION WITH NONMEDICAL SERVICE PROVIDERS

You will most likely have occasion to refer to and consult with service providers who are not medical professionals. Examples of these providers might be attorneys, financial management counselors, teachers and educational tutors, rabbis, pastors, ministers, and priests. The most important consideration in referring and consulting with these providers, besides having signed permission to release information in each specific situation, is to engender an atmosphere of collegial respect. It can be harmful to clients when two different service providers handle referral and consultation situations with a competitive attitude. Part of respecting your client is the attitude and approach you take with other professionals he or she has or may choose to consult. You are in dangerous territory if you approach client concerns as if you are the only professional with which he or she needs to consult. This type of arrogance leaves clients in a position of having to choose with whom they will confide and invest their trust. An important part of our professional position is to allow clients to direct their own lives through the choices they make in consulting various professional resources.

Clients will inevitably have concerns that they discuss in therapy which could best benefit from the client consulting one of these types of providers. You must not allow a client to try to use you as a source of legal, financial, educational, or spiritual advice. Again, we are not saying that clients should not discuss these concerns, nor that you should have absolutely nothing to say about such concerns. It is vital that you recognize the defined area of your profession and expertise. It can be very damaging to a client for you to either present yourself as competent outside your profession or be "seduced" into providing advice in an area in which the client should be consulting a more appropriate professional.

Overall, the competent marriage and family therapist is in the best professional position when he or she is familiar with the broadest range of treatment modalities, tools, and professionals, and is comfortable utilizing them as needed. We recommend continuing your training to obtain this level of breadth so that your clients may be all the more well served. Now, we turn to one of the most often ignored mundanities yet absolute essentials of professional practice: documentation. Be ready to take notes . . .

Chapter 9

Documentation and Case Management: The Job Ain't Done Till . . .

The dramatic and exciting work of marriage and family therapy is described in great detail in every teaching videotape, every training workshop, every class, and every written work on the subject. What is rarely, if ever, presented is the less-than-breathtaking endeavors of documentation and case management. Admittedly, discussion about documentation and case management and the actual practice of them are about as effective at inducing sleep as a serious dose of sodium pentathol (When was the last time you heard about an exciting weekend workshop at some world-famous resort where the topic to be examined was how to write case notes?). The problem with this lack of attention is that documentation is as critically important in your professional work as *anything* else you do. In the real world of clinical practice, it is a greater concern that your clinical documentation be done correctly and in a timely fashion than whether you have read the latest book or journal dealing with snazzy treatment techniques. Case management concerns are what can make or break a therapist over the long haul; therapists who learn to handle their cases efficiently and effectively are much less likely to burn out or make critical blunders than are therapists who never learn to manage cases well.

As the subtitle of this chapter hints, "the job ain't done until the paperwork is finished." This means that the documentation must be completed thoroughly, competently, and on time to ensure that the rights of the client and the requirements of the agency and funding sources are safeguarded, not to mention that your performance (and that of your supervisor) clinically can be shown to stand up to the professional standard of scrutiny. No matter how good a job you may do in providing clinical services, your work (and hence, your professional reputation) will always be suspect and vulnerable if it has not been appropriately documented. You can be the most gifted therapist on the planet, but if your paperwork and record-keeping skills are underdeveloped, you will be at risk to numerous hazards.

DOCUMENTATION

Unfortunately, if your training is like that of many clinicians, the time you spent focused on documentation during your professional preparation is only slightly more than that spent on discussing the merits of using blue versus pink paper for forms. This is a very large drawback with several potentially life-changing ramifications. The management that you provide to a therapy case extends beyond simply conducting therapy sessions. It is ultimately judged by the careful documentation of all the services you provide for that case, and this is why the job's completion is a function of finished paperwork. A service is defined as any and all of the following: a session with a client and/or his or her family members, a consultation (written, verbally in person, or by phone) with another professional, a consultation (written, verbally in person, or by phone) with a nonprofessional relevant to the client (family members, a spouse, significant other, employer), and any emergency contacts with clients and related parties. In short, anything you do as a marriage and family therapy professional on behalf of a client can be considered a service, and each service must be documented adequately.

The implications for inappropriate or inaccurate documentation are very serious for a therapist. Do not make the grave error of taking them lightly. If a particular service is not documented in the client chart or case file, then it technically did not happen; thus, the phone call you had for two minutes yesterday from the school counselor who told you Suzie Q. Client was kicked out of school and is pregnant never occurred if there is no note about it in the file. This may appear merely annoying, and it is, but there is much more to be concerned with than that.

There are two obvious reasons for why failing to take adequate time and attention to documentation should give you a nasty rash: *liability* and *money*. The thoughtful steps you took at the end of your session last Thursday to ensure that Mr. Huttlestutz was not actively homicidal or suicidal and thus did not require hospitalization count for nothing if they are not included in the file. If he takes over the local Pizzas 'R Us Saturday night with a gun and puts a lot of holes in the citizenry, or if he swan dives off the town water tower, your actions to protect him, the public, and yourself had better be in the file. If they are not, they did not happen, and you are in more trouble than you could ever imagine. Your effort to replace missing documentation with your verbal recollection and report of the service is a legal nightmare. Your competence and judgment as a professional as a result are suspect and would surely be in serious question if you ever ended up in a court proceeding in which you are subpoenaed to testify. Obviously, liability concerns in these situations are scary, and only adequate documentation can afford you some measure of protection.

Another reason for precise and thorough documentation pertains to reimbursement. Anything not in the file cannot be clinically or legally recognized or reimbursed. If you had a two-hour phone call with Mrs. Cornflake during a family crisis, or the Cornflakes came in for an unexpected emergency session, you might like to be reimbursed for that time. Without the proper documentation, you cannot bill anyone for this service. Conversely, sometimes third-party payers like to see some documentation for billed services, and so the file had better accurately reflect the log of services delivered. If a discrepancy is discovered during an internal or external quality assurance review, unpleasant repercussions will ensue, and there may even be demands for the return of previously disbursed funds. You do not want to end up owing your employer money because a third-party payer demanded the return of insurance payments that were ruled fraudulent as a result of inadequate documentation (and this might be the least of your troubles).

INSURANCE INFORMATION

The range of all the necessary documentation that accompanies a typical therapy case can be staggering. Even before the first session begins, you or the agency support staff must first gather client demographic information on some type of intake form. You must also obtain clients' insurance information, which usually includes a copy of their insurance card(s) and signed permission to communicate with their insurance company regarding authorizations for services and claims payment. Most insurance companies will accept standard HCFA-1500 forms for claims submission, but sometimes they will have their own specialized claim forms that require documentation by the therapist rather than just the billing clerk. All phone calls with insurance companies to verify benefits or discuss clinical information for authorization or precertification of sessions must be documented. You must be able to substantiate your contacts to ensure that the billing of services proceeds without delay and to verify to your client that the necessary and appropriate contacts with his or her insurance company have occurred.

CONSENT FORMS

During the initial session, you must obtain the client's consent, in writing, for the various activities in therapy in which they will be involved. Simply put, you need to be sure you have permission to do what you are doing before you begin doing it. Generally, this would involve at the least a consent for treatment form that gives you and the agency permission to provide clinical services to the client. Additionally, there may be a need for signed release of information forms for any professional resources (previous treatment providers, referring professionals, concurrent treatment providers, etc.) with whom you may have contact about the client. If you are under close supervision, meaning that your therapy with a client will be observed live or on videotape by your supervisor and/or colleagues, then you will need to have the client(s) give permission for the observation and taping involved in the supervision. If you are planning to use any data from the client's therapy in any type of research, you must also obtain their permission for their case data to be utilized in such a fashion. An excellent source for examples of every type of form you may use would be the *AAMFT Forms Book* (Piercy, Laswell, and Brock, 1989), which is available directly from AAMFT in Washington, DC.

You may find that clients have little or no problem with the simple consent for treatment form, but as you increase the number of forms to sign, clients become more curious, cautious, and/or reluctant, especially when terms such as "videotape" or "research" are mentioned. We suggest that you train yourself to utilize the forms as standard operating procedures that are accompanied by the activities they disclose. If you intend to use videotape or live supervision regularly, get in the habit of mentioning to clients the benefits they will receive as a result—more professionals who are there to help at no additional charge, the opportunity to review your sessions with them for more focus, etc. Treat the various forms as normal parts of getting therapy started, but do not railroad clients or move more quickly than they are comfortable. Answer honestly and respectfully any questions or concerns they may have, and do your best to accommodate any requests they may make with regard to the different forms and procedures.

DIAGNOSIS, TREATMENT PLANNING, AND TREATMENT SUMMARIES

The specific documentation of the therapy begins with the initial diagnostic assessment discussed in Chapter 4. A case has not been appropriately opened until it has a written assessment that includes a description of the presenting problem, relevant historical information, a diagnosis, and a treatment plan. The treatment plan is a document of growing importance in this era of managed care (see Chapter 10). This documentation requires that you identify the particular goals of the treatment, including specific short- and long-term objectives, the prognosis and specific timelines for these objectives, and the types of treatment modalities and interventions you plan to utilize. You will often develop a treatment plan early in your professional practice with your supervisor, whose signature will be required, and who may continue to sign off on treatment plans as long as she is your boss. Collaborating to develop a treatment plan is usually a very good idea and very helpful for the therapist, so do not view it as a necessary annoyance (it also gives your supervisor a sense of your own clinical skill and ability).

The treatment plan is not to be viewed as a document carved in stone, but rather a game plan for therapy that can and will most likely be revised as therapy progresses and develops (as we discussed in Chapter 6). Most agencies, accrediting bodies, and reimbursement sources require a written update and summary of the treatment plan at ninety-day intervals while the case is still active. These documents should summarize the treatment over the past ninety days, with specific attention to what has been described in the treatment plan. This would include describing specific progress or lack thereof, justification for continuing the current treatment plan, or the proposal of changes and revisions to the plan. In some cases where there has been either significant progress or no progress at all, you will need to justify whether services should be continued for the case.

When you terminate a case, a treatment summary report must be generated in order for the case to be closed. Just as a case is not properly opened without the treatment plan, so it is not properly closed without the treatment summary. The summary documents what was done in therapy and the results of therapy in terms of progress, and it may include recommendations for follow-up or subsequent services and a prognosis regarding the potential for relapse. Whether the specific goals outlined in the treatment plan were met and the degree to which they were should be delineated. A good treatment summary should serve more or less the same function as a good journal article abstract—it lets you know what happened to whom and how in a short and succinct way.

DOCUMENTING INDIVIDUAL THERAPY SESSIONS

The specific record of each therapy session, typically called a case note or a progress note, is probably the most difficult documentation for therapists to do and the easiest for therapists to procrastinate about doing. (In our experience, the most frequently used rationalization for procrastination is that the entire range of documents the therapist is required to produce and keep updated is the worst enemy, leading down the path to burnout.) Case notes should always reflect a focus consistent with what has been outlined in the treatment plan although a high degree of variability is not unusual in terms of how directly what you are doing in a given session relates to the problem being addressed. The obvious exception to this is when the treatment focus explicitly changes consequent to a new perspective or new information presented by the client during that particular session. These changes should be described very clearly and then included in the treatment plan via an addendum or the next scheduled ninety-day review.

Many formats for case notes exist, and you should adopt one that suits you well and use it consistently. Additionally, an increasing number of new computer software packages for producing complete clinical records for easy access and managed care compatibility are becoming available. You may be free to make your choice from among these. However, most agencies will have a format that they have administratively and clinically determined most appropriate for themselves, and so you should use that one and become proficient with it.

Despite all the effort to make therapy's documentation very objective and organized in nature, it remains a challenging task to capture on paper not only the "nuts and bolts" facts and data, but also the essence of the complex intrapersonal and interpersonal dynamics of a fifty-minute session. A major part of the difficulty is the fact that this activity is supposed to be accomplished immediately after the session you just had (and before your next session begins ten minutes later) so as to eliminate the possibility that you will "lose" (through innocent forgetfulness) the important facts and impressions of the session. The time crunch can be a problem, especially if you or your clients start running late. Furthermore, as you may have already found, a therapist has many thoughts about a session well after the session is finished. Some of our best observations and insights come days later, particularly after supervision sessions or peer consultation sessions with our colleagues. Nonetheless, case note entries are best taken care of shortly after a session for both the clinical and legal implications that are the basis of all documentation.

Case notes need to be the "right" length, meaning long enough to contain all the essential facts and impressions for you (or another therapist) to follow the flow of the case, and short enough to not be cumbersome and cluttered. The case note length should be balanced, as too brief a note leaves you vulnerable when it is reviewed or cited, and too long a note makes it less useful because the reader must go "excavating" to find the important points of what took place. Learning to write good case notes that are the "right" length with the "right" information requires practice, and you will find yourself getting better at it if you pay attention to what you are doing.

One way that we have discovered to begin thinking about writing case notes is to make use of the SOAP method, an acronym that stands for subjective, objective, action, and plan. The subjective component of the note is your clinical observations and impressions of what happened in session, and that may include your hypotheses about intrapsychic functioning, or system dynamics, or whatever your thoughts are. The objective component is what is actually seen and heard in the session—just the facts, so to speak, and the language used to reflect this should remind you of a rather boring newspaper article: "Hilda stated that she was angry at George, and reported that she had locked him out of the bedroom four nights last week. George laughed out loud at this point, and Hilda became enraged and cursed at him." The action component of the note is the part in which describe the interventions or therapeutic moves you made in session and their effects, and the plan component should reflect how the session relates to the treatment plan, as well as updates in terms of what will be on the agenda for the next session. These four components can be written together, or they can be written in separate sections, although this tends to reduce their readability. In any event, following this general format should start you on the way toward writing good case notes. In any case, notes should be written as soon as possible after a session, definitely on the same day.

DOCUMENTING COLLATERAL COMMUNICATIONS

Another area of case management that gets short shrift in most therapists' training is collateral communication. Collateral communications involve contacts in person and by telephone with either professionals or nonprofessionals directly involved with the case, both within as well as outside the agency. Examples might be a child's teacher, a spouse's attorney, a previous therapist, a physician currently treating the client for a medical problem, a probation officer, an extended family member, or a managed care case manager. These contacts are just as important as case notes in achieving a complete and accurate documentation of a case, and so they must be included with equal care. While it may not seem crucial at first glance, you will understand and appreciate the importance of documenting these contacts the first time you (and the chart) are subpoenaed to court. A thoroughly documented chart is a therapist's best friend when faced with questions and cross-examination in a courtroom. A poorly documented chart can be a therapist's worst nightmare, and it can lead to the termination of employment, license suspensions or revocations, lawsuits, and even jail.

THERAPIST ACCESSIBILITY

The issue of therapist accessibility is a major one with regard to case management because you often have a larger say in it than in other areas of professional practice. Therapist accessibility is an area in which you have to contend with the policies and procedures of the agency that employs you while making your own decisions about the management of your personal and professional lives. How you end up deciding to work this out will have some considerable consequences for most, if not all, areas of your life, and it is a good idea to begin thinking about it sooner than later.

Most agencies employ some type of after-business-hours coverage to handle emergencies presented by clients being treated at the agency. This typically involves a rotation for the therapists, where each clinician periodically is "on call" (to respond to emergencies) for a specified time period (anywhere from two to seven twenty-four-hour days in a row). A beginning therapist may not be involved in this type of rotation at the start of his or her employment depending on licensure considerations and agency policy, but sooner or later, everyone takes a turn. In other instances, beginning therapists are included in this rotation, with supervisory backup available at all times. In these situations you are most often required to wear a pager and remain within a specified distance of the agency so that the pager can receive the signal and you can respond to an emergency in person if necessary. In addition to wearing the pager, when you are "on call," you will most likely be contacted by an answering service at home during the hours when you would be asleep. This scenario is fairly common in all mental health settings; thus, accommodating the demands of your position (i.e., the required invasion of your privacy) in this area is not usually negotiable.

The issue of receiving phone calls at home, however, is also worthy of studied consideration. A question you will need to contemplate is whether or not you would give your home phone number to a client so he or she might call you in an emergency or crisis. Some agencies have policies prohibiting this practice, while some require it, and still other agencies leave this decision in the hands of the therapist. This is a judgment call on your part, and you may want to find out about a given agency's policy on this issue as part of your interviewing process.

There may be times when you determine that it would be therapeutically wise and appropriate to give your home phone number to a client who may need it and, in your judgment, would not abuse it. At other times, you may determine just the opposite—that the client in question would not make reasonable use of having your home phone number and would likely abuse the privilege to compromise the therapeutic process and appropriate therapist-client boundaries. Beyond these key issues, however, are ones pertaining to the effect that allowing clients access to you at home may have on your personal life and relationships. Your spouse, for instance, may not be very excited about answering telephone calls from frenzied clients, or conversely, may attempt to "counsel" them if you are not home when they call. Either response is not desirable, and in fact can lead to severe outcomes for clients and for therapists and their families.

In our experience, an interesting phenomenon has been to watch how various clinicians seem to have clients that call or page them regularly while other therapists are rarely ever paged or called. While we have done no scientific study on this observation and are aware of none that examine it elsewhere (another thesis or dissertation topic ripe for the doing), we suspect that those therapists whose clients "keep them busy" may actually subtly give signals that indicate an openness to contact at home. We are not saying these therapists like it, but rather that they may not be as firm in maintaining professional boundaries as they could be. Nor are we saying that therapists who are not often paged or called at home are better therapists because they may give off signals of unapproachability. Our suggestion in this regard is to be clear and firm, but not hostile or punishing, about clients' permission to contact you away from the office. You as a therapist may want to keep in mind that "it is easier to give up ground than to take it back," whereas clients may think in terms of "it being easier to get forgiveness than permission."

These issues are quite thorny and require some careful reflection. In our view, they are best handled through discussion with your supervisor who, until you are independently licensed, is clinically and legally responsible for your work with clients. In all instances, contact involving emergencies after business hours should be documented in exactly the same way as case notes and collateral contacts are documented during regular working hours. Just because you are "off-duty" does not mean you have the luxury of becoming sloppy. One lawsuit can ruin your whole day, and even longer.

Chapter 10

Dealing with Money Issues Impacting Treatment: Insurance, Managed Care, and Fees

One of the areas in which many marriage and family therapists coming out of training programs find themselves quite confused is financial matters pertaining to their delivery of services. A reason for this confusion lies in the fact that the rate of change in the financial world of medical service, of which psychotherapy is a part, is highly similar to the computer industry—what is most up to date and cutting edge today is old news and nonapplicable tomorrow. In this chapter we will examine the complex and ever-changing world of money matters that impact treatment in mental health services. The three important areas for our consideration are (1) insurance reimbursement for mental health services, (2) the use of managed care organizations in the administration of mental health services reimbursement, and (3) fees paid directly by clients for the services they receive.

In our experience, handling money matters in general is quite uncomfortable for beginning therapists. Some causes for this discomfort include the following: the understandable lack of confidence experienced by beginning therapists in having clients pay for the services they provide ("How could I expect someone to actually pay for therapy from me?"); the anxiety of exposing their work to the scrutiny of a managed care company or insurance reviewer ("They will probably ask more and more questions until I don't give the right answer"); or a complication with their newly discovered and underlying belief system about helping another human being ("People in pain shouldn't be subjected to the stress of paying for help," or "If I really cared about people, I would do this for free"). Understandably, dealing with money matters impacting treatment can present numerous challenges for the new clinician. Another hurdle therapists find particularly intimidating about the financial aspect of therapy is that money issues usually are dealt with early in treatment, and they are not something that can be put off until later. The "money thing" presents itself very quickly in one's professional work. Whether you are ready or not, it is there.

INSURANCE: WHAT IT USED TO BE, WHAT IT IS, AND WHERE IT IS GOING

Health insurance is one of the "hottest" issues on the national political scene these days. There are the conflicting and sometimes competing voices of the millions without health care coverage who ask how they can survive, and the millions who ask where the money will come from for anything close to universal health care for all citizens. This issue will most likely remain a focal point in political campaigns for years to come until a workable solution is developed. Also, one person's workable solution will likely be someone else's intolerable situation.

Be that as it may, the general public is now coming to better understand what medical insurance really is and what it is not. One thing for sure is that it is not the way it used to be. In the past, a client with insurance coverage through his or her employer (or government entitlement like Medicaid) would expect it as a benefit of his or her job (or situation in life) without any cost to them. They would also expect to be able to consult any provider of their choosing (for medical or psychological reasons), to have 90 percent or more of each charge payable by their insurance company, and to have a yearly limit set so high that they could almost go once a week or once every two weeks for services for the entire calendar year. This was the "golden age" of medical insurance coverage for both consumers and providers. Clients had very generous coverage with maximum control in decisions about services, and mental health professionals could generally have a sufficient volume of clients and a very substantial reimbursement rate so as to enjoy much financial comfort and security. Understandably, such a cozy system fostered a tremendous temptation to abuse it, and part of where we are today is a result of abuse of the system. The golden age view would best be described, in 1997, as what insurance is *not*—that is, not anymore.

OK, you say, so what is the insurance story nowadays? The description of what insurance is these days is very difficult to pin down because it might very well have changed during the time it takes you to read this book. Nevertheless, we will give it a try, based on our current knowledge.

Today, clients with insurance coverage through their employer can expect that, although a benefit of their job, they will have to make a sizable monthly contribution to secure the coverage for themselves individually and a substantially larger contribution if they desire coverage for their family. They can also expect that the specific insurance carrier with which their employer contracts may change as often as once a year as the employer finds a less expensive rate for an insurance plan. The coverage may not remain consistent as the employer switches plans so that what services are covered, what deductibles are due, and what percentage of covered services will be paid changes as well. You can see the beginnings of a real whopper of a headache here. But wait, there is more.

In addition to keeping track of who one's insurance company is and what is covered at what rates and what is not, most insurance plans now involve the use of HMOs (health maintenance organizations) or PPOs (preferred provider organizations), of which the clients are considered members. This development means that the client members cannot consult any provider of their choosing, but rather must follow specific procedures if the services are to be covered to any degree. In other words, one must also keep track of which professionals are on which provider lists as acceptable sources of services. Provider lists are continually updated, with additions and deletions occurring all the time, and there is of course bureaucratic lag time between providers' application to the list and their acceptance. The long and short of it is that clients are responsible to know a great deal more about their insurance today, and so it should be no surprise that many clients are seriously confused and cannot do much but confuse you, the clinician.

Differences also exist not only in the way insurance coverage works today, but also in the process of obtaining services. In a typical HMO, members will have a PCP (primary care physician, not the drug!) who is their first contact in almost all instances of seeking medical care. This provider decides whether services by mental health specialists (such as a psychiatrist, psychologist, counselor, social worker, or marriage and family therapist) will be authorized to be provided and reimbursed. If authorized by the PCP, the services must be chosen from among the approved list of specific providers for that HMO, i.e., those providers who have met credentialing requirements and contracted with the company to accept their rates for various services. The PCP may determine the number of sessions a client can attend for mental health services. In some cases, a separate managed care company specializing in behavioral health care will be the "gatekeeper" for deciding the provider, amount, and frequency of services.

In the PPO scenario, the client is given a list of the "preferred providers" (again those providers who have met credentialing requirements and contracted with the company to accept their rates) from whom to choose for services. The amount and frequency of services available are set by the insurance plan. With all services there will be a charge the individual has to pay up-front at each appointment called a copayment or copay, and with many services, there will be a minimum deductible amount that the individual must pay before their insurance will begin to reimburse for services rendered. Needless to say, the amount of services a client could receive in the past was significantly greater than the amount allowed under both of these current insurance plans.

What is left is the question of the future trend of health insurance. If we could readily answer that question, we would not be writing this book. Instead, we would be conducting very expensive seminars to health care professionals on how to be prepared to succeed under the new game and new rules. Because we do not know, we can only speculate that we will see more of the current structure for managing health care until it is no longer profitable for the companies controlling the funds. Fiscal and treatment accountability provided the rationale for the changes into the era of managed care. The sad but true fact is that, in an effort to control health care costs, we have allowed these companies to flourish and make a profit by controlling expenditures.

"Where do these profits come from?" you may ask. The ability to deny services or slow down the frequency at which these services are provided is the core function of these entities. They endeavor ultimately to pay out less than members pay in. The question of whether each denial or delay is appropriate and ethical is at the forefront of the daily battles between providers and managed care companies. In the end, this confrontational process creates less money flowing out to providers to render services to clients and more money flowing back to the managed care company in the form of profits, and it seriously alienates many professionals and clients. Unfortunately, the client gets hit hardest and most immediately by the fallout. The combination of uproar by consumers and professionals and diminishing profits for these companies will hopefully press our political leaders to find some form of government and private sector collaboration to provide ethical and effective health care services as we begin the next century.

WORKING EFFECTIVELY UNDER MANAGED CARE

As we have seen that managed care is a strong and growing force in mental health services, what are the implications for our clients and ourselves as providers? We will examine the responsibilities of the therapist with managed care and the understanding of responsibilities for the client with their managed care-driven treatment.

Therapists, both experienced and beginners, are adjusting to the transition of working within a managed care system. Understanding the basic premise of managed care is important if you want to make this transition successfully. With the historical lack of external controls on clients and therapists "administrating" mental health treatment, managed care aims at establishing standards for determining the necessity for and the quality of the mental health services being provided. This alone sounds like—and is—a laudable goal.

In establishing credentialing procedures and standards, a managed care company is first attempting to gain some control over quality by admitting only those providers who have the licensure, experience, specialization, and geographic location they believe appropriate and necessary for their operation. The use of professional references and association with major hospitals and clinics are also used in determining admittance to a panel. In addition, a provider's pattern of treatment sequences (average number of sessions used from intake to termination of previously treated cases) may also be used to determine if a provider remains on a panel in the future. The tension between finding a well-trained professional who does good work and finding a professional who does things quickly is readily apparent.

The next step is monitoring the necessity of services requested and the quality and effectiveness of those services after they have been authorized. The process of acquiring authorized services (precertification of initial treatment and recertification of subsequent treatment) with a managed care company usually takes one of three forms. In one form, the client contacts his or her PCP for an office or phone visit to discuss the request for services. The PCP gives initial authorization, if the necessity according to company standards is met, and often refers the client to a specific provider with which the PCP is familiar. Subsequent treatment must be cleared through the PCP who will most likely require a written progress report and/or phone consultation with the provider before authorizing these additional sessions.

A second form provides clients with anywhere from one to six sessions after calling and presenting their request for services to the managed care company intake department via a conference over the phone with a case manager or utilization review specialist. If the request appears to be within the company's and specific insurance plan's guidelines, the initial authorizations for a specific provider are granted in some form (some specific plans allow marital therapy while others do not; some plans require treatment of children and adolescents to include family therapy while others do not—all of this even when both plans might be managed by the same company). The client may already have a provider in mind or can be given choices from the company provider list according to the presenting problem and provider's specialties, preference of the provider's gender, and geographical location.

A third form permits a client to go to any provider on the approved list for one session after which an OTR (outpatient treatment review) document must be completed, submitted, and possibly discussed over the phone with a case manager or utilization review specialist before any further sessions will be authorized.

Precertification of services is where the company is basically stating, "Let's not begin treatment until we are sure there is sufficient and appropriate necessity for services." The provider's (i.e., your) presentation for services after an initial diagnostic session (or the client's presentation to request initial services) is examined from a brief solution-focused time-limited therapy perspective relative to the specific symptoms and severity described in the presentation. In this initial authorization, the company is basically asking you to describe your view of the case and noting the compatibility of your view with one of the perspectives previously noted. The company wants you to specify goals that are practical, individualized, behaviorally stated, and symptom-driven. They will also require a prognosis from you indicating the number of sessions you are requesting over what period of time (usually three, six, or nine months). Recertification for continuing treatment involves the company examining whether or not the case is progressing, what the behavioral evidence of the progress is, whether you have remained solution- and treatment goal-focused (or wandered from your goals), whether further services should be authorized versus termination of the treatment, and the patient should be transfered to another provider if the need for treatment remains but treatment progress is not evident.

An important part of your job is to assist clients in understanding their responsibilities in managed care-driven treatment. Clients need to understand the basics of how obtaining services is achieved, including the process, procedures, and limitations of their specific insurance plan and managed care company. Just because this information is available in their policy manual does not mean they have read or understand it. You need to impress the client with the collaborative intent of the managed care approach. A treatment plan with specific symptoms, goals, and prognosis outlined needs to be developed with the client. In other words, the client has the right to know what the managed care company is examining and how the potential course of treatment is determined. The client must understand the limited scope and length of his or her treatment in order to keep treatment expectations in proportion with what the managed care company will likely allow.

The pitfalls here are obvious and disturbing. Will clients edit or censor their presentations in sessions because they fear sharing too much and "getting caught out on an emotional limb" if managed care stops their treatment too soon? Will therapists compromise their therapeutic intuition because they fear getting into territory requiring more intensive treatment a managed care company might not authorize, but where they remain legally and ethically responsible for the client's emotional well-being even if further treatment is denied? Will the therapy process become too impersonal and mechanical with the limited symptom-solution focus approach potentially overriding the personhood and the story of the client? No easy answers or quick solutions are available for these and other troubling questions presented by both therapists and clients. A vital part of helping a client understand managed care is addressing these concerns either as an introduction to treatment during the initial session or at the first indication that they may emerge as part of the treatment dynamics.

FEES: THE REAL AND SYMBOLIC VALUES

The issue of money paid directly by clients for their therapy has become increasingly complex with the advent of managed care. The copay due at the time of service can vary in terms of set amount versus percentage of the UCR (usual, customary, and reasonable charge for a specific service), as well as between insurance companies and specific plans within the same company. This amount can also change periodically as employer groups negotiate better contracts with insurance carriers to decrease the cost to themselves and their employees. These variations in fees, coupled with the outdated mode of thinking that says "the insurance takes care of all of it," can create both confusion and resentment in clients.

As a therapist you will be required to discuss financial issues with clients in most every setting. Examples would include discussing the specific financial conditions of a client's insurance coverage, collecting copays and deductibles from clients when clerical staff is unavailable, confronting the business and treatment issue of a client avoiding or ignoring responsibility to pay his or her copay for services rendered, or discussing treatment decisions and alternatives when a client's benefits are exhausted for the calendar year or their coverage is terminated due to a job loss or change of job. An additional problem frequently encountered involves the "preexisting condition clause" in most policies, which requires a client who has been receiving treatment and who changes jobs—and hence insurance plans—to wait six to twelve months before he or she can use mental health coverage under the new plan.

Another perspective on the issue of money is the value a client may receive from therapy when he or she is required to pay some portion of the fee with each session (Bishop and Eppolito, 1992). This idea is as old as Freud, existing long before the complexities of health insurance and managed care, and is intertwined in the concept of the transference between client and therapist as a major force in the working therapeutic alliance. The logic states that the financial investment a client makes with each session enhances the emotional investment in each session and the treatment process as a whole. The same logic stated in reverse might be that "free advice is worth about as much as it costs," raising the concern that clients would take the therapy process less seriously if they received it free of charge. In the end, it is hoped that this financial investment on the part of the client joins with your commitment as a therapist to assist in making this serious endeavor called psychotherapy a profound experience that has lasting results.

SECTION III:
ALONG THE WAY

We have now discussed many elements that organize the professional practice world, and we hope that your perspective has been broadened in a useful way. We now turn to a variety of issues that you will need to consider on an ongoing basis, ranging from the concrete practical to the philosophical to the somewhat esoteric. In this section, we will begin with an examination of the basis from which you determine health and normalcy, that is, your values. Then we will look at dual relationships, something that remains a controversy in the marriage and family therapy field. The next two chapters will return to the stuff of practical clinical work, as we look at treatment impasses and then termination. We will turn then to a discussion of the legal world and how marriage and family therapists interface with it. The final three chapters will address aspects of practice pertaining to burnout, job changes, and specializing in a particular area of your choice within the discipline, respectively.

Chapter 11

Values Conflicts:
Who Knows What Is Best for Whom?

"You can't legislate morality." This statement has reverberated through American culture for the last few decades and has been a rallying cry for numerous social movements. We still hear it all the time on campus as students, both undergraduate and graduate, from various groups debate controversial topics in classrooms, dorms, and public forums. For many people in society at large as well, the statement is taken as an axiom of life. There is only one problem: It is an incandescently flaming demonstration of a tremendous ignorance of the nature of law and morality's relationship.

Now, before you wonder where you left the book on practicing marriage and family therapy in the real world and how this philosophical and editorial-sounding tone took its place, give us a moment to make some sense out of this for you. We do not wish to suggest that we are philosophers par excellence, or that we have some gnostic brilliance that we want to let you in on in the form of lessons about the true nature of morality or law (or anything else). However, we do believe that intellectual integrity must be preserved; therefore, professionals of all disciplines including this one need to be able to get their minds dirty down in the philosophical mud. First, let us return to the argument. The belief that morality cannot be legislated is a huge intellectual error. Why? Simply put, all legislation *is* morality! It is merely a question of *whose* morality is being legislated.

Let us present a rather benign but clear example. Our society has numerous traffic laws, dictating everything from how to stop and go, how to turn, where on the road to drive, what speed limits to follow, what insurance you must carry, if you must wear seatbelts, which approved car seats children must ride in. Each of these springs from an underlying moral imperative about the value of keeping people safe, which really is indicative of an even more general moral law holding that human beings are valuable and should not be harmed. Somewhere along the line, the belief that people are inherently valuable was developed. This is a moral position, and must be accepted as such.

The law insisting that you cannot drive over sixty-five miles per hour exists because human safety is a moral value to which society as a whole subscribes. The people of this nation have consented formally to subject themselves to the morality of not running over people, and so to reduce the likelihood that your driving one hundred miles per hour just because you want to will harm you and/or someone else, laws have been passed to say that sixty-five miles per hour is as fast as you can go without getting in trouble. Thus, the interdependence between morality and law should begin to become clear.

"So what does this have to do with practicing marriage and family therapy?" you may ask justifiably. The answer is that, in just the same way that people fail to see the connection between morality and law, so have marriage and family therapists failed to see the connection between values and therapy. With a little intellectual exercise, you should be able to begin to see how you can substitute "values" and "therapy" for "morality" and "law" in the previous discussion.

Therapy is fundamentally about values. There has been a long-standing myth in the mental health professions that therapy needs to be value-free, and this myth is still being promulgated in many individually oriented counseling professions and training programs (Doherty and Boss, 1991; Doherty, 1995). What this has meant historically is that the competent clinician should avoid value judgments of any kind when working: there is no right or wrong answer, no right or wrong action, no right or wrong motivation, etc. To put it bluntly, therapists' values supposedly need to be kept out of their clinical work.

This myth is problematic from several vantage points. First, to avoid using one's values is impossible. People view all of life through the value "lenses" they have, and the best they can do is be aware of those lenses and try to decide under what conditions to allow them to operate unrestrained—and even this decision-making process is value-governed. Second, it is undesirable to keep values out of therapeutic work. Clients come to professional therapists because they have problems they want help in solving, and part of developing workable solutions lies in determining what is *wrong*, and what might make it *better*. The very idea of problem/solution begs the importance of values that provide direction, and like it or not, the values of the therapist will have a significant impact on the development of goals for treatment and the direction therapy takes.

Third, and most important for our purposes in this chapter, trying to keep values out of therapy is irresponsible, especially for marriage and family therapists. Marriage and family therapists are trained to work with relationships and the people having them (Goldenberg and Goldenberg, 1996). The focus is on what happens between individuals and not solely on the individuals themselves. The moral imperative for the marriage and family therapist is to pay balanced attention to both ends of the continuum—the well-being of individuals *and* the well-being of relationships, which have profound implications for individuals.

William Doherty (1994, 1995), at the University of Minnesota, and other scholars (e.g., Lageman, 1993) have argued most persuasively that the moral imperatives underlying marriage and family therapy are in direct contrast to the moral positions taken within other mental health disciplines, at least from a historical perspective. Doherty points out that, beginning with Freud, therapists have had the purpose of liberating individuals from the toxic constraints of family, society, and religion; his critique, and what we take as important to note herein, is that in the last few decades some therapists have taken that purpose to the point of irresponsibility, advocating willy-nilly for individual entitlements without appropriate regard to their consequences for those with whom the individuals are involved or for the communities in which they live.

As an example, Doherty notes that it is almost a cliché that therapists of all stripes (but particularly those trained individualistically) ask clients things such as, "What do you need to do for yourself?" and "How can you take care of your own needs?" Or they admonishingly say things such as, "You're *should-ing* yourself again" when a client expresses a sense of obligation, guilt, or culpability. Marriage and family therapy, in contrast, substantially includes a component that recognizes the interdependence of and tension between individuals such that relationships can be maintained, changed, and improved. The sense of entitlement for individuals that is sometimes so strongly emphasized in the mental health disciplines is clearly counterbalanced within the marriage and family therapy field by a strong focus on obligation to (and rewards from) others with whom the individual is involved. Saying things to the effect of, "Spending more time with your spouse and children is a good idea; you should try it," which is obviously a value-laden statement, is something that the typical marriage and family therapist will have plenty of occasions to do. Whether the therapist ever says those things, however, is another story.

Unfortunately, marriage and family therapists as a whole have not done very well in taking on their moral responsibility; instead they have bowed to the implicit value-free assumption other disciplines have emphasized to therapists and the culture at large (Doherty, 1995). Undoubtedly, one of the major reasons why family therapists have not taken on their responsibility regarding morals and values very well is the fact that what is attempted to be done in family therapy is in an ongoing, dynamic tension with the cultural norms governing people's lives. Individuality and independence are hallmarks of our culture, and the person who has reached his or her true potential is said to be "self-actualized" (Maslow, 1954). There is no reference to being "other actualized," and in fact, people who regularly accommodate to the wishes and suggestions of others with little difficulty run the risk of being labeled "codependent." In direct contrast to this is the task of the marriage and family therapist to help members of relationships find ways to make their relationships work better, which inevitably requires accommodation to the needs, wants, and quirks of others. So, on the one hand, marriage and family therapists are directed by cultural norms to advocate for the importance of independence, self-direction, and freedom of choice for individuals, and on the other hand, they are simultaneously told by the nature of their profession to advocate for the development of communality, accommodation, commitment, and compromise so that ongoing relationships can be maintained and enhanced. This results in being caught between a rough rock and a very hard place—trying to balance individuation and belonging (which—surprise surprise—is the main struggle that many of our clients have).

A second source contributing to the difficulty of handling values in therapy is that no universally accepted standards exist for what the optimally healthy individual, marriage or couple relationship, or family is like. There is no picture or map that everyone agrees on, and so what Therapist A thinks is the "perfect relationship" may be startlingly different than what Therapist B would say. If, for example, the Deefendorfers went to both therapists with the same presenting problem (like the client in the old Gloria tapes—tapes in which a woman was interviewed by Carl Rogers, Fritz Perls, and Albert Ellis, three *very* different therapists, on the same day), the theoretical conceptualization may be quite different (no surprise, of course), but the course of action and moral implications for that action may be tremendously different. This needs to be considered carefully.

Let us say that the presenting problem is the classic uninvolved, unemotional, and peripheral husband and the nagging, frustrated, and overburdened wife, complete with the stereotyped traditional gender roles of the Cleaver family—he works and she stays home with the kids. As we discussed in the section on agendas in Chapter 1, the feminist-informed therapist who has an eye for power imbalances may be struck most by the apparent implicit oppression of Mrs. Deefendorfer and act with the priority of addressing that as the solution to the problem. However, the pronatalistically oriented therapist with a child development background will be struck most by the lack of involvement of Mr. Deefendorfer with his children and act to address that as a priority that may solve the problem. Neither of these per se is necessarily problematic, but if you imagine the implications of the intensity of each approach's emphasis being raised (i.e., the therapist's priority of attending to the "real" problem as he or she perceives it becomes a bigger and bigger deal), the possibility for values conflicts becomes readily apparent. There are moral consequences of the potentially very different outcomes as well.

Third, the increasing influence of postmodernism in the field of marriage and family therapy over the last decade in some ways has further confused the values issue. Specifically, ideas pertaining to right, wrong, and truth are no longer in vogue at anything more general than an individual level (except for a few hot-button issues such as abuse). With postmodernism's emphasis on nonhierarchical relationships and the equal validity of all points of view, therapists have been pushed further away from the position of acknowledging their purposeful influence in favor of viewing all that they do as the collaborative cocreation of meaningful narratives. This may sound philosophically quite appealing, and it has spawned a great deal of therapeutic creativity, but it fails to adequately recognize the inherent power that therapists have by virtue of their socially defined position as experts on people and relationships. If clients did not believe we have something to offer hurting people, they would not come to us; if there were no hierarchy, there would be no need for licensure, credentialing, or thorough documentation. That the law ignores postmodern assumptions is something that you need to take into account as you approach your clinical work—if you act negligently, philosophically stimulating arguments about collaboration and cocreating meaningful narratives will probably annoy the judge more than impress her. Postmodernism's inadvertent contribution to the values issue has pragmatically resulted in the further justification for therapists' tendency toward the abdication of moral authority in clients' lives.

IDENTIFYING YOUR OWN VALUES AND VALUE BIASES

In Chapter 1, we raised the issue of agendas, which you may recall were defined as the often covert or hard to see reasons we have for getting into this field in the first place. We argued that it is absolutely essential for you to become aware of your agenda as thoroughly as possible because it is what underlies your views on health and functionality. In this section, we want to discuss further the importance of having you become increasingly aware of your own values and value biases that emanate from your agenda. We also hope to offer you the opportunity to do some thinking to examine some of them more closely.

As you approach clinical work from the perspective of an educated professional, what in your educational, professional, and personal experience tells you what a healthy person looks like? Take a moment to think about "the perfect person" (and we are not talking about any Hollywood celebrities here!). What characteristics describe this person, in terms of their way of being, individually and in relationships? In what order do descriptors such as creative, assertive, caring, strong, sensitive, responsible, gentle, etc., come to mind as you think about this person? It may be useful to note who the person is that you are describing—is this someone you know personally, a historical figure, a mentor, someone in your own family, or a fictional character you or someone else invented?

Another key question to ask here is this: How closely do you match the description you have? On the one hand, it is desirable for each of us to actively seek to improve ourselves according to a standard that we strive to meet, but on the other hand, if we find that our perfect person's description closely matches ourselves, then we had better be pretty darn impressive! More likely, an arrogance may exist that needs to be addressed. We believe honesty demands that each of us acknowledge our own bent toward arrogance; if we did not believe that the way we thought about things and did things was the best way, we would choose a different way. The risk is that we may begin to expect that the lives of others would automatically be improved by their adopting our views of things. This is a definite "no-no."

In any event, it is likely that if you showed your description of the perfect person to a hundred people at random, most would agree with you to the extent that whomever is being described sounds like an admirable person. However, this general consensus is probably about as far as it goes, and this can be demonstrated easily if you then ask these hundred people for their descriptions of the perfect couple, the perfect person, and the perfect family.

Again, take a few minutes to try to describe the ideal couple relationship and then the ideal family relationship. How do you weigh various factors such as communication patterns, autonomy, sacrifice, emotional bondedness, commitment, power and authority, closeness/distance, etc.? Make your description as concrete as you can. Should both parents work? When? How much? Under what conditions is divorce acceptable, and does it matter whether there are children involved. If so, do their ages make a difference? Should they have cable TV? Should they go to church? How do decisions about feeding the dog get made? Should marital swinging be tried, and how should spouses go about attempting to influence each other to have sex, go out to eat, put braces on Junior's teeth, and buy the Ford versus the Chevy? Where do they spend holidays, or should they even observe them? How are children best disciplined—should corporal punishment ever be applied, or should we let parents just decide? Obviously, we are trying to force concreteness out of the abstract, but it is absolutely critical to be able answer these questions with a minimum number of "it depends." It depends on what?

To several of the previous questions you may answer with some exasperation that it does not matter what you think, but rather what the clients think. But it *does* matter what you think, for three reasons. First, the clients think that what you think matters (if not, why do they want to meet with you, let alone pay you?). Second, in all likelihood, you have opinions on all of these questions. They may not be strong opinions (you might even think you have no opinion), but your opinions exist and will come out to the degree that they are important to you. Also, what your clients may choose differs from what you would choose. As an example, if clients decide that the children should take care of feeding the dog, you may be fine with that; if, however, the assignment of responsibility for the dog extends to the payment of veterinary services, food, and grooming, you may find yourself uncomfortable with that and want to intervene. Your values then will influence your work more overtly. Third, there are some situations about which what you think is extremely important for legal and/or ethical reasons—e.g., is child abuse happening, or is a duty-to-warn issue arising—or for reasons that are unique to your agenda, e.g., perhaps the abused spouse described in Chapter 1 wants to remain in the marriage. In either of these scenarios, your thoughts and actions will have significant bearing on the outcome because you are *obliged* to influence, either by law or because you want to. What values you have cannot (and should not) be ignored.

You need to be sufficiently aware of your values and value biases so that when you are in a concrete clinical situation, you know which direction you want to go (it will be hard for you to not go there, even if you try). To say "it depends" is to acknowledge complexity, to be sure, but it is also a convenient cop-out that avoids necessary therapist responsibility. You are an influential person as a therapist, and you need to be ready to be responsible for your influence. We will return to discuss the pragmatic and appropriate use of your values in therapy later in this chapter, but right now we want to switch gears a bit to take a look at values of a different but no less important sort.

IDENTIFYING INSTITUTIONAL AND PROFESSIONAL VALUES

In addition to your own values, the values held by your employer and by your profession will affect how you practice. Not surprisingly, each agency has its own values concerning health and functionality, as well as values pertaining to how to treat clients and staff, financial matters, and public relations. You will find it necessary to become familiar with the values that permeate your place of employment, and you will also discover fairly quickly how well your own values match those of your employer. It will be a most uncomfortable work environment if a lack of fit exists.

Many institutions providing mental health service have some general common values. Unfortunately, on the surface anyway, some of these values lack a degree of nobility that you may have hoped for when you began your training. Among the more commonly held values of this type are the desire to reduce liability and costs, the urge to increase client referrals, and the need to avoid negative publicity. Some more positive-sounding values are held about clients' needs being met, staff being maintained with decent morale and facilities, and a real positive difference being made in people's lives. Great variability exists in the degree to which these values affect the day-to-day operation of mental health settings, and the nexus of this variability is where ideals and pragmatics collide.

Depending on the nature of the agency—e.g., for-profit versus community mental health versus religiously sponsored—different values will be held in priority. The for-profit institution may have a strong value on admissions and the full use of insurance coverage prior to treatment termination whereas the community mental health agency may prioritize keeping clients out of scarce beds in inpatient settings, and the religiously sponsored agency may be inclined to place an emphasis on the idea of ministry as much as or more than on treatment. Each of these examples manifests different practical realities: the for-profit site may be guilty of looking at clients more with an eye for what their insurance coverage will pay for than for what they need; the community mental health agency may overmedicate clients and underplay their severity in order to keep them outpatient; and the religiously sponsored site may be more interested in obtaining converts or providing free counseling in the name of ministry than in providing quality care by qualified professionals. It would be very wise of you to investigate as much as possible the various values that govern the agencies at which you apply to work.

The particular profession in which you are trained also has its values. Many of you reading this book are being or have been trained systemically as marriage and family therapists, but some have not had similar training. These people have been trained primarily in another discipline, such as social work, psychology, or counseling. Your specific discipline will steer you to emphasize some things as highly important while deemphasizing other things as anything from less important to nonexistent. Among marriage and family therapists, for example, there are still many purists out there for whom individual symptoms or diagnosis is irrelevant at best and seriously harmful at worst (Doherty and Boss, 1991). Similarly, within specific marriage and family therapy schools, certain concepts and beliefs are emphasized at the expense of other concepts. For example, communications (e.g., Segal, 1991; Watzlawick, Weakland, and Fisch, 1974) or strategic therapists (e.g., Haley, 1987), may be prone to overemphasize interaction patterns of a paradoxical nature at the expense of examining family-of-origin dynamics and connections. Professionals trained in other disciplines have values that are strongly emphasized to them as well, and it is vital that these usually implicit beliefs be made explicit and examined.

LISTENING FOR CLIENTS' VALUES

Beyond your own values, those of your profession, and those of your employer or agency, one other critical source of values in therapy must be accounted for as you approach treatment: the values of clients. Bluntly, these values are arguably *the* most important ones to pay attention to in therapy. They are also sometimes the hardest ones to detect for a variety of reasons. First, clients may be reluctant to overtly share their values because they may view them as one source of their problem. They also may feel some anxiety, embarrassment, or shame concerning the values they hold, especially if they do not match those of the popular culture (for example, the young twentysomething couple that decides to abstain from sex because of religious and/or other personal reasons may be afraid that the therapist will think they have a hang-up about sex that needs addressing). It is also possible that clients may not be very aware of their own values, perhaps because they have never spent much time examining them, having not had cause. Another reason clients' values can be overlooked is that therapists sometimes do not make much effort to observe their clients' values, instead being transfixed by their own agendas or distracted by obvious things such as appearance (e.g., clients who appear slovenly may be judged automatically and inaccurately to be less intelligent, less motivated, more sexist, etc., when they may have just left work at the farm and came directly to their appointment). Sometimes, therapists bypass thinking about values at all in favor of pursuing their therapeutic model of choice's theoretical or practical assumptions and techniques. In any event, clients' values often get short shrift in therapy, and this can and does lead to untoward outcomes (Odell and Stewart, 1993).

Fortunately, this is a problem that usually is easily rectified once therapists get into the habit of attending to clients' values. The first way in which marriage and family therapists can begin to train themselves to think respectfully about clients' values is, of course, to be aware of their own and to practice observing their own processes in which their values influence them. Beyond this, though, values-sensitive therapists need to listen for client values in the conversations they have with them. When clients use words such as "should," "ought," "guilt," "right," "wrong," "pride," "shame," etc., they usually are indicating the values they hold; this does not mean they like their values, necessarily, but it does suggest what their values are. We need to carefully guard against allowing our apparently automatic "therapeutic" responses (e.g., "you did what you needed to do," etc.) to drown out clients' values statements (Doherty, 1995). The typical therapist's desire to remove clients' subjective suffering from guilt and other cognitions and/or emotions needs to be tempered with both the desire to understand how clients' values operate and the willingness to consider that such suffering may be necessary at times.

Sometimes, asking clients about their values is the easiest and quickest way to get them out in the open, and to make yours known as well. This type of conversation may happen more readily during therapy in which a relationship's viability may be in question, such as when a married couple is dealing with infidelity. Under these circumstances, determining the values that govern whether both members of the couple will engage in therapy to the degree necessary to heal the betrayal of trust is essential—if someone wants to continue to have the affair, then a values fit between the clients and therapy for the purpose of saving the marriage is almost certain to fail, as is the marriage itself.

Finally, clients' values can be accessed to a degree by observing them. Happening into the waiting room where your client family is waiting and hearing the mother verbally rip apart her four-year-old daughter can give you a good look at some values governing their practical daily living. Even if they make a great deal of noise about how important respect is in their family in therapy sessions, the values that tend to operate for some members may be quite the opposite, and you can see how mixed messages may contribute to whatever presenting problem(s) they may have.

MENTAL HEALTH VALUES, RELIGIOUS VALUES, YOUR CLIENTS, AND YOU

Though we have spent considerable time examining values from several vantage points, you may find yourself still wondering what to do with values in treatment. You know you are supposed to be aware of your own values, those of your profession and employer, and those of your clients. You know that keeping your values out of therapy is neither possible nor desirable, but you also know that you cannot just start pushing certain values down clients' throats. So what are you supposed to do?

Honestly, there are no easy formulaic answers that remove the precariousness of judgment or simplify the incredible complexity involved. But there are, however, some ways to think about approaching values in therapy that increase the chance of treating them in an appropriate, sensitive, and ethical manner. One way, suggested by Alan Tjeltveit (1986) and echoed by some others, is to examine values and classify them according to their type. Values, he says, can be thought of as applying more or less to particular areas of people's lives, and therefore, it may be useful to view clients as asking for help with some values and not others.

It can be argued that there are mental health values and there are religious values (Tjeltveit, 1986). They have a connection to each other that should not be underestimated, but they are not usually the same (although there are situations in which they appear identical). Mental health values direct day-to-day living with respect to normative behaviors and attitudes, and they may be seen most easily as the usually covert assumptions underlying clients' normative ways of being. This may include the expectations and assumptions that are held regarding relationships and family roles, modes of communication, and rules about ways of treating others in intimate environments (or elsewhere). Religious values, in contrast, have more to do with philosophical and existential questions about God, nature, humanity, morality, and the meaning of life; they usually can be overtly asserted with minimal effort, and they are the ultimate source of truth and purpose in people's lives. For some people, religious values inform mental health values rather closely and the latter flow smoothly from the former; in other people, two do not connect.

Clients coming to therapists usually have difficulties that require intervention at the mental health value level; more rarely, they are looking for help from us also at the religious or spiritual level. It may be surprising for you to realize that in many places, pastors, priests, and ministers do far more counseling than mental health professionals do (Chalfant et al., 1990) and that, by and large, clergy are not hesitant to refer people to mental health professionals when they feel it is appropriate (Worthington, 1986). Clergy often are the first contact persons for the emotionally, psychologically, and relationally troubled, and evidence indicates they see the same problems and same levels of severity as mental health professionals (Worthington et al., 1996). While it is common for clergy to pass to professional therapists those with severe symptoms and those not dealing with explicitly spiritual or religious issues, the latter do not generally return the favor. Clergy may be more likely to voluntarily limit their influence to areas in which their role is clearly appropriate, and we suggest strongly that therapists do the same as a general rule (the obvious exception is the situation in which a therapist is billing him or herself as a *religious* therapist).

Unfortunately, having therapists stay out of religious and spiritual values is easier said than done. The problem herein concerns the fact that at some levels religion and psychotherapy both attempt to provide guidance and answers to the problems of life. These answers inevitably compete with each other at points, and psychotherapy's originally hostile stance toward religion, starting with Freud, has not made it any easier. Therapists' views of religion historically have ranged from seeing it as a constraining, guilt-inducing, anxiety-increasing, and unnecessary source of pathology that people would do well to be without, to seeing it as a tangential source of comfort, security, and community (Bergin, 1980). Only recently has religion begun to be accepted at some level by the majority of clinicians, although how welcome it is in treatment is highly variable (Worthington et al., 1996).

As a result, therapists on the whole have not made significant and coherent efforts over the years to integrate religion and spirituality with psychotherapeutic treatment very well. Rather, they have tended to treat religion with a degree of uncertainty, usually by not explicitly addressing it at all. At the same time, however, because of the inevitable competition between religious and psychological models of health, therapists generally have not been hesitant to address issues that were once within the purview of religion but they now believe psychotherapy offers an answer (presumably a better one). For therapists, when religion and psychotherapy have competed in providing answers, the former has usually lost.

Recently, however, this position has been softened to an extent, and the importance of spirituality (not necessarily religiousness in the traditional sense) has been increasingly emphasized among the mental health cognoscenti (e.g., Stander et al., 1994; Worthington et al., 1996). Despite this development, though, the fact is that although many therapists today recognize the importance of spirituality in people's lives, their view of spirituality is˙less likely to include or endorse "institutionalized" religions. Some research, for instance, has shown that psychotherapists as a group hold "orthodox" religious views less and "liberal" religious views or alternative religious worldviews more than the rest of the population (Worthington et al., 1996). Clients, on the other hand, come from that population and tend to be more inclined to be "institutionally religious." The lack of fit between therapists' values and clients' values may be unsuspected by clients and capitalized on by those therapists who hold particularly unfavorable views toward religion (or certain religions). Bluntly, therapists who denigrate the religious answers a client's beliefs offer in favor of psychotherapeutic answers without a careful and examined discussion with the client, and preferably with a supervisor, are operating in a realm outside their expertise. Therapists who do this are acting unethically (AAMFT, 1991).

Another difficulty for therapists in staying out of religious values has to do with the fact that it is sometimes hard to tell mental health values and religious values apart. When the two are closely aligned in a client, for example when a client's religious views dictate that women should not be in the labor force, it may be very difficult to separate treating a mental health value from a religious one. In these cases, we suggest including or at least consulting with a religious expert who the client has some confidence in to increase both your effectiveness and your sensitivity.

A more tricky issue of a related nature concerns situations in which religious values and mental health values are for practical purposes the same. A good example of this would be the client presenting with issues related to homosexuality. Most therapists today accept homosexuality as a viable lifestyle choice. The general population, in contrast, is less accepting, and as one might expect, homosexuality is even less well-received among many religious groups. Let us suppose the client's religious views include the rejection of homosexuality, and so he is wrestling with what he feels drawn toward vis-à-vis what he believes is wrong morally. The therapist may automatically suggest that the religious teachings that prohibit homosexuality are wrong, narrow, homophobic, or culturally specific, and that the client should not allow erroneous religious ideas to induce guilt on him for something that seems quite natural and normal for him.

However, we suggest that this may not be an appropriate or ethical course of action. Such a point of view on the part of the therapist may be quite comfortable for him or her, but it may vastly underappreciate the weight of such a position for the client. The therapist may not fully understand the implications of "freeing" such a client, and to merely assert that the client needs sufficient education to get over whatever difficulties he may face as a result is to be remarkably insensitive to the core beliefs the client has. We suggest the therapist do something much more difficult: help the client recognize that he is in a dilemma, offer him a great deal of support, and help him see the potential implications that will accompany whatever choice he makes—everything from effects on his relationships, his philosophy of life, and his health. In our view, this is the most ethical way to proceed in that it preserves the client's integrity, and it does not denigrate his religious values; in fact, it allows, or perhaps more accurately forces, him to evaluate the degree to which he is committed to those values.

We have made the case that therapists by and large should stay within their areas of expertise, i.e., mental health values, and stay away from addressing religious values. We have also stressed that doing so is sometimes very difficult. However, there are some situations, albeit comparatively rare, in which a therapist may be free to address issues of a spiritual or religious nature in addition to mental health values. One possibility that comes to mind is when the client and the therapist are of the same religion and *agree* to include that realm as one possible area in which to work. This must be an explicit decision and not an implicit assumption on the part of only one party. Another instance may be when a therapist has credentials that qualify him or her to address religious concepts and values; a therapist with a Master's in Divinity or other seminary training may be competent from a training perspective to work with some clients' religious values. Apart from these circumstances, though, we believe that therapists need to vigilantly remain where they are trained and qualified to work, and that is in the realm of mental health values.

ADOPTING MORAL POSITIONS IN THERAPY

Even with all the above said, you are not out of the woods yet when considering values and morality. At some point in your work, you will come upon a situation where there are no apparent religious values on the part of the client to worry about, and yet you have a morally pregnant problem. As we stated earlier, marriage and family therapists have not taken hold of their moral authority very well for numerous reasons. Principally, however, the most salient reason may be because it is extremely difficult to perform well, without going to any extreme.

Let us look at an example of a situation in which religious values per se are not on the table, but issues of a moral nature are. You have a client who is married and has children, and he is considering leaving them to pursue a "more free" lifestyle. He is concerned that he will have a difficult time with guilt, but he also does not want to continue to feel trapped in an unhappy marriage and burdensome family. As before, some therapists would say that there is nothing particularly worrisome here and that the client just needs to "take care of himself" by getting out and moving on with his life. We believe this is shortsighted because it fails to account for the consequences of the choices he makes that will be felt tangibly in the lives of his family, as well as for the potential consequences for society at large. Some would argue that the man's individual freedom must be of primary importance, but we challenge that belief because he has responsibilities and commitments to consider.

For example, is it morally acceptable for him to leave a wife and three children for whom the state will have to provide funds for daily living? Is it morally acceptable for him to abdicate his parental responsibilities just because he does not like them? It may be that the guilt he does not want to experience more acutely is precisely what keeps him from engaging not only in affairs and whatnot, but also what prevents him from gunning down his neighbors or setting the local factory on fire. The point is that there are legitimate instances in which guilt should be expected and even encouraged (certainly perpetrators of abuse qualify). The larger point is that arguments can be made for both the importance of the man's happiness and for the importance of his not abandoning a wife and children, and therapists need to be able to evaluate these arguments and adopt a morally defensible position that balances both of them. In our view, too many errors are made in favor of the individual's concerns. Controversial as it may be, the most ethically and morally responsible course of action may be for the therapist to impress upon the man the fact that he is considering things that have profound implications for himself, his family, and society, and accordingly to advocate more for his obligations to others than for his entitlements to himself. It may be that he needs to experience meeting what he perceives as unpleasant but critical responsibilities and/or restraining guilt as a facilitator of his own personal growth. We all need to learn that life is neither fair nor easy all of the time.

Therapists who operate regularly from a morally informed framework must be prepared to be unpopular with some colleagues and clients because they may highlight issues that therapists typically have been trained to ignore or about which to even take a contrary position. Additionally, we do not want to be taken as saying that we have *the* answer, or that one exists out there to be discovered. A single answer or moral position is vastly oversimplified, and we want to discourage our argument being used as permission to take the moral high ground in service to anyone's agendas. But we do want to underscore how critical it is that therapists think hard about issues such as these and be able to assume a position of moral authority when necessary. This does not necessarily involve telling clients explicitly what to do, but it does involve making very clear the moral, relational, personal, and societal consequences of their choices.

In any event, we hope that this discussion has provoked you to think pointedly about values in therapy, specifically about your own and how you will and do use them in your work with clients. You may not agree with some of what has been said, but at the very least you owe your clients the obligation of attending to their values and being prepared to handle them well. It is our hope that we have helped stimulate you to evaluate the whole values arena thoroughly, and we hope that you will return in an ongoing fashion to wrangle further in this controversial domain.

Chapter 12

Inevitable Dual-Relationship Issues

Professional marriage and family therapists are trained to work with people's relationships, but there are certain situations in which the going becomes extraordinarily sticky. Over the course of your career, you will repeatedly encounter relationships in which the boundaries are very blurry concerning various roles in the relationships. The manifold relational connections inherent in professional practice all lend themselves to overlap quite easily: therapists can become close friends, or sometimes even more, with their supervisors and colleagues; therapists in training can develop a mentor relationship with a faculty supervisor that includes social elements such as attending parties; clients can view their therapists as friends and may invite them to special occasions such as weddings, graduations, etc.; and therapists commonly develop strong feelings of attachment to some of their clients. These relationships, however, need to be carefully evaluated because of the risk of problematic dual, or multiple, relationships. And, as you will note, these relationship connections can become exceedingly complex. In this chapter, we will examine some of the more typical situations in which dual relationship issues become salient, focusing on therapist-client relationships, collegial relationships, and supervisor-supervisee relationships.

The ethical principles for therapists in all types of professional organizations address the issue of dual relationships. Generally, there are strict prohibitions against them under the circumstances wherein a relationship comprises the therapeutic process and/or well-being of the client (or person in a less powerful position, like a client, trainee, or supervisee). AAMFT's (1991) Code of Ethics addresses them in Principles 1.2, 3.5, and 4.1, which we will not quote here.

Despite these rules, reports of therapists establishing dual relationships with clients (often including sexual relations) and then being censured and even removed from the profession as a result are still surprisingly common (for instance, ethics violations and consequences are regularly included in *The Family Therapy News*). This suggests that either therapists are willfully throwing their professional codes of ethics aside (and some are), they are stupid (and some are), they have poor judgment (and some do), or they sometimes lose their bearings in the complexity that therapy develops with regard to relationships and end up in bad situations. We tend to believe that most therapists who get into dual relationships do so innocently enough although they do bear culpability in not taking adequate steps to prevent it. This underscores the fact that there are going to be those kinds of challenging relationships—some of which will become unethical dual relationships and some of which will need ongoing attention to remain on the correct side of the boundary between appropriate and inappropriate. These are challenges that you will confront both in and out of your professional role throughout your career.

The common element that exists in these relationships is the development of warm personal feelings between individuals who work together, whether they are clients, therapists, colleagues, or supervisors. These feelings tend to occur quite naturally in the course of one's daily work as a consequence of "being" together, beyond mere propinquity. Working on an assembly line just does not naturally by itself foster the potential development of the same kind of intimacy that discussing issues of a highly personal nature does. It is very important to develop a professional demeanor in your daily work, but doing so is not enough by itself. It would be foolish to believe that personal liking and attraction, collegial camaraderie, and professional caring can easily remain separate and manageable in every instance. Rather, these complex interpersonal affinities need your apt attention and careful consideration to remain appropriate and allow you to keep your professional focus. It is also true that these affinities need to be monitored when they are negative rather than positive.

PROFESSIONAL THERAPISTS VS. SOCIAL THERAPISTS

In examining the area of dual relationships between therapists and clients, it is useful to look at the role distinctions of a *professional therapist* who works with clients and a *social therapist* who functions as an attentive friend in personal relationships. You may ask why these distinctions are important to you because, after all, you are (or are training to be) a professional therapist, not a social one. It is, nonetheless, valuable to understand the distinction between and the importance of the roles of professional and social therapist. The fact is, you are both a professional and social therapist. You just cannot be both to the same person at the same time.

Almost all human beings have moments when they are social therapists to their family and friends, and professional therapists are certainly to be counted in this group (probably more than most). In fact, our experience suggests that many professional therapists' backgrounds as social therapists to their friends and family contributes significantly to their decision to become professional therapists. An old cliché in the field is that therapists are simply paid, professional friends. While this is a somewhat insulting oversimplification, most professional therapists recognize the grain of truth in it and have utilized their own social therapists (i.e., family and friends) during times of stress and confusion.

Although therapeutic conversation is most certainly a possibility whenever two people interact, it is important to recognize the differences that are designed to be in place between a professional and social therapist. Many clients have an experience with a social therapist prior to consulting a professional therapist. This would be the friend or family member they meet for conversation or with whom they spend long periods on the phone. This person is their confidant, with whom they can share their secrets and their struggles with life. The social therapist usually offers encouragement, validation, advice (sometimes some very *good* advice), and a willingness to help in perhaps concrete ways (e.g., watching their children, giving them the use of their car, etc.). Their interaction is characterized by overall support. There is also the normative expectation of some degree of reciprocation; the social therapist role usually is switched between the two persons with some frequency. Finally, the social therapist role is a little ambiguous in that tomorrow the same people may meet to play a game of tennis, to watch a movie, or to take a trip together. There are several other possibilities available to them if they both so choose.

The role of the professional therapist is both similar and starkly different. The commonalities include much of the supportive nature of the social therapist. The interactions common to social therapy that mark the beginnings of significant self-disclosure and the risk-taking are necessary and can be very helpful if the individual decides to proceed into a professional therapy experience. A professional therapist may be the follow-up to a social therapy experience or may be the first effort a person makes to share problems and concerns with anyone. In either case, a context favorable to the self-disclosure of personal data, including secrets and struggles, must be developed with the professional therapist.

Unlike the social therapist, the professional therapist is paid to listen with some purpose in mind—there is a problem to solve, an issue to consider, or a personal habit or characteristic to be examined. They will tend to be less free in sharing their personal opinions, and they will render judgment in a different manner than the social therapist. The professional therapist is also constrained as a matter of course to keep the information the client shares absolutely confidential. Most important, however, the professional therapist is working at the direction of the client and is there *for the client's benefit*. The professional therapist does not expect to switch roles with the client, and certainly will not show up tomorrow to play tennis, watch a movie, or take a trip together.

Finally, the professional therapist can be terminated from his or her special position by the client at any time. People tend to fire their social therapists comparatively infrequently. (A good thing to remember: if clients feel that receiving contradictory input from multiple sources is too uncomfortable and thus they must choose between firing family, friends, or social therapists and firing professional therapists, the one that sends the bill usually gets the boot.) This generally allows the client a freedom not available with friends and family (social therapists) who represent an ongoing part of the client's real world and who might be offended or shocked as a result of his or her self-disclosure. The sense of shame and the accompanying fear that can be present for clients will often, in the end, make a professional therapist seem like a safer choice than the social therapist whom they will face on a daily/weekly basis long after the need to share a particular struggle has passed.

NONCLIENTS REQUESTING PROFESSIONAL THERAPY

Professional therapists have a natural pitfall that "civilians" usually are able to avoid, and you probably have already experienced it. As a professional therapist, you are viewed as a much more attractive option as a social therapist to your family, friends, and acquaintances because you have that "something extra," which is your professional training. People tend to think, "Why settle for free advice from just any friend when I can get convenient, friendly, professional expertise at no cost at all?" This is especially true if you were their social therapist of choice before you started professional preparation; now you have "real" training and can be expected to be even more helpful.

The obvious hazard that we are pointing out is that some people (nonclients) may try to use you as a professional therapist with many dubious expectations. This is trouble from the outset, for two major reasons. First, friends and family members usually know nothing and care even less about transference or loss of professional objectivity, let alone the ethical prohibitions against providing professional services to them. Because of this, they may not understand why you are not as eager to help them as you may have been before, and they may become angry and hurt that you refuse to engage with them as they request. This has implications for your social relationships with them. Second, friends can call you virtually anytime at no charge (we hope!) because the boundaries are much looser and different than with clients, who are required to schedule and pay for appointments and respect the firmer boundary of the therapist-client relationship. In this way people can try to get the benefit of your professional talent while sidestepping the financial cost, the serious emotional commitment, and the rules of the therapist-client relationship that come with consulting a professional therapist.

This does not mean that you must give up being the type of support to your friends and family that you have been in the past. It does mean that you must watch carefully to assess the issues, needs, and requests being presented to you as a social therapist. It will be your responsibility, as a professional therapist, to set limits in your role as a social therapist and make appropriate recommendations when your friend or family member presents concerns of a type or magnitude that belong in the domain of a professional therapist. The line between social and professional therapist must be respected, including a healthy appreciation for how easy it is to start sliding down a very slippery slope once you take the first step over that line.

CLIENTS REQUESTING SOCIAL THERAPY OR RELATIONSHIPS

Because the work of psychotherapy can be a very intense, very personal, and very intimate endeavor, there is the other side of this situation where the client wishes that the positive feelings he or she has for you would not have to be restricted by the rules of a therapist-client relationship. They experience you as a trusted friend rather than as a detached and inaccessible professional, in reaction to their experience of your nearly inexhaustible genuine concern for their well-being and your appropriate and occasional self-disclosure about your personal life that you use for its well-timed therapeutic value. Nonetheless, they may see you as the parent figure/sibling/friend they have never had but have always wanted in their life. They may have a "crush" on you and find you sexually attractive. These are fairly common client responses to therapists about whom they feel good that do not necessarily signify a problem.

A problem is on the horizon, however, when the client attempts to take steps commensurate with social therapy. This can be done in ways that range from naive honesty to scary manipulation. Clients may have crises that require/demand additional contact with you outside of therapy appointments and regular business hours. They may ask why you could not simply have sessions over lunch or exchange lengthy phone calls during and after business hours rather than be constrained to scheduled appointments. They may try to involve you in a parallel relationship such as soliciting you to be a customer for something they are selling or as an investor or participant in a business venture. They may make similar attempts by becoming a student in a class you are teaching or workshop you are attending. Whatever the particulars, they may want that friendly, trusted feeling with you as a professional therapist to cross the ethical boundary line of a concerned and compassionate professional into their real social world where you can become their "real life" personal friend/primary support relationship/romantic interest. These situations require that you recognize them quickly, consult with your supervisor immediately, and clearly convey and reinforce to the client the ethical boundaries they are attempting to have you breach.

There are also those situations in which *your* feelings may seem to move out of the professional domain and complicate or compromise your functioning and the therapeutic relationship. A therapist can be personally and sexually attracted to a client. If you do not believe you are susceptible to such feelings, you are trying to live in Oz, and you are more at risk because of your denial. The specifics of this type of situation may range from somewhat innocent and occasionally predictable to dangerously distorted and seriously unethical. On the one hand, this could be a situation in which you wonder if, in addition to the rewards of working with this person as a client, this person would be attractive as a personal interest to you in your real social world if he or she were not a client to whom you must remain a professional. This might simply be called "liking your clients as persons, too." You should be willing to accommodate the possibility that you might actually like some of your clients or at least have a genuine respect for them as persons.

On the other hand, this could be a situation that results in your becoming distracted and preoccupied by your feelings toward and attraction to a client and having a personal relationship with him or her. This might be called "losing professional role responsibilities through making a client an object of your personal need gratification." Signs that this type of situation may be developing include increasingly warm and personal validation of clients, compliments of a highly specific nature that you typically would make to a friend or a person to whom you are attracted, a willingness to blur some boundaries (e.g., giving your home telephone number and telling the client to call anytime), a willingness to go "the extra mile" or more (e.g., holding longer or more frequent sessions, waiving fees, etc.), and actually considering the development of other roles.

In both these situations you need to take some serious steps and fast—to recognize these feelings quickly, consult with your supervisor immediately, and clearly confront *yourself* with the ethical boundaries you are or might be crossing. Any hesitance you have to do that is often a good indicator that you are in over your head already; grab the life preserver of supervision and hold on tight. In the latter and most grave of situations, you would be best advised to find a therapist for your own personal therapy, and you would do well to consider referring the client. This type of situation always indicates that you are letting your personal issues "spill" into your professional responsibilities. Even if you are only dealing with persistent thoughts about this type of unethical behavior, you are already demonstrating a form of "acting out" that requires professional assistance to protect your clients, your emotional well-being, your professional reputation, and your ability to remain in this profession.

COLLEGIAL RELATIONSHIPS

As we have indicated, the work of psychotherapy can be a very intense, very personal, and very intimate endeavor, and this applies to your interactions with your colleagues as well. The dual-relationship concerns raised about clients are much murkier with colleagues. As a professional therapist, you will share in the professional life stories of your colleagues in their work with their clients as well as their personal life stories as you interact in the work setting over the course of time. This may range from casual conversations about daily events in life to informal consultations/peer supervision on troubling cases that challenge your perceptions and assessments of yourself as a therapist or to the serious personal and professional events that affect your coping abilities and require support and understanding from your colleagues. The question for us is how to manage these relationships and interactions so as to not compromise your professional functioning. What do you do when these feelings in professional friendships seem very much like the feelings you have for your personal friends? What do you do when, in the midst of being a professional therapist, you find yourself strongly liking and being attracted to one of those persons with whom you must maintain a professional and collegial relationship?

We are not saying that all relationships with colleagues must retain the characteristics of your relationships with clients, but neither can we say that your work relationships can always be on the same plane as your deeply personal relationships with intimates, friends, and family. Although important friendships do develop in your work relationships, you must remember that you always have a responsibility to your professional role that cannot be compromised by your personal relationships in the work setting (we suggest taking a look at Ryder and Hepworth's (1990) provocative article on dual relationships). The same warning given regarding clients becoming an object of your personal need gratification should remain in your awareness regarding relationships with colleagues.

A fine line can exist between a strong personal *and* professional relationship that nurtures and supports your personal self in the professional role and an overly intense personal relationship that overshadows the professional role responsibilities that you are paid to perform. As is the case with these issues in therapist-client relationships, you will have to examine the extent to which this situation compromises your professional functioning. If you find yourself feeling uncertain or uncomfortable regarding this type of boundary issue, it can be useful to consult your supervisor, your social therapy network (trusted friends and family members), your personal therapist, or all of the above.

SUPERVISOR-SUPERVISEE RELATIONSHIPS

A particularly complex type of collegial relationship is the supervisor-supervisee relationship. As these relationships are essentially collegial, our previous section applies in full. However, because of the hierarchical dynamic of the supervisor-supervisee relationship, there is the quality that mirrors the therapist-client relationship. In addition, the supervisor may also have the position of evaluator of performance, checksigner, and overall "boss." The supervisor may wear many hats, but the underlying commonality remains the difference in hierarchical status.

Isomorphically to therapy, the power and influence of the supervisor and the supervisee's desire/need to learn have the same quality as the power of transference in the therapeutic alliance between the influential helping therapist and troubled searching client. The development of warmth and respect in the personal feelings between supervisor and supervisee can be, and hopefully is, a natural and positive outcome in a supervisory relationship. However, when these feelings (in fantasy or behavior) cross the line into the supervisor or supervisee becoming an object of the other's personal need gratification, then the supervisory relationship must address and confront this ethical dilemma and, if necessary, request appropriate consultation from a competent senior colleague or program director.

The difficulty with being able to manage these situations easily lies in the multiplicity of roles that both participants have with each other. As you most likely will be a supervisee before you become a supervisor, our focus here is on concerns that may be more likely to surface for you in the former role. If the supervisee senses that the supervisor holds a particularly fond view of him or her, this may elicit several competing feelings. In this instance, you as the supervisee may feel flattered both personally ("I must be a special person") and professionally ("My supervisor is very impressed with my work"), or the feeling may be ambivalence ("Is there a hidden agenda here—even though I might be able to exploit my position of favor?"), or even fear ("What if my supervisor pushes to have a more personal relationship than I want? Will I lose my job if I refuse?"). Conversely, the supervisee may believe that the supervisor has a very negative feeling toward him or her and receives insulting, condescending, or otherwise inappropriate behavior. An uncomfortable mix of feelings results here, too. Given that many agency structures place the supervisor in both clinical and administrative positions, finding someone in the agency who is out of the loop sufficiently to approach for counsel and feedback may be very difficult. In this instance, it may be useful to return to your training supervisor if you can. That person may have some ideas or resources of which you can make good use. Ultimately, however, the professional ethics board and/or state licensing board can be a source of help if needed. Beware, though, that the price both professionally and personally may be very high.

Our advice to you is to get in the habit of addressing dual relationship issues overtly wherever you see the *potential* for them to develop. Unchecked and implicit assumptions, misperceptions, and erroneous attributions of others' and your own words and actions can make a normally complex situation into an impenetrable morass of confusion. The results of these dual relationships have implications and consequences for your professional and personal lives, as well as for those of your clients. Handle them carefully.

Chapter 13

Treatment Impasses:
Revitalizing Stalled Therapy

There is no shortage of books, articles, journals, and workshops about what to do in therapy at almost every point (the notable exception is termination, which we will discuss in the next chapter). Advice can be found for almost any situation, and all it takes to obtain some is a short trip to a colleague's or a supervisor's office, the local university library, or even the World Wide Web. Given the plethora of sources out there just waiting for your eager discovery, we want to spend a comparatively small amount of time examining one area of clinical practice that every clinician experiences from time to time: stalled therapy, also known as being stuck.

The old joke about impotence (it happens to everyone sometime) could easily apply to treatment impasses in marriage and family therapy—everyone gets stuck sometime. And, similar to impotence, how one handles it tends to define it. If you take it as a traumatic disaster of epic proportions and allow it to call into question your entire sense of ability, making you doubt your skills and sense of confidence, then getting stuck will be a pretty bad thing. You will want to avoid it like a root canal. Thus, such situations will dictate more and more how you operate as a therapist, causing you to avoid issues you are afraid of and the clients that tend to have them until the fear overwhelms you and you *do* lose your competence to some degree.

On the other hand, if you view it as a matter of inevitability that is an interesting and growth-producing challenge for you, getting stuck will not be nearly as bad. You might view it wisely as an opportunity to develop greater maturity as a therapist. You may even come to anticipate it a little bit like the rock climber anticipates a particularly dangerous route; it makes you both anxious and exhilarated. If you do not experience peak emotions when you think about therapy, by the way, consider yourself normal. And you can still be a very good therapist, too. The point about stalled therapy is that it is not uncommon, it *is* frustrating (at times severely so), and sometimes you can do something about it and sometimes you cannot.

HOW DO YOU KNOW WHEN THERAPY IS STALLED?

Although the above question sounds like the beginning of a lousy therapy joke (one possible—and lousy—answer is "when you have to ask the utilization review officer for more sessions"), it is really an important question to be able to answer. This issue also is something that is less commonly discussed in the therapy literature. The fact is that it is not always easy to tell when you are stalled. Being able to discern stalled cases reliably is, surprisingly, an acquired skill that needs to be deliberately developed. The obviously stalled cases you will spot rather easily, but the less obvious ones are particularly difficult to recognize and also the most difficult to restart.

Treatment impasses, as getting stuck is more formally known, occur at virtually any point in therapy although they are more common after a few sessions have occurred than at the outset; after all, some inertial movement must occur before stuckness can happen; otherwise, you never got out of the blocks. For many new cases, something of a "honeymoon" period occurs during which time the therapist and client are both interested in getting off to a good start together. For the first few sessions, positive feelings are more common, motivation may be a bit higher, and optimism may abound. Sometimes, too, changes occur fairly rapidly and some positive movement is noticed. Sometimes, though, none of this is seen and sometimes high initial expectations fail to be met. In any case, either or both of these sorts of cases have a very good chance of stalling somewhere along the way, irrespective of how they started out.

Regardless of the particulars, it is the comparatively rare case that comes in and proceeds through a course of treatment without any significant bumps, burps, backfires, or blowups at some point. You should come to expect every case to throw you an impressive curveball sometime during the course of treatment, and if you do not get one, consider yourself fortunate (just a minute ago we were saying how great being challenged is, but it is true that the smooth and seamless case feels very good so when you get one, enjoy it). In fact, if you find yourself very rarely getting stuck in treatment, with clients coming in and out of your caseload in a nice, comfortable, and orderly fashion, we would suggest you examine the degree to which you are being effective. It may be that your effectiveness as you see it (i.e., not getting stuck much) is really a better indicator of your lack of taking risks or a willingness to overlook important but potentially sidetracking or therapy-derailing issues. We admit these are strong words, but experience has shown them to be wise ones as well.

Simply put, treatment impasses occur in cybernetic terms when a homeostatic mechanism kicks in that blocks further change in the system (Hoffman, 1981). Speaking more humanly, impasses are a result of fear and the misdirected, maladaptive attempts to cope with that fear. What varies is what the fear is of, who has it, and who, if anyone, realizes it. Transference is always bilateral, and it becomes increasingly complex as the cooperative relationship between client and therapist develops over the course of shared emotional experience. Therapy is a personal encounter that cannot help but become emotionally complex for all parties, arguably more for the typical client than the therapist, but important to both nonetheless. The therapist's own history of personal experiences are as much at play and as important as those of the client, but therapists usually tend not to see that as easily. When therapists lose sight of how they are impacted both internally (i.e., personally) and externally (how their professional conduct is subtly directed), they tend to be more susceptible to getting stuck. In other words, therapists are mostly ordinary people who had scraped knees in their childhood and also who are not Teflon-coated (Campbell, Doane, and Guinan, 1983). It does not take an obvious crisis to slow them down or trip them up. In our experience, most therapists tend to err toward . . . either.

Being afraid in therapy is part and parcel of the enterprise, and in training, most therapists get a good dose of that understanding in terms of expecting their clients to balk from time to time. It is less common for therapists in training to routinely examine how they become afraid also. A hallmark of good supervision is the attendance of the supervisor to the supervisee's own internal processes that influence how he or she handles a case. When trainees come to supervision with a stalled case, it is usually a good idea to examine not only the potential fears the clients may be experiencing, but also the fears the therapist is experiencing (Campbell, Doane, and Guinan, 1983; Quinn, Atkinson, and Hood, 1985). When both parties are afraid together, you get the therapeutic equivalent of cement galoshes— nobody is going to go anywhere, except maybe home permanently.

The difficulty with managing the fear is that often it is almost imperceptible to everyone in the therapy room. Conversations, homework assignments, and various interventions are made, and therapy continues for perhaps several sessions, but very little happens. If pressed, the clients may say that they are working hard and so is the therapist, but right now not much improvement is occurring. The therapist may also say that everyone is working diligently, but that a very entrenched system is being addressed, and so overcoming systemic inertia takes time. Someone may comment that what is being worked on is a chronic problem which may never be seriously improved by therapy. Perhaps.

It may be, though, that either or both the clients and the therapist have encountered a systemic rule that some or all of them are unwilling to examine or break. They are afraid, and so they avoid addressing the rule, or they provide a decoy, or even a crisis, on which to focus (Quinn, Atkinson, and Hood, 1985). At the same time, clients in particular often *really want* change to occur at the level at which that rule operates, so they tend not to drop out of therapy at the first sign of danger, but rather stick with it, hoping that somehow something can be done without having to directly address or break the rule in question. The client and therapist may become stuck trying to solve a particular problem (or set of problems) with various interventions, etc., but it cannot be solved without dealing with the underlying rule. To apply a quote from cartoon character Foghorn Leghorn, "You're doing a lot of chopping, but no chips are flying." This is because the ax is not hitting the tree.

SOONER OR LATER YOU WILL KNOW YOU ARE STUCK WHEN . . .

So, how do you know when you have arrived at the point in treatment when you really are stuck—even if you may not feel like it? There is no single, surefire answer (perhaps other than the client, colleague, or supervisor who says, "Nothing is happening and nothing has happened for a while—this is a stuck case"), but there are a number of subtle or not-so-subtle signs which suggest that you may be at risk soon for getting stuck, or that you may already be stuck.

You Are Still Working on the Same Problem

One of the first things to look for as a sign of being stuck is determining what is being focused on in therapy. If after several weeks of regular work, you are still dealing with the same issue that brought the clients in and nothing has changed, you are most probably stuck. Fortunately, most people do not have to be rocket scientists to discern this, and it comes as no surprise to anyone. As the stuck therapist, you may feel embarrassed or frustrated, but the clients may feel some of the same things. Fortunately, though, at least everyone in this situation is aware of what is and is not happening.

It is not always quite so obvious that the same problem is indeed the focus of treatment. One way to tell if you are still working on the same problem is to determine if there is any sense of déjà vu—i.e., you have had some of the same conversations before, and maybe have tried the same class of intervention before. This is not the sort of thing that you will tend to notice from week to week, of course. More likely, you will find that you have already explored this or that issue about two months or so ago, and your notes reflect it. In the meantime, you have addressed several other issues of import, some or all of which were at least tangentially connected to the point of origin, or perhaps none were. For some of these other issues, you may have felt that you were making some decent progress until you got derailed onto yet another important topic. As you trace your treatment path, in fact, it may be quite unclear as to how you have managed to return to the same place. Nevertheless, there you are.

A Small Change Has Been Made

A variation on the "same problem" is when a small change has been made (i.e., a first-order change [Hoffman, 1981]), but things are not where the client would like them to be, and more and greater change is desired (i.e., a second-order change [Hoffman, 1981]). Perhaps the small change is one piece of the whole troublesome picture (e.g., a fifteen-year-old son has become more willing to participate in household chores, but his schoolwork remains problematic and he is still staying out after curfew). It is often the case that clients will make a small change, but then therapy stalls when they are faced with the prospect of larger, systemic change. Somewhere, a major homeostatic system rule may be operating.

A Problem Substitution Has Been Made: Different Symptom, Same Problem

Another version of the "small change/same problem" motif is symptom substitution. The original presenting problem is improved, but a new problem, usually of the same class but hard to recognize as such, arises. An example that is fairly obvious would be the fifteen-year-old son who has begun obeying his curfew, but is now skipping school. The particular complaint has been helped, but the class of problem—the son's acting out—remains and manifests itself now in the form of truancy. A less obvious example is the couple whose fights have become much more civil and are exemplary demonstrations of excellent communication skills, but who now complain that their sex life has evaporated. Their conflict may have gone underground as their communication patterns in arguing were changed, but the underlying system dynamics pertaining to control or the like were untouched. In either case, therapy has stalled.

Clients Are Unwilling to Follow Through with Directives

Another fairly obvious sign of stuckness is when you discover that clients are regularly disregarding therapeutic directives or homework assignments. Most clients are not out to "defeat" their therapists; thus, in these instances you should not take their apparent lack of cooperation as a personal affront. It is much more likely that they are just not ready to go where you have asked them to. This can be exceedingly frustrating, because sometimes the solutions seem so obvious (to you, anyway) that you cannot fathom *why* anyone would not follow through with them. In simple terms, however, their fear, of which they may be completely unaware, keeps them from movement.

There are other ways of thinking about it. Perhaps you have not yet found the way to cooperate with them. The way you want them to proceed springs from your fears; perhaps you are concerned with your effectiveness, and so you push them for change in a particular direction and at a pace that is commensurate with how you might want it done if you were the client. Their system, however, just does not work the same way, and so they appear to "resist" you by not following your directives. It may be that what you want for them as the solution to their problems does not fit with what they want as the solution. For example, you may feel that Mom needs to spend more time with the fifteen-year-old son to help him stay current on his schoolwork, but the family rule is to keep Dad at the center of the family and in control—even though they all want the son to get his act together at school. When your goals and those of the clients' are ostensibly the same, but how to attain them is at cross-purposes, you have a very high probability of getting stuck.

Everyone Feels Too Comfortable

Being stuck is not always frustrating, annoying, or uncomfortable. In fact, there is a great deal of seductiveness involved in some cases wherein getting stuck feels very nice. Everyone feels good about everyone else, and a pervasive sense that *some* progress is being made occurs, and yet concrete evidence of substantive change is elusive. The clients come to therapy regularly, they talk and engage with both you and each other, they do their homework (at least they make an effort), they pay, they seem motivated, and they think the world of you, their dedicated and caring therapist. Yet, the system is very analogous to a tarpit; it is warm and placid, but movement is nearly impossible. The difficult thing is that it can take a very long time to finally shake off the stupor and realize that therapy is stalled. If you find yourself becoming a bit bored or thinking that a particular case is blandly nice, or you have not taken any risks with a given case of late, you may have been seduced into a comfort zone of stuckness. Escaping from one of these cases and going on to do significant clinical work with it is no small feat.

You Are Fresh Out of Ideas

Every therapist occasionally finds him or herself running low on creative energy. Part of what makes therapists effective is their ability to help clients create a new way of thinking or behaving that makes a difference. It should be expected, then, that there will be sessions where the creativity on the part of the therapist is not up to its usual level, and so not much exciting will happen. It is an indicator of being stuck, however, if you find yourself consistently "out of creative gas" with a given case. Once you have taken your best clinical shots and have seen them disappear into the client system's black hole of homeostasis, you will find yourself empty of additional ideas. When you find yourself celebrating a certain client's cancellation or no-show, you may want to look hard to see if you are stuck. Parenthetically, if you find yourself celebrating cancellations and no-shows regularly, regardless of which cases they are, you are either working with a very difficult treatment population, or more likely, you may be struggling with burnout, which we will discuss in Chapter 16.

You Are Working Too Hard

Finally, a very good indicator of stalled therapy is how hard you believe you are working with a particular client. Therapy is both hard work and fun, and like any challenging activity, coming out pooped at the end of the day should not be all that unusual. Certain cases, however, will prove to be particularly draining, and if you find yourself mentally and emotionally exhausted after most sessions with someone, you may be stuck. If you need an hour or two break after seeing a given case, or you find yourself wanting to schedule them at the end of the day on a more regular basis, therapy may have stalled.

SOME STRATEGIES FOR REVITALIZING THERAPY

In any event, you *will* get stuck with your cases with some regularity. This is not so much an indicator of some deficiency in your skills, but more a measure of the difficulty of working with some human problems. Once you settle with yourself that it is okay to be stuck, you have already taken the first step toward getting unstuck. There is another step that you must take, however, before you begin strategizing about how to get started again. This step is the appropriate handling of your frustration. Stuck therapy cases can be exquisitely maddening if you allow them to penetrate your person. Our advice to you is to try to become somewhat detached personally as you approach cases professionally. If you find yourself cursing clients in your mind, thinking pejorative things about them, using their Axis II labels as descriptors that explain why they are stuck, or being even close to disrespectful or brusque with them, you need to get some breathing room.

If you cannot do this, you will develop an increasingly adversarial mind-set toward them, and you will lose your effectiveness, not to mention begin to sour your view of clients in general. This is a good recipe for clinical burnout, and you do not want to experience that. The price is too high for you and for those with whom you work. You must learn to handle your frustration in appropriate and effective ways. One way, of course, is to become more adept at getting stalled cases moving again. To this end, we would like to offer some ideas on how you might overcome therapeutic impasses; again, we offer no magic bullets or guaranteed strategies, but we have found some of the following to be fairly effective at restarting some stalled cases.

What Is the Hidden Rule?

As we have mentioned, often a treatment impasse results when a systemic rule is in danger of being violated, and someone important in the system is afraid of allowing that to happen. This important person could be a parent, a spouse, an identified patient child, even a therapist, or any combination of them. When therapy stalls, one of the first things to look for is the hidden rule. Ask yourself questions such as, "What is it that I do not feel I should do? What area am I supposed to stay out of? Who do I want to keep from getting angry, suicidal, or more depressed?" Your answers may be less cognitively generated than perceptible through your intuition or emotions—that is, it may be more useful to access your gut-level hunches and feelings than to analyze the case from a purely theoretical or cognitive level.

Approaching a supervisor or colleague about the case and having him or her ask you hypothetical questions (e.g., "What do you think would happen if you really pushed Dad?" "What do you think would happen if you asked Grandma to stay home next session?" "What do you think would happen if you egged Junior into a tantrum and then laughed at him?", etc.) can be a good way to try to make the rule more discernible. Your answers that make you uncomfortable, or answers that you would be particularly hesitant to enact, may indicate precisely the next step you should try to dislodge a stuck case. You also may benefit from thinking about what you would be thinking if you and your family were the client.

It is also important to recognize that dealing with systemic rules that clients (or you, or both) are very antsy about confronting or altering, or even making explicit, is risky business. The mere fact that you unearth a hidden rule is no guarantee that the result will be therapeutic. It could get quite messy. Therefore, you must do some thinking and strategizing beforehand about what you will do given particular responses. For example, if you really push Dad and he gets mad and says that he is leaving or that the family will not be returning, you need to be prepared to deal with that eventuality. You may not be able to prevent him from leaving, but you do need to make the effort to find some way to keep the family engaged; perhaps pushing him hard but humorously or leaving him an acceptable "out" so that his dignity can be preserved a little might work.

Shuffle the Players

You may or may not be able to discover explicitly the hidden rule or rules, but one way to affect them potentially, and hence to revitalize a stalled case, is to shuffle the participants. Changing who comes for sessions can make a substantial difference in what a system does and how it can be changed. Our suggestion is that the first shuffle usually should entail increasing the number of players. Get more people in (remember Chapter 7) so that there will be a greater number of access points into the system and more leverage with which to work. Additional persons, by the way, do not necessarily have to become permanent members of treatment. The second shuffle, if it is necessary, or when you are already starting with a large number participants, is to *eliminate* some participants on a temporary or perhaps permanent basis (and we do not mean eliminate them as "Hide the bodies!" You do have to watch your frustration level!). A third shuffle is to change combinations of participants: bring Dad and the children in together, and let Mom stay home or out in the waiting room. You can also bring in another therapist, a supervisor, a team, or if you have one-way mirror and observation room facilities, you can do any number of variations on live supervision or observation. This can be done on a one-time or ongoing basis.

Shuffle the Timetable

Another way to revitalize stalled therapy is to shuffle the spacing between sessions or even the length of individual sessions. The Milan team, prior to their breakup (we will forgo the musical group metaphors . . .), were very effective in drawing out treatment over the course of several months to a year by having marathon sessions once a month (Selvini Palazzoli et al., 1978). It may be that offering a stuck case that is accustomed to a fifty-minute weekly session a three- or four-hour session every few weeks, complete with an observing team, might be enough to get things moving again. It may be that the prospect of having that much time under the therapeutic microscope may prove to be too much for systemic inertia to dampen; of course, *you* also have to be ready and willing to experience the marathon session. Another less complex way to shuffle the timetable is simply to schedule a stuck case a few weeks between sessions, with the rationale that change takes time and there is no need to hurry. This may engender greater motivation on the part of clients to make something happen.

Be Provocative

Sometimes stalled therapy requires a more calculated but very dynamic action. This is especially true if you have stalled in a comfortable way, as previously discussed. You can try to be provocative by detonating a totally different theoretical approach on the client. Let us say you have been working from a solution-focused point of view (e.g., de Shazer, 1985), but the clients are just not able to note much improvement, few positive exceptions, and even their answer to the miracle question is anemic. Suddenly altering frameworks to some other approach, for example, an experiential one (e.g., Whitaker and Keith, 1981), may bring about something new and different. Doing some family sculpting (Constantine, 1978; Duhl, Kantor, and Duhl, 1973), or psychodrama (Moreno, 1952), or some such activity may catch clients off guard enough to make a change happen.

There are many ways to be provocative. Only one needs to work at it. Strategic interventions often are quite provocative; thus, if you are not prone to using them during most "normal" therapy, they may offer just the ticket to getting some stuck clients unstuck. Humor is another way to approach hidden rules that may underlie stalled therapy, thus allowing you to say and do things that restart treatment. You can also try to get some clients to take care of you—sometimes, clients care greatly for their therapists and do not wish to see them feel bad, so letting them know that you are beginning to feel like a failure with them may engender some movement from them on your behalf.

Consider Referral or Termination

Finally, you can sometimes get stuck cases moving again by considering out loud with them the possibility of referring them to another professional or even of terminating treatment. For the purposes of referral, you may simply suggest that the problem is beyond your ability and that it is time for them to try someone else, or that you just are not a good therapeutic "fit" with them. With regard to termination, it can be framed as "this problem is just a normal problem of living that you will have to deal with," or "it is obviously not so bad that it needs to be changed." We advise against implying to most clients, though, that they are "bad clients." A compassionate and benign spin is much more likely to encourage them to seek another clinician, or to keep the door open for them to return to therapy, either with you or with someone else should they indeed terminate.

With some cases, clients feel very strongly that they need their therapist's continuing involvement, even though no progress to speak of has been made. With these sorts of cases, announcing that a referral may be in order or that therapy may no longer be necessary can have a very strong motivating effect. Too, there are cases wherein termination becomes itself a therapeutic issue, and we will discuss this in more detail in the next chapter.

The stalled therapy case is a natural part of every clinician's professional life. Learning to accept that and deal as effectively as possible with these cases is a major part of developing as a mature and experienced practitioner. There will always be cases that you cannot restart, too, and treating them as "learning cases" is far wiser than looking at them as therapeutic failures for which you (or the clients) should be blamed. As you gain experience, you will develop your own tried and true methods for recognizing and revitalizing stalled therapy. Do not be shy about sharing them with your colleagues and supervisors. We all need as much help as we can get.

Chapter 14

Terminating When It Is Time

Finishing up a case in a planned and deliberate fashion is rarely ever the topic of an exciting workshop, article, or book, as we have mentioned. Termination as a subject just does not seem to grab many professionals' fancy very well. This is somewhat surprising in that, for some clients, termination done deliberately at the end of a successful course of treatment is something akin to a graduation. They may have feelings of accomplishment and pride, not to mention that they may be enjoying the benefits of having made the changes that they desired when they first began treatment.

A few writers have discussed how to conduct terminations at least to some degree (e.g., Lebow, 1995; Nichols, 1996; Worden, 1994), but it remains arguably one of the least well-investigated areas in the marriage and family therapy field. This lack of attention from researchers and theorists alike is the result of a number of factors, the most obvious being that terminations are not done deliberately nearly as often for the average clinician as they are done by de facto client decisions (Edwards, 1990; Phillips, 1987). Clients just stop coming, either ending with a no-show, a cancellation, or with "leaving it up in the air" when and if they will schedule their next appointment.

We believe, however, that many of these unilateral terminations could be avoided with a little preparatory effort on the part of therapists, and that there would be several benefits gained in so doing. Part of practicing good therapy includes terminating cases well as much as possible. It is true that no matter how good you are or will become, a percentage of your clients will terminate treatment unilaterally and you will be the last to know, finding out in the standard no-show or cancellation fashion. We believe that with some deliberate attention devoted to setting up the whole process of therapy with clients, including termination, you will do them and yourself a favor in terms of streamlining and tidying up the way therapy works as a matter of course.

PREPARING CLIENTS FOR TERMINATION

Termination begins long before you have a final session, write your treatment summary, or close a case. The process of wrapping up a case successfully is something that begins at the intake, and it requires some architectural work. Laying a firm foundation with clients on which all of therapy, including its conclusion, will be built will greatly increase the likelihood of ending well. We recommend that you open therapy with an eye for finishing it, and let clients know that therapy is not forever. Informing them that your expectation is to work yourself out of a job can give them a sense of hope that things are likely to change and that there will be an end to whatever struggles they may encounter during therapy. It also sends a clear message that you expect that they will take full responsibility for their own lives, culminating in disengaging from your helpful hand at the appropriate time.

Pragmatically, starting therapy with the inclusion of issues pertaining to termination is usually not difficult. In fact, it is not uncommon for consent for treatment forms to include something about the clients' right to know what therapy will consist of and how long they may expect treatment to last. Of course, the difficulty with this is that it is not usually very easy to predict at the beginning what therapy with a given case will involve or how long it will take. Even veteran clinicians lack the crystal ball for making highly accurate predictions of this nature, but they at least make the honest effort and are often not very far off the mark. The other important aspect is that many of these practitioners *do* make it a priority to give clients their best estimate about therapy's particulars and length. You should get in the habit of doing it, too.

Many clients will make having that discussion quite easy. For some clients, termination should have been yesterday, and they will not be shy in sharing their feelings about it with you. They are not particularly excited about being in therapy anyway; thus, in their minds, the sooner they can get done, the better. Court-ordered or otherwise-mandated clients often present this kind of attitude. You can do much to smooth their ruffled feathers by quickly moving to discuss finishing up therapy and what will be required to make that happen. Placing the responsibility for achieving the necessary results required to complete therapy on them along with the clear understanding that you will do all you can to help will likely increase their motivation. It will also help them to avoid seeing you as a pawn of the state or whomever it was that mandated their therapy.

For other clients, a major concern has to do with money, especially for those clients with minimal or no insurance coverage, and so discussing termination again may be very natural. Therapy can be pretty expensive; whenever you forget that, just imagine adding to your monthly budget four weekly therapy sessions at even the much lower than average cost of $50 each. Not too many people have an extra $200 a month to play with, and so committing to therapy with no idea about whether it will be three months or three years is asking clients for a great deal of trust. Not addressing their financial concerns explicitly can make you seem a bit on the greedy side, too (clients do not know where all the money goes; they assume that you get whatever they pay). After all, you are asking them to pay you a pretty penny regularly for a service that you and they both know has no guarantees for an undetermined amount of time. Change the service to, say, dry cleaning, and it is unlikely your shop would stay open very long.

You can do much to assuage clients' financial fears by letting them know up front that therapy is not going to last forever. You may want to contract with them informally to have conversations every few sessions about how things are going, how much longer you think therapy will go, and whether they want to continue. This gives them the most input into the decision, and it greatly increases the chances that termination will not be a surprise. It also will dispel any erroneous assumptions they may have that you are their only possible source of treatment, and instead will free them up to seek a referral should that become necessary (and on occasion it will).

For those clients who have some insurance coverage, too, financial matters still are salient, and issues pertaining to termination again may come up early on their own. For instance, managed care may dictate that you have four or six or ten sessions in which to work, and after that, it may seem like you need a note from the President himself to justify additional sessions. Clients may be understandably concerned that therapy will require more time and more sessions than they have coverage for; therefore, making the necessary effort to explain how you will work with their managed care company or insurance plan can make a big difference. Certainly included in this explanation should be some discussion of termination. You may want to pay particular attention to how things will be managed if insurance coverage runs out before therapy's end arrives; do not participate in the further denigration of the field's integrity by pronouncing them "cured" at about the same time as their insurance coverage is exhausted. To leave them hanging with no reasonable alternatives because they no longer have coverage is unethical (AAMFT, 1991). Any concerns they may have pertaining to this should be addressed long before that reality appears—if it ever does.

For some other clients, the very idea of termination is rather foreign, and although they may not have any difficulty discussing it with you at therapy's outset, they are not likely to broach the topic of their own initiative. These clients may be "therapy veterans" or "therapy junkies" who have been in and out of treatment for a long time and who tend to view therapy as an ongoing part of normal life rather than as a fairly goal-directed endeavor. The idea that therapy should have some more or less formal sequence of termination may not be very appealing to them because they have never experienced it before. Rather, it is possible that having moved from therapist to therapist much like a grazing animal samples a variety of pastures—stopping to browse here and there for a while and then moving on—they have never stopped to consider therapy as a "get in, get something done, and get out" process. Instead, they have moved into one therapist's office for a course of treatment, and then perhaps just petered out with that one, and then a while later, picked up with another one, basically addressing the same issues. Their therapy may have started formally several times, but ending has been a very blurry process, and because they have returned yet again to another therapist (or even the same one), they have never come to expect it to be different.

Discussing the proper purpose of termination with these clients is very important, unless you see no problem with them participating in therapy like someone participates in a hobby—it is something they have done, like to do, and want to continue to do, even if it is only on occasion or sporadic. There may be some clients for whom this way of operating is best, but we would argue that the risk among the majority of clients of encouraging their overdependence by continuing in this manner is too great to ignore. You must be prepared for clients for whom this is an accurate description to not be very excited about working with you; they may be more interested in a therapist "flavor of the month" than in approaching therapy with an eye for making significant, goal-driven changes.

WRAPPING UP THE SUCCESSFUL CASE

Putting the finishing touches on a successful therapy case is almost always a very nice feeling. It is a little bit like completing an elaborate and ornate sand castle, or placing the last piece on a ship built in a bottle (although we recognize the failure of these metaphors to adequately capture the clients' essential participation—therapy is done with clients, not to them). There is a feeling of pride in having done solid and challenging work, but there is also often a lurking sense of anxiety about the potential fragility of that work. You do not want someone or something to come along out of the blue at the last moment and wreck what has been so carefully and laboriously constructed.

In any event, the first step to wrapping up the successful case is making sure the whole idea of termination is placed on the table at the beginning. Once therapy is under way, it is always a good idea to periodically discuss finishing up. This is a useful way of monitoring the case's progress and also of staying focused on the issue(s) being worked on. Therapy that loses its sense of direction often stalls, and if that happens, clients are more likely to drop out and you, as the therapist, will feel the inevitable missing sense of closure. Having too many of these cases will eventually take a toll on you.

At the point in treatment when the goals set at the beginning are appreciably closer to being met, planning for termination needs to begin in earnest. The clients should be able to say in some form or fashion how much progress they have experienced and how much more they want, and you should be able to give them an estimate of how much longer therapy will need to continue to meet their goal(s). In the end, though, clients will know when they have come far enough, and you should avoid "being smarter" than they are and telling them that they are wrong, even if your theory directs you to question their assessment. You may raise concerns you have (in fact, you have that obligation), but you must recognize clients' right to make the decision finally for themselves.

A good termination of a successful case will usually include several key elements. First, it is often quite validating to both clients and therapists to spend some time reviewing the case's progress. Some clinicians with videotaping capabilities like to show a tape of an early session as a concrete reminder of where the clients were when they came in and as a poignant indicator of how different they may be now. Doing this sort of thing can help clients crystallize their belief in the changes they have made and give them a firmer resolve to maintain their accomplishments.

A second component of a good termination is the deliberate attention to giving genuine congratulations and compliments to the clients. They have worked hard and experienced success for which they bear the primary responsibility, and they deserve proper recognition. It is not uncommon for clients to do this among themselves, but it can be particularly meaningful when it comes from the clinician. Some therapists prefer to ritualize the last session into a time of reviewing gains and paying compliments, but it remains a very personal encounter. Like a proud parent, the therapist is giving his or her explicit approval for the clients' having terminated therapy after successfully addressing a serious issue.

Clients also usually appreciate being given the opportunity to pay their therapists compliments and express their gratitude. It is important that therapists learn how to take these positive strokes from clients well—it can be very disconcerting for clients' genuine feelings of appreciation, admiration, and thanks to be taken lightly or discounted. Doing so even runs the risk of undermining some of their progress. At the same time, it is not a good idea to overplay your significance or to go fishing for compliments. Your clients' gratuitous feelings about you should be allowed to just be what they are and to be expressed as such.

A third important element is having a discussion regarding the clients' expectations for the future vis-à-vis what therapy was about. Clients need to be prepared for the possibility of at least partial "relapse," or a return of the problem to a degree, either temporarily or on occasion. If they are terminating with the problem not "completely resolved," handling this concern is much simpler because they realize that the problem is not totally gone, or may never be. One way to mitigate the impact of relapse is to space out the last few sessions over longer and longer periods of time—up to several months—so that the clients experience something of normal, post-treatment life, including likely but small relapses, without coming apart. They will discover that they can still have difficulties in life without needing to continue formal treatment.

It is also often wise to explicitly leave the door open for clients to return, should they deem it necessary. Termination does not have to mean permanence, and clients need to know that although they may have "graduated," that does not mean they are not permitted to return for periodic "refreshers" as needed. In fact, normalizing the reappearance of symptoms will be a healthy dose of preventive medicine. Giving them the option to return as well reduces any pressure they may feel to avoid relapse, and it helps them keep from imbuing relapse with the stigma of total failure.

Another element common to good terminations is discussing the pragmatics of maintaining and continuing change. Beyond letting them know that some relapse is normal, clients can benefit greatly from being given prescriptions for what to do after therapy ends that can help them maintain their gains and perhaps even continue to make more progress. Giving them sources of help, such as recommended books for further reading, advocacy and support groups, psychoeducational opportunities, and the like, is a very good way to keep your successful cases successful after they are no longer seeing you.

It will be very common, however, for you to broach the topic of termination with clients only to find that they are not quite ready. Clients who experience some success in working with you on their presenting issues are apt to bring up a new problem or concern that they wish to work on. You should welcome the opportunity, and address it in the same way you did with their presenting complaint—by giving them your best estimate of approximately how long therapy may be expected to take and what might be involved. In these instances, you may consider treatment to be more like a new case than a continuing one.

There is a significant caveat to bear in mind in these instances, however. You need to learn to discern genuine appeals to address new issues from some clients' fears of letting go and their subsequent "invention" of additional therapeutic issues. This is not easy to do, and we recommend that you regularly give clients the benefit of the doubt when they say they have something else to work on with you. The difference will likely become more apparent over time, as the case begins to resemble more and more the comfortably stalled cases discussed in Chapter 13—different issue, same class of problem. When this happens, you may need to take more directive and controversial-sounding actions.

FIRING CLIENTS—YES, YOU CAN (AND MAY HAVE TO) DO IT

Every therapist's caseload sooner or later includes a "case that will not end." Therapy is stuck, and probably has been for some time. You have exhausted yourself and become either very frustrated or very complacent, glumly accepting their regularly scheduled sessions like a visit from obnoxious or boring relatives who, because of your family duty, you cannot disown. You may have been absorbed into the client system's homeostasis or repeatedly rebuffed from accessing parts you believe to be crucial to making something happen. In any case, therapy is going nowhere, but the clients do not seem to be interested in discontinuing or doing anything different.

In these cases, you have to take action that from your training would be considered drastic or perhaps even unthinkable. It may be that your clients are just not going to be successful working with *you.* Then again, they may not be successful with anyone, but you will not ever know that for certain, and you and they should definitely consider giving another professional a try. The best course of action for you to take with such cases after you have exhausted a variety of strategies is to refer them to someone else, but in any event, you should discontinue seeing them. Bluntly, you may have to "fire" your clients.

In situations where such an action is warranted, it needs to be handled carefully. First, the clients may not see that therapy is stuck, or they may not want to. If so, you will need to help them to see the dearth of observable progress and explain to them that perhaps it is time to move on. Making it clear that you perceive yourself to be primarily responsible for the lack of action will help them hear you and more readily accept your suggestions about how to proceed.

However you find yourself having to dismiss clients, they need to be informed in such a way that they do not come away feeling as if they are in some way defective. They, in fact, do bear some responsibility for therapy's failure (and success), but it is not a good idea to emphasize that fact. Instead, you should emphasize both your responsibility for therapy's lack of progress and your concern that they be in the best possible position to obtain help. Suggesting referral at this point is quite logical, and if you have any specific professionals in mind, now is the time to reveal them. It is sometimes the case that some clients either need to move on to someone else or try later, and if you explain this to clients, they are much more likely to be open to doing so.

There are some situations, however, in which firing clients is necessary for other reasons. Clients can on occasion become rather attached to their therapists and to being in therapy, and they will be most reluctant to disengage from treatment even when it appears that there are few good reasons to continue. Simply put, some clients stay in treatment because they become overly dependent on it. Clinicians that allow these clients to stay in therapy without ever addressing the dependence issue do a grave disservice to them, even though it may be a flattering feeling to be so important to someone that he or she does not want to sever the ties. The fact is that unless you plan to see a client for the rest of his or her life, you only prevent him or her from becoming self-sufficient by allowing the person to remain in therapy longer than is necessary.

Overly dependent clients are not usually too hard to spot once you have had some experience with them. They tend to be very genuinely appreciative of all your help to them, and they are usually not stingy with compliments and thank-yous. They also tend to be motivated for therapy and to openly self-disclose with little hesitation. Very often they have some prior experience being in therapy and tend to place a high value on it. In short, at the start of therapy they look like the type of clients therapists like to have.

It usually takes a while before the question of overdependence enters the therapist's mind. Indicators to watch for include the addition of issues whenever some progress in a given area is noted; this may be framed as "there is always something to work on." Many therapists tend to agree with or appreciate this mind-set; therefore, they tend to not look twice for any patterns to show that there may be a dependency fostered that is not in the client's best interests. Another sign of overdependence is the prevalence of minor relapses after progress has been made. These reappearances of symptoms are not so serious as to elicit questions of complete failure, but they are significant enough for the client and therapist to agree that treatment needs to continue. Another sign of possible overdependence is the uncanny timing of crises that occur just as the reality of termination becomes more clear; these crises may be unrelated to therapy's focus or they may be quite relevant to it. In any case, these crisis events are justification to stay in therapy "just until things settle down a bit." The problem is that these little extensions of treatment may end up lasting for months. If you find that you were expecting to terminate a given case several months ago and yet issues keep delaying that, you may have a problem of overdependence on your hands.

Perhaps the most difficult thing about overdependence is that it is very hard to discern where a legitimate reason for therapy ends and an overdependence reason begins. We recommend that you pay attention to your own hunches, but that you also seek supervision to obtain an alternative perspective. One way to assess overdependence is to schedule clients' sessions a little bit less often or with more time between them and see if they still continue, especially if you frame the scheduling as your confidence that they need therapy less and less. If they continue to come and never say that they feel like they are getting close to stopping, they are likely overdependent.

The second real difficulty with overly dependent clients is that they can be extremely hard to uproot. If these cases were plants, they would be dandelions! You may be surprised at how blunt you may have to be with clients to make it clear that you do not believe continuing therapy is good for them. In some of these cases, you may only be able to get them to terminate by either giving them an assignment you know they will probably not do and stipulating that they cannot return until they do it (and if they do it, it requires a second-order change), or putting so much pressure on them through provocative interventions that it is easier to discontinue treatment than to continue. Neither of these strategies is particularly enjoyable.

You may find it necessary on rare occasions to fire some other kinds of clients also. Among those that may prove to need such a strong hand are dangerous clients, unethical clients, and clients who refuse to pay their bills. Dangerous or hostile clients are those that repeatedly put you in untenable situations as a result of their refusal to abandon potentially risky activities. Clear examples would be the court-ordered spouse-abusing client who refuses to abide by the court's terms for dealing with the partner and who tells you so, or the substance abuser who refuses to participate in a recovery group despite his or her likelihood for relapse. In our view, it would be better for you to inform these types of clients of your unwillingness to continue to work with them unless they comply with the directives of the court, yourself, or to whomever they are accountable. If you do not make this clear and somebody is seriously injured or dies while under your care, you may be in for some very uncomfortable times, even if you are ultimately not liable. Requiring compliance with whatever rules are set up for clients also sends the clear message that you are there to help them, but you will not brook any shenanigans. If they are not serious, you are telling them to go elsewhere.

Unethical clients are also problematic because they put you in a position in which you must choose between doing what they want (however therapeutic or benign it may seem) and maintaining ethical standards. Clients who insist on pursuing multiple relationships with you that could be avoided with little difficulty are members of this group. These relationships could be social, business-related (like Amway), recreational, or whatever, but they all share the problem of duality of relationship in which the possibility of exploitation of them or you exists, as was discussed in Chapter 12. Another unethical client situation that you may have the experience of facing at some point in your career is being the target of a client's attempted seduction. We would advise that you get as far away from that client as possible with microscopically detailed documentation of the whole process. A client who repeatedly pushes your boundaries must be set straight or terminated. Neither you nor they can afford the risk of ethical violations or their consequences.

Clients who run up a large bill and make no effort to pay must also be terminated. This may seem to be a rather cruel thing for a professional helper to do, but you will probably not think that for long once your creditors start bothering you for payments you are late making because your clients have not made theirs. You are a professional who deserves fair compensation for rendered services, and clients who take unjust advantage of the caring nature of the field need to be jettisoned quickly. Paying bills can easily become a therapeutic issue, but we would advise you address it as soon as it appears rather than later. If it is necessary to terminate a client for nonpayment, make sure that you have all your bases covered and inform the client in several ways repeatedly of the situation before termination is actually done (it is likely the agency for whom you work has a policy to take care of these occurrences; if so, follow it closely).

If you develop practice habits that attend to every phase of treatment from beginning to end, you will be a better clinician, pure and simple. Termination is an easy area to overlook, but it can be a very critical period in therapy that, when done well, makes a big difference. It is said that people tend to remember best the first part and last part of an activity or event; if so, a strong memorable termination can help clients maintain their gains and also make them more likely to think highly of you. This can be important in terms of generating new referrals and developing a respected reputation as a professional marriage and family therapist. To a degree, in therapy, "all is well that ends well." Learn to make that happen regularly.

Chapter 15

Here Comes the Judge . . . and Attorneys: Some Pragmatic Advice for Typical Situations Involving the Legal System

One area that produces great discomfort for not only beginning therapists but also for veteran therapists is dealing with the legal system. Comparatively few therapists develop much legal experience and choose to actually specialize in performing various legal system-related services. This rare breed's typical functions tend to center around playing the role of recognized expert in making evaluations pertaining to divorce actions, child custody disputes, child abuse and neglect cases, foster care placement decisions, adoptive parent and family home studies, domestic violence assessments, and other marriage- and family-related matters. For most "regular" therapists, however, their sole desire is generally to do therapy and stay as far away from the legal system as possible.

Nevertheless, most therapists will see the inside of a courtroom as a professional or "expert" witness at one time or another in their career. The variety of ways in which you may find yourself tangled up with some aspect of the legal system cannot be underplayed. Going to court may turn out to be routinely relatively unexciting (and that is not a bad way to go), but you should not be surprised to experience a court visit at some point as a most memorable happening (positively or negatively). It is important to recognize that a degree of influence over the direction of court appearances can be had if you take the necessary time and effort to prepare for them, and like most aspects of clinical practice, it is wise to do that sooner than later. (We strongly recommend Charles Huber's *Ethical, Legal, and Professional Issues in the Practice of Marriage and Family*

Therapy [1994, second edition] as an excellent primer on dealing with the legal system.)

Preparation for this eventuality should be undertaken in several ways. First, you must understand both the ethical principles of your particular professional discipline and the legal mandates for various mental health professionals set down by state and federal courts. They are not the same for everybody; in fact, laws vary from state to state in ways that sometimes boggle the mind. Additionally, laws change regularly as new court decisions are made. Taking a course on professional ethics and legal issues as part of your graduate program is a very good way to become familiar with the legal particulars of your state, and most clinical training programs include a required course in this area. If, however, you do not have such a class in your course of study (or have graduated already without having taken one), we urge you to rectify the situation as soon as possible via formal course work or at least through several workshops or conferences pertaining to these subjects.

Second, your supervisors can be an important source of wisdom as a result of their experiences in court and with the legal system in general. Case reviews, formal and informal, can be extremely useful in grasping how the system really works (and it is not like it is portrayed on television shows). Such reviews can also help you see how therapists are often viewed by the legal system and how they can get in trouble when they stray from keeping adequate documentation, acknowledging their professional limitations, or maintaining competent practice. Accompanying your supervisor or another senior clinician to a court hearing or trial can provide you with a feel for the territory. Third, consulting with a legal assistance program set up by your professional organization (such as the AAMFT Legal and Risk Management Plan) can give you up-to-the-minute information on legal issues you may be likely to encounter.

It is not our intent to try to discuss herein the formalities of working in the legal system, but rather to give you some brief advice on a few typical situations you may find yourself faced with from time to time. We will look at situations in which clients may be looking for your professional expertise as a weapon in the courtroom, attorneys solicit your testimony for a case that you may or may not have treated, situations may elicit strong feelings about vouching for a client, and you must deal with legal threats made against you.

CLIENTS LOOKING FOR PROFESSIONAL THERAPIST COURTROOM "MUSCLE"

First, keeping in mind that the legal system is very often an adversarial environment where the goal is winning (or getting the best deal in a compromise or settlement) is essential. Therapeutic issues usually are not at the forefront of anyone's mind. Therefore, things can and often do get rather messy, and the risk of clients being harmed in some way during the course of the proceedings is significant. Clients often do not adequately appreciate the degree of difficulty that going to court can produce, for both themselves and for the therapist. In our view, it is a far better option in many and arguably most situations for clients to work out their difficulties via some type of mediation services rather than the more emotionally and financially damaging route of formal legal action. Despite what you would like to believe about the pursuit of truth and justice in the legal system, you must recognize the reality of how the system works, with all its flaws, inequities, loopholes, absurdities, and manipulations.

You should begin to think about the possibility of your being requested to participate in legal proceedings as early as the intake session. With the vast majority of your cases, legal issues will be at most peripheral, and for many, there will be nothing at all about which you need to be concerned. Fortunately, most cases do not end up finding their way into courts, pursuing litigation against anyone.

On the other hand, in some clinical situations, it pays to be vigilant about potential legal repercussions from the beginning. For instance, clients coming in for marital therapy are possible divorce cases, and you may find yourself being pulled in different directions by them. Couples that state during the initial session that they each have an attorney on retainer not only give you insight into their marital relationship but also the possibility that you might be slated, in the mind of one or both of them, as a potential weapon in court. In cases such as this, it is advisable to inform clients at the beginning of treatment, or at least as early in therapy as possible, that should they attempt to involve you in some legal action, everything they communicate to you can be made fair game if you are called into court as a weapon for either of them. This may seem like a poor way to begin a relationship that has the legal protection of confidentiality, and it is awkward, sending them a message that acknowledges their marriage's plight and implying that it may not be solvable. However, if legal action appears to be a possibility on the horizon, it is best to be clear. Otherwise you may have them coming to you later inquiring about and requesting that your testimony be tailored to their need to win in court.

We have found that a good way to stay out of court altogether is to be very clear about what is likely to happen if you are brought into the courtroom to offer testimony about their case. First, you can mention that you will probably end up having both positive and negative things to say about each of them from the therapy experience, and even remind them of specific areas in which they may have some culpability. You also should let them know that each of their attorneys will have complete freedom to ask and probe about most anything about them, from your professional point of view as gleaned from treatment, once the clients decide to open up their Pandora's box in a courtroom. You can even underscore the potential risks each of them engages as a consequence of involving you by helping them see what potential effects information you may reveal could have on their case. They need to be made aware that their wisest choice may be to keep you out of the courtroom altogether.

Despite your best efforts to protect their interests, it sometimes works out that clients do not believe the risks outweigh the potential benefits, and so you will be brought to the stand. If they mutually choose to sign release of information consent forms to fight it out in court using the "turf" of their therapy sessions, then they lose control of their privilege to have confidentiality maintained. This is consistent with the notion of the mutual responsibility clients have for what they make of their relationships. It is also helpful for you because their consent for you to testify means you have to tell the whole story as objectively as you can and not just the way each of them would like to remember it.

Another frequent type of case in which legal concerns are apparent at intake is where one of the parents, in a postdivorce situation, brings the children in for therapy because they seem unhappy or disobedient. When you inquire about the other parent you might hear, "My ex-spouse wouldn't be interested in participating, and in fact he (she) is the reason I have to bring the kids in for counseling." This may be a clue regarding an anticipated court action where one parent may be trying to gain custody from or restrict the visitation privileges of his or her ex-spouse. Alarm bells should go off in your head when you encounter such a case. A married person seeking individual treatment may also have divorce or custody matters in mind with hopes of using you as an advocate in court in the near future.

In postdivorce situations, you should require clients to provide you with a copy of the divorce papers as an addition to the consent for treatment they must sign. This will enable you to be clear on who has what kind of custody (sole, joint, or shared) or visitation (none by choice, none by court order, attempting to secure it through this request for therapy, every other weekend and one weeknight, or whatever possible based on the schedules of the two parents). It is also a way to determine who is actually (rather than reportedly) responsible for what part of the therapy fee. (We advise you against taking a client's word on it, having been stiffed on more than a few occasions.) It is also valuable to have the nonparticipating parent either involved through invitation to a session or by signing a consent for treatment form indicating his or her awareness of the therapy and his or her rights to consult with you.

The skill that you will develop as you mature as a therapist is to most often "sniff" these situations out during a preappointment telephone consultation or very shortly after clients enter treatment. This is not to say that you should be overly suspicious, but that it is wise to listen for words and statements that may indicate an underlying agenda with legal or court implications. While you would understandably want to assume that any client who comes to see you is coming for therapeutic treatment, you must be wary that you may present a very attractive weapon for interpersonal warfare in the courts.

ATTORNEYS SEEKING AN EXPERT: "HOW'D YA LIKE TO BE ON OUR SIDE?"

Without giving in to the temptation to begin this section with a lawyer joke (it *is* difficult), we will discuss the tricky business of attorneys approaching you to be involved in a case. This may be a case you are currently treating or one you have worked with in the past, but the underlying rationale in either instance is to present you as the best source for a professional opinion because you are or were the therapist involved in treating the case in question. The logic of this approach does not require an inordinate amount of brain power to appreciate. Another possibility may be the situation where you receive a request to do some short-term evaluation or treatment with one of the attorney's cases so that you can be brought in for the purpose of offering testimony on "their side." The rationale here is to qualify you with the court as an "expert witness" as a way to get your opinion in the court record. In this situation, you would be brought in as a "hired gun."

As a beginning therapist, it is highly unlikely that you will be in the latter "hired gun" situation anytime soon. In fact, your "newness" to the field probably makes you less of an expert to attorneys and the court. Thus, being called into court early in your career is likely a sign that you may be viewed more as a vulnerable target, not an expert, by one party in an adversarial case. As you develop experience, however, especially as you may develop a reputation for a particular area of specialization, the likelihood of your being called upon to provide expert testimony is greater. All in all, it is more likely that your first encounter with the legal system will be within the context of a case for which you are or were the therapist. Therefore, it is important to understand the process you will encounter.

Attorneys can be varied in their style of presentation when approaching you to be involved in a court case. They may have had their client prepare you about the anticipated action or they may call you up out of the blue. They may be quite pleasant and ask about both your willingness to participate and any concerns you may have about participating in the legal process. They may demonstrate some degree of understanding of mental health treatment. They may solicit your input or advice about the case. And they may do all of this after having secured and forwarded to you the properly signed release of information forms.

However, it should be no surprise that some attorneys approach you very differently. Some attorneys may be aggressive and bullying, treating you as if you are one of their many subordinates. They may present you with a demand (or threat of subpoena) that you participate in the court proceedings. They may tell you what is going on with the case without any interest in or regard for your observations. And they may do this all with an attitude that a properly completed release of information form is a requirement for everyone else in the world except attorneys. And, of course, there will be all the various degrees between these two extremes and combinations of these and other characteristics (with many twists and turns) that you will encounter during your career.

As a beginning therapist, it is important to be aware of how you might be intimidated when approached by an attorney. With their effort to win for their client (maybe at any cost), they are not necessarily concerned (or familiar) with the ethical standards of your particular profession nor the dynamics of the client's clinical situation that may suggest many different options or viewpoints than the ones on which the attorney is focused. This can very much be the case where the custody of children is involved. The attorneys are hired by the adult clients, and of course, all the adults profess to have the best interests of the children as their first priority. In reality, the clients can be out to defeat each other, exact revenge, or just make life a little more complicated for their former partner, and their attorneys are hired to win for them. In the meantime, the children can be left out of the loop unless a guardian *ad litem* is appointed to represent them in the proceedings.

For just these types of situations, you must remain grounded in the laws and ethical principles that govern your work. You must guard against being pushed, cajoled, coerced, or manipulated into behaving outside these principles by an attorney simply bent on orchestrating his or her client's "victory" in court. It is not unusual for clients themselves to be pushed or manipulated away from their own feelings and positions on a legal matter in deference to the view of an aggressive "professional attorney" (after all, who knows best?) who may be thinking more about the size of his or her fee and the "thrill of the kill" in the heightened hostility of a more intense legal dispute. We do not wish to imply that lawyers are all despicable characters (calling to mind the idea that the difference between a lawyer and a shark is that one is a bloodthirsty, ruthless, bottom-dweller and the other is a fish—see, we just could not contain ourselves!); in fact, some attorneys are very sensitive and careful when dealing with therapy clients. Unfortunately, however, some are quite the opposite, and we believe it is important to be heedful of that as you encounter attorneys with reference to clients.

Inevitably, you will encounter attorneys in the course of your professional duties, and there are a few important points to remember regarding contacts with them. A paramount concern is to make sure all communication occurs only after all the necessary signed release of information forms have been executed and exchanged. This is fairly straightforward when you are discussing an individual client with whom you have worked, but it is a bit more complicated in those situations where you have treated a couple or family. The more people involved, the hairier it gets. In these cases, you must have the written permission of all the adult clients involved (not just the one associated with the attorney who contacts you), as well as that of any other adults with legal rights (e.g., a former spouse, parent, or other legal guardian not in treatment with joint custody of any of the children being seen) before discussing the case.

Another serious thing for you to keep in mind concerns being cognizant of the potential consequences for the client of legal action involving him or her. Remember that your contract is with the client, and your first priority is to be therapeutically responsive to the goals you and they together have formulated in treatment. This way of viewing your case should not be overshadowed by the legal agenda of the attorney—or even the client. As always, you should thoroughly document these contacts with attorneys as well as discuss them with the client both before and after they occur.

VOUCHING FOR YOUR CLIENTS

Another point of contact with the legal system will occur in those instances in which you have cases that enter the legal arena and you will hold a very strong desire to advocate for your client. These may be cases in which the person(s) with whom your client is at odds has had no contact with you. You may have worked with the client as an individual (albeit from a systemic perspective) because of one or more of a number of reasons: no family members were willing or able to participate, the client desired to work individually on very sensitive issues before involving family members, and/or the client may be estranged from his or her spouse/children/family of origin. The particular issues of the therapy, such as sexual abuse or uncertainty about sexual orientation, may also be a determining factor in the decision for individual therapy. In any case, you may find your client embroiled in a legal battle and feel that due to the work you have done with this client, he or she needs and deserves your support in the form of court testimony.

If your client and his or her attorney decide that they want your participation, they will generally be able to secure it through a subpoena. However, in many situations the client and attorney will want to know beforehand how you would testify via a preliminary consultation in which the attorney will question you about your observations and opinions. The strength of your responses in this consultation will determine whether the attorney will deem you helpful to the case, in part, due to your answers to the questions already posed and the potential vulnerability in exposing you to the opposing attorney's cross-examination. It is at this juncture that your feelings about your observations and opinions will come into play, that is, your feelings that you want to vouch for your client. Whereas your professional opinion is what is being offered in court, it is your empathic and personal feelings about your client and your work with him or her that can have an important influence on whether an attorney deems you a useful witness. For these reasons you should carefully examine, with the help of your supervisor, your personal issues and your feelings about your client to be sure they are not unduly influencing how you would present your professional observations and opinions.

There will also be cases in which you have worked with both parties and feel that your professional evaluation/opinion clearly is and should be more supportive to one of the parties. In these situations, you will be viewed as taking sides between two clients whom have been in treatment with you. This can be a very difficult decision, and it has great potential to result in the other client feeling betrayed by you. These are vexing experiences in which you feel compelled to choose a side in an adversarial process that is diametrically opposed to your role as a marriage and family therapist.

Situations such as these often mirror those times in therapy when you say something to a client that he or she really does not want to hear. The outcome can go either way. The client may either become defensive and withdraw from you or may reflect on what you have said in a way to allow it to sink in and hit home if it is on the mark. As you experience more of these kinds of moments as a therapist, you will gain a sense of how to handle the more intense situation in which what the client does not want to hear comes in the form of court testimony.

An example might be a postdivorce custody dispute in which you have treated the family both prior to and after the divorce. You have a fairly good sense about the children and their feelings, you have watched the custodial parent function pretty solidly, and you have observed the noncustodial parent remain hooked on a need to get revenge with regard to the ex-spouse. You can see how much this anger and need for revenge taints the reasoning offered in therapy and in court by the noncustodial parent for the proposed custody change. While on the one hand, you may empathize very deeply for this parent and the loss he or she experiences in not having daily contact with his or her children, at the same time you observe how the custody change proposed would better serve the emotional needs of the noncustodial parent's transition through divorce than it would serve the needs of the children. Your role in a situation like this one is not easy or comfortable, but your participation is nonetheless necessary when considering the needs of all the family members, but particularly those of the children who must live with less decision-making power than their parents who chose divorce as a solution. And as before, you should examine your issues and feelings carefully to be sure they are not unduly influencing how you would present your professional observations and opinions.

DEALING WITH LEGAL THREATS

There may be times, especially in the situations we have just discussed, where someone will not be very happy with you because of your testimony in a case. This may be a client, one of the client's family members, or a client's friend/significant other who feels compelled to express his or her dissatisfaction. A statement you might hear could be, "These blankety-blank professionals think they have the right to tell people how to run their lives; who do they think they are, anyway?" These statements in part come out of frustration with the court system, in which the legal process takes away some of clients' power to make decisions in their own lives.

At any rate, you will experience some of other people's unhappiness in the form of hostility. Some people will strike out at you verbally in an effort to dissuade you from giving your testimony or to try to vent the anger that can come with disappointment in losing and the accompanying feelings of helplessness. This may involve a threat of legal action against you ("I am going to sue you for everything you have and your license to practice"), or, on a rare occasion, a threat of physical harm toward you. These situations, though not your everyday occurrence in professional practice (thankfully!), can nonetheless be very traumatizing for a therapist. It is best to process any of these with your supervisor as soon as possible, for your own mental health and because of the potential legal ramifications for the supervisor and agency. In agency work, you will find that each institution will have an attorney on retainer for purposes of legal discussions on all kinds of questions and situations that may arise. You can utilize these services through your supervisor as well as the services of your professional organization's legal assistance program.

If you have your own personal attorney, it would also be advisable to at least notify him or her of a legal or personal threat against you, so he or she would be aware of the situation if services might be needed. It may be that your attorney, who does terrific wills and mortgage closings, would much rather refer you to a colleague who has greater expertise in these types of situations. In any case, if any threats actually are followed through, then you will need the assistance of your supervisor, the agency attorney, and possibly your own personal attorney.

Numerous other situations will arise in which you may have some contact with the legal system, and one of the unfortunate things about that is that you can only prepare so far. The rest will have to come with time and sometimes painful or annoying experience. Do not fear it, but do respect it. As with most other components of professional therapists' work, dealing comfortably and competently with the legal system is a skill that will be developed over the course of your career.

Chapter 16

Avoiding Clinical Burnout

The term "burnout" has become widely overused in our culture and, like many other words, has lost some of its ability to impart meaning. In the world of clinical practice, it is often overused to express a mixture of tiredness, boredom, frustration, and waning enthusiasm (Farber, 1990). Still, it is a word that requires attention when it is mentioned because it has serious implications when it is an accurate assessment of a given therapist's condition. All therapists experience on occasion some of the above feelings, and they should be considered normal in such a context. What is not normal and is a cause for concern, however, is when these feelings are not occasional, but instead accurately describe a therapist's regular state of mind.

Our experience of feeling clinically "burnt out" can be easily conveyed through the metaphor of taking care of a car. A car ceases to function in any number of ways, including when it runs out of gas, a tire blows, or when the engine overheats. All of these are troubles that can usually be avoided by paying attention to routine preventive and remedial maintenance; cars inevitably break down without it. In the same way, therapists have a limited amount of physical, emotional, and psychological energy with which to do psychotherapy, and if they do psychotherapy without sufficient professional and personal support and nurturance (regular maintenance), a breakdown will ensue. And, with both cars and therapists, the costs of allowing a breakdown to occur are much more egregious than are those required to perform routine maintenance. In this chapter we will look at some ways therapists move in the direction of clinical burnout, usually unknowingly. We will also discuss some ways for you to take care of yourself, both professionally and personally, so that you may not only survive but flourish.

CLINICAL BURNOUT 101: BLURRING BOUNDARIES

The world of clinical practice can be very exciting and stimulating. As therapists start their paid professional experience, much is both intriguing and challenging, so much so that many often feel they want to learn it all and do it all right away. They are driven both by this natural "newcomer's" feeling and by the desire to accumulate some real experiences so that they feel a stronger sense of competence, or at least less confused and incompetent. As the "new kids on the block" in their first agency position, they generally want to make a good impression, to fit in, and to feel like one of the team. This combination of natural enthusiasm and self-induced pressure to perform is often what drives some of new therapists' best work.

In the rush to become professionally established, however, many marriage and family therapists forget the first and most important rule of being a therapist: Keep a clear distinction or boundary as much as possible between one's personal self and one's professional role as a therapist—involve your whole person in your role, but do not "do your own work" in other people's therapy (Aponte, 1992). Many novice practitioners consciously or unconsciously overwhelm themselves by trying to do too much, sometimes for some questionable reasons, in an effort to prove to themselves (and their employers) that the agency director did not make a mistake in hiring them. The two areas in which this can easily arise are with therapists' schedules and client caseloads.

Therapists have some of the stranger-looking schedules compared to many professions. Contrary to the stereotypical media portrayal of the private practitioner (the old Bob Newhart TV series from the 1970s, for instance), most mental health professionals do not have ultimate control over their schedules and do not make scads of money in the meantime. In fact, the typical agency clinician has one of the most demanding schedules around. For starters, productivity standards must be considered.

All agencies have productivity standards, which refer to the number of therapy sessions a clinician must do each week to justify his or her salary. The percentage of a forty-hour work week required to meet one's productivity standard can range anywhere from 50 percent (twenty sessions) to 70 percent (twenty-eight sessions). Just taking the time and energy to conduct that many sessions regularly each week is no small feat—it is a full-time caseload that some clinicians never develop the stamina to handle on an ongoing basis. However, beyond these twenty to twenty-eight client contact hours, during the remaining hours each week, therapists are not twiddling their thumbs, either. These hours are taken up with the other essential, nonnegotiable components of clinical work: telephone calls (they never end), documentation (it *really* never ends), meetings (ranging from critically important to seemingly downright pointless), informal collegial interaction ("Can we talk about the family I just saw?"), and supervision (both individual and group/case conference). Each therapist may also have public relations, community service, or other regular duties. We therapists tend to stay pretty busy.

As if this normal level of craziness is not enough, there is more. It is also standard practice that evening hours (usually two evenings a week) and/or some Saturday time be available in the therapist's schedule for the convenience of clients who work 9 to 5, Monday through Friday. There are also the inevitable emergencies that some of the more fragile and at-risk clients have, which usually seem to come at the most inconvenient times (during the work day in the middle of a session, in the evening during anything relaxing and enjoyable, or in the middle of the night during a terrific dream). Added to these responsibilities is often a strong sense of needing to remain current with the literature of the field as a means by which to become more competent. You now may expect a work week consisting of a minimum of two twelve-hour days and two eight-hour days at the agency, time at home for professional reading, and an occasional weekend conference or workshop (often out of town) to sharpen your skills and meet continuing education credits for your license and credentials. This all adds up in both hours and energy, and it continues week after week, month after month (clinical mental health practice in the real world does not operate on semesters or quarters with comfortable two-week breaks in-between and a lighter load during the summer). Are you feeling tired yet?

It is clear that in the course of simply performing your regular duties at the typical agency, you run the risk of getting seriously drained. Add to that the natural enthusiasm that accompanies your first clinical job, and it is frighteningly easy to see how you can be carried into being/becoming a therapist to the unintentional exclusion of your personal self. It is not unusual, too, that clients sometimes expect therapists to be like the emergency room—always open and available, twenty-four hours a day, seven days a week. You may work for an agency that, in an effort to be very customer-friendly, will also expect you to be accessible beyond your forty scheduled hours. Last, but certainly not least, is your own striving to be a good therapist to your clients and in the estimation of your employer. All of these factors easily if unintentionally conspire to prepare you for an unpleasant trip toward burnout. And if you forget that your personal "self" and your therapist "role" need to be clearly separate, you are only being your own worst enemy. Not only will you be increasing greatly the risk of untoward outcomes for yourself in all areas of your life, but you will also be placing your clients, the very ones you are trying so hard to serve well, at risk as well.

CLINICAL BURNOUT 201: EGO, ROLE, IDENTITY, AND CONFUSION

Just like clients, professional therapists have egos that can be, at times, both a solid asset and a tremendous liability to their work. The responsibility of being a therapist alone can weigh heavily on you, but it is often compounded by the intense (and good) desire many therapists have to be maximally helpful to those who come to them. This strong sense of responsibility can bring with it great difficulties vis-à-vis your confidence. The normal fears about not being smart enough or creative enough or just really good enough, when left unchecked, can tear at your insides and make self-doubt a constant and unwanted companion.

At other times, the prestige that comes with being a therapist can act as a stimulant or intoxicant for an ego yearning to be inflated. A therapist can become quite full of him or herself and how important he or she is because others seek out (and pay) for his or her services. Therapists can be seduced by the power of the position and use it, quite unconsciously, to hide their immature side and act out their darker impulses and unresolved issues. Dealing with their personal history, the "story" that is their life, is work that cannot be ignored (Titelman, 1987). To paraphrase that famous quotation about history as it would apply to a therapist, "If you do not learn about your own issues, you will be condemned to act them out in your work." This may seem harsh and overgeneralized, but we believe it to be true.

The depth of your responsibility as a therapist is not only in paying very close attention to your clients, but in paying very close attention to your own self. If you do not make self-examination a regular part of your life, your ego becomes susceptible to the perils of self-absorption. You can become hounded or paralyzed by self-doubt or you can be lost without awareness in inflating a false self. Neither of these outcomes is healthy—for you or for your clients.

Therapists must remember that being a therapist is a *role,* even though it requires much energy and genuineness. Being a therapist is what we do, not who we are. It is true that your clinical work can be a profound force in your personal development, and it is also true that you should learn from your clients. You can be challenged by their questions and pushed by their pain. This is a priceless reward available to you if you invest in your work and let it teach you each day.

At the same time, however, your work cannot be your life in toto. Your clients cannot be your friends and significant others. Your personal identity cannot be only your professional role. To do this is to try to fool yourself into playing the game with your clients called "Do as I say, not as I do." Your work as a therapist is to help others become their own persons, to examine their lives and live them honestly and to the fullest level of satisfaction possible. If you try to make your work be your entire self, you will create a personal space that may appear impressive but will always ring somewhat hollow.

Is this separation of role and identity an easy task? Absolutely not, at least for the therapist who cares, who feels called to the work more than to simply having a job. The caring and dedication are precisely what can contribute to the times of confusion. If you did not care, you would not get confused. This is a task all clinicians must work on repeatedly: to care enough about their work to make a genuine difference while caring enough about themselves to not lose track and get lost.

CLINICAL BURNOUT 301: FACING THE INEVITABLE—
FAILURES, IMPASSES, AND TRAGEDIES

The greatest hazard that comes with caring about your work as a therapist is your vulnerability to your clients' pain, confusion, and sadness. Clients' experiences are often the measures many therapists, especially at the beginning of their careers, tend to use as the standards by which they evaluate their performance. Happy and well-adjusted clients are seen as evidence of competence, whereas maladjusted clients tend to be used as indicators of failure. Problematically, it is this reliance on clients' experiences as the principal assessment of competence that can strike at you and haunt you in the tragedies you witness.

As we have discussed throughout this book, it behooves you to approach your clinical work from a realistic perspective. This includes being pragmatic about how your cases turn out; some get better (and some of these you might say did so *despite* what you did or did not do), some do not seem to do much of anything, and some get worse. Despite your continuing goal to be successful with clients, failure and uncertainty will always make an appearance among your efforts. Like the baseball player who considers one hit in three times at bat a good day's work, you must be realistic in how you evaluate your work, even as you strive to get a hit each time you step up to the plate.

No matter how flawless therapy may appear in the edited case studies and theoretical descriptions pervasive in the literature, it just does not ordinarily work that way. You will have many experiences of feeling lost and stuck and of groping to find your way. You will struggle with impasses because the complexity of clients, yourself, the therapeutic process, and life itself all come together so uniquely time and time again. You should not become resigned so that you give up at the first sign of an impasse. Instead, try to hang in and do your best, to consult with your supervisors and colleagues, to read and contemplate, and to try your best yet again. Some impasses will be resolved through your collaborative efforts with your clients, some will magically and mysteriously resolve on their own, and some will remain and bring the work to a halt.

The most trying experiences therapists have are the tragedies they witness from the intimate position the therapy process creates. These tragedies are the losses clients inevitably experience through such things as separation, divorce, custody disputes, chronic medical conditions, terminal illnesses, and death. These situations demand that clients accept what is painful, tolerate what seems intolerable, and continue with their lives when they feel overwhelmed with hopelessness and despair. Some situations must be endured only until they pass whereas others will never pass but instead reshape the client's life forever. A tragedy may give some warning or it may strike like lightning, but either way it shakes clients to the core. These experiences challenge them to both summon all their resources and to grow beyond what they have previously believed they could overcome.

In these tragic experiences you will find that you resonate with your clients' pain. It is a most intense sensation, unlike virtually any other position in which you have found yourself. You must accompany them on their lonely and uncertain journey of encountering their worst fears. You will feel for them *and* feel for yourself in your empathic relationship with them. Their pain can resurrect your own fears and tragedies, and in so doing demand that you face them once again. To be able to be with your clients most efficaciously, you must make sure you attend to what stirs in you and use it appropriately in the therapeutic relationship—without confusing what belongs to you and what is their experience.

The most painful of all these tragedies is the suicide of a client—one of your clients. It is said that there are two kinds of therapists: those who have had a client commit suicide and those who will have a client commit suicide. The event may be the predictable outcome of a client's long and tortured struggle with depression, failure, and hopelessness. In such cases, you may feel a keen sense of a cruel betrayal, discovering that despite your hard work with the client, it was not enough. You may have even believed that the client had moved past the crisis of heightened self-destructive impulses, and so the suicide's impact on you is all the more devastating. Alternatively, the suicide can be so unexpected that the shock and disbelief seem like they will never end, and you are left wondering how the client could have reached such an extreme state without warning. Neither type of suicide is any easier to deal with.

When you have a client commit suicide, you are required, for malpractice reasons, to review your documentation of treatment and determine if you have any vulnerability to legal action. Did you document all contacts (sessions, phone calls, meetings with other professionals and family members)? Did you respond appropriately to any mention or sign of suicidal ideation? These questions, however, usually pale before the more personally challenging ones that accompany a suicide. Over and over again, you may ask yourself, "What could I have done differently?" "Did I miss something that would have told me what the client needed from me to retain some hopefulness about life?" "How do I understand this, make sense of it, so I can keep on believing in myself as a therapist?" These are some of the many doubts and questions about yourself as a therapist and as a person you must process again and again before you can accept this special tragedy and then go on.

At this point, you may begin to wonder how a therapist can practice for ten, twenty, or fifty years and *not* become burned out. We think that it is important for you to realize that this is a very good question—there are not that many folks out there who can stand up to and even thrive in these sorts of conditions over the course of many years. It is foundationally a gift, nurtured and developed through training and guided with the increasing wisdom that comes from experience, that makes it possible. It is not an easy road. You may want to think hard regarding your long-term career goals if you doubt your fit with this kind of professional life.

MENTAL HEALTH 101:
FAMILY, FRIENDS, HOBBIES, AND HUMOR

Obviously, mental health, either as a field of endeavor or a state of mind to be achieved, is not always easy, but that does not mean that no strategies and activities exist that can make it more doable. The first part of the task is to recognize how difficult being a therapist is. Being a therapist does present many risks and complications to a person's health—physical, social, emotional, spiritual, and mental. Perhaps the most common question we are asked by people who do not work in this field is, "Don't you get really depressed listening to people talk about their problems all day long?" Some days we try to answer in such a way that we convey how our work is much more complicated and rewarding than their question implies, and then some days we recognize how on target their question really is.

Therapists do a lot of listening to problems. They can become sponges that absorb clients' pain and frustration, and they can add their own to that. At the end of a session and the end of a day, therapists may feel as if they need to wring themselves out, to dispose of what they have absorbed while listening so patiently and caringly to clients. Appreciating the difficulty of being in this role so much is a good start, but we would like to focus in on three sources of support that can keep a therapist operating well or, if they are unavailable or underutilized, will be sorely missed.

Therapists' significant others, family, and friends can provide the support system that helps them keep their perspective and their sanity. Having hobbies, activities sufficiently different and separate from doing therapy, provides a similar respite. Last but certainly not least, the development of a solid sense of humor can help to keep professional helpers from depressing themselves right out of action.

Family and Friends

As a marriage and family therapist, you are in the business of helping couples and families become healthier and more functional. This may mean helping them to become closer or sufficiently separate, more expressive or better listeners (probably both), more responsive and concerned, or less intrusive and overprotective. The list grows with each case you treat.

You must recognize the healing potential of the family unit for the whole as well as the parts. It is very important to remember that you, too, are a member of your own families, both family of origin and current family; you are not *only* a therapist. It is, of course, unethical to be the therapist for a member of your own family (AAMFT, 1991). Nevertheless, you must be aware of how you may automatically try to operate as your family's therapist. When you accept that role, no matter how innocently, you run the risk of losing your place as a family member who needs the companionship and support of the family. You can also alienate those you love by inadvertently playing therapist rather than being their loved one.

Therapists are sometimes notorious for neglecting their family life in the pursuit of their own careers. If you forget to be a person in your family, then you lose and your family loses a most important part of life—feeling connected to and loved by those most dear. Your family can help you remember who you are as a person beyond a professional role, and remind you that you need everything possible from your family experience just as you teach your clients that they need the same from theirs.

Friends are another critical component in sustaining your own mental health. You can receive support from friends just as you do with your family, but with something else. With friends, you have the luxury of not holding the types of expectations that typically are made among family members. The intensity is not as great; thus, you can sometimes feel more freedom to express yourself without fear of disappointing or being disappointed.

Because your work involves all the emotions a family elicits, you can sometimes find your situation with your own family to be quite intense. Personal issues are stirred by working with clients, and working with clients stirs personal issues with your family. When these feelings arise and challenge you, your friends can be the primary support system to utilize. In a way, friends provide brief vacations from clients, from your family-of-origin role, and from your current family role. You can share with friends without all the intensity that family dynamics, either professional or personal, can generate.

Hobbies

Despite the urge you probably will feel to become more competent, it is not advisable to make professional reading your primary hobby (for some readers, this may never have been much of a worry!). As much as it is good to broaden your understanding about therapy, it is important that you have activities in which to be involved that have nothing to do with therapy. These activities, which should both invigorate and relax, are crucial to maintaining your mental health, your internal compass where you keep a balanced perspective on work and play in your life. Hobbies come in many shapes and sizes. Which one you choose is unimportant. What is important is that the hobby takes you some place mentally and emotionally that is different enough from your "work self" to be nourishing and rejuvenating to your "personal self."

Humor

The work of being a therapist is mentally and emotionally very intense. Therapy is serious business. You are invited regularly into people's lives in such a way that your words and actions can be profoundly influential. While not forgetting the seriousness of what you do, you must also attend to the danger of taking yourself too seriously and letting the seriousness become an oppressive weight on your psyche.

We find the use of humor to be an excellent antidote for pathological seriousness. While it must always be appropriate in terms of respect for clients, a good measure of humor in the recipe can keep a therapist alive and cooking. The absurdity of life is abundantly present in therapy, and it offers the makings of much wit and wisdom. To find the humor in the absurdities of your work and personal life can allow you the freedom to laugh, to look anew, to release and relax, and to grow in your appreciation of life's complexities without succumbing to terminal seriousness. Additionally, your clients will be greatly benefited.

MENTAL HEALTH 201:
COLLEGIAL SUPPORT AND SUPERVISION

Psychotherapy is a very isolating form of professional practice. Therapists spend great amounts of time alone with persons whom they serve, in part, by putting themselves and their needs aside. Between appointments, paperwork, and phone calls, therapists are usually behind a closed door trying to stay focused on the task at hand. The brief periods of time when they get coffee, pick up messages, and check the appointment book (all on the way to and from the restroom) allow for only fleeting moments with colleagues.

It is vitally important that you not become swallowed up in this isolating type of professional existence. Your colleagues can be a tremendous source of support to you because they know the frustrations, doubts, and concerns you have so very well; they share them. You need your colleagues and they need you. You can support each other through professional consulting on difficult cases, informal "talking shop," or having lunch or coffee and relating personally about anything but doing therapy. Sharing your family news and experiences with colleagues can help you to remember, again, that you are persons first and therapists second.

The appropriate formal usage of collegial support is through regular supervision. We do not believe that any therapist ever outgrows the need for supervision. For six years, one of us (CEC) traveled to Cincinnati, Ohio for a bimonthly consultation group for seasoned therapists with the late Carl Whitaker, MD. We would regularly hear Carl ask for our help in listening to him present a case he found troublesome. It was genuine, yet strange, when Carl would thank us for helping him feel unstuck with his case.

Supervision, at its best, is in many ways like a good therapist-client relationship (Liddle and Saba, 1984). There is an alliance developed with the supervisor and you come to feel his or her interest in helping you become a better therapist. The supervisor can listen patiently, sympathize, support, challenge, confront, interpret, and struggle through the rough spots just like you do with your clients. To avoid having supervision or to "sleepwalk" through it via some routine deprives you of the help you need to keep examining your work. When therapists believe that they do not need supervision any longer, they are in danger of hurting their clients and themselves.

Your work is very intense, very emotional, and very serious. Without a supervisor to help you in self-examination, you risk taking this work for granted, and that is an open invitation for all sorts of trouble. Insecurity, pride, self-doubt, grandiosity, cynicism, arrogance, confusion, tunnel vision, fear, blind spots, and other spells to which your ego may be susceptible can surely overwhelm you.

MENTAL HEALTH 301: PERSONAL THERAPY

At times in your professional life, you may find yourself lost and hurting in ways you cannot seem to overcome. These times may relate to issues and events in your personal life, uncertainties and tragedies you encounter in your professional work, or a combination of the two. During these times, you are better off to consider the possibility that personal therapy for yourself may be the most appropriate intervention.

Curiously, some therapists have a real problem accepting that course of action. They will tell clients and nonclients alike that seeking therapy is not a sign of weakness, but a sign of wisdom that shows a recognition of the need for help. Yet, therapists sometimes are not able to use their own wisdom very well. Regardless, it is the responsible thing to do—for themselves, their spouses, their family, and their clients.

Therapy for the therapist, when you really think about it, makes perfect sense. Marriage and family therapists are mentally and emotionally quite vulnerable by virtue of how much stress they are exposed to in the daily juggling of their roles as "therapist" and "person." When most people have the flu, for example, they try to give themselves the care that is needed to recuperate. They also try to give themselves adequate space to recover while they also protect others from their germs. In the same way, recognizing that their mental health is as important as their physical health, therapists have the responsibility to act in ways that safeguard themselves and their clients. This can and should include a willingness to pursue personal therapy.

In conclusion, you should have a deep appreciation for the challenge that professional clinical work affords, including the risks and rewards inherent. Some days will be more rewarding, and some days will be more risk-promoting. We strongly urge you to pay close attention to how you handle the stresses, strains, and rewards. With this done wisely, you can look forward to many years of fulfilling and interesting professional work making a difference in people's lives. On the other hand, if this is done foolishly, it is a ticket to disaster at both the professional and personal level. Burnout is not something to risk; do everything you can to prevent it.

Chapter 17

Changing Focus: Jobs, Settings, Populations, Careers

It might seem odd to have a chapter discussing a change of professional focus in a book for beginning therapists. However, we believe that this is the best time to be thinking about where you may decide to go from either graduate school ("Hey, I'll just settle for a job that pays something more than my graduate assistantship or my part-time job at the mall") or after you have obtained your first job in the field of marriage and family therapy ("Hey, let's not push it—I wasn't sure the first place was even going to hire me"). With all the changes in the field of mental health services, from reimbursement to mergers to highly specialized delivery programs, it is very likely that you will not work at one job for the same agency for your entire career. In addition, as we will discuss in Chapter 18, you may choose a treatment modality and/or client population of professional interest that will become your specialty as you become a more mature and seasoned therapist. Also, after some time in this field, you may decide to work in a career that is somewhat related to marriage and family therapy but is nonetheless a significant departure from what you are doing now. For these reasons, we will discuss the realities of the job market and professional experience, the variety of settings and the challenges of the different client populations in mental health services, and the business of changing careers.

REALITIES OF THE JOB MARKET AND PAYING YOUR DUES

We would like to be able to say that there are millions of jobs for therapists in every conceivable setting so that everybody could get whatever job they might like. However, quite bluntly, we cannot say that, and must also admit that the job market is more questionable in the mid-to-late-1990s than it has been at times in the past. In some parts of the country, particularly on the East and West coasts, there are estimated to be many more therapists than the population can support (Woods, 1995). The constant state of transition with managed care seems to be pushing both private and public agencies into various more efficient (not necessarily more effective) and economical service delivery strategies that, in turn, affect the specific size and profile of the staff needed to provide services. With all of these considerations, it is best to expect that you will have to present yourself very well to be hired, as the competition will be substantial for most any position, and even more so for entry-level positions. You will probably find yourself applying for positions that do not necessarily strike you as the job of your dreams but can provide a beginning for your career.

We want to point out that, just like the phrase goes with musicians, "you have to pay your dues." Working in agency settings is an excellent means of gaining experience and exposure to the range of professional activities in which therapists engage. The more experiences you participate in and are exposed to, as well as the more supervision you receive, the better you will be prepared to make the necessary transitions to remain employed in this ever-changing market. It takes time to do this well.

All too often, we hear graduate students and beginning therapists talk about working in an agency for "a few years" and then wanting to go into their own private practice. Frankly, this is not a very realistic way of thinking about your career, for several reasons. Your professional experience is one of your most valuable commodities, and it takes more than just a few years to become a mature and competent therapist. Even for an experienced and capable therapist with a reputation for quality work, it is quite a jump to go from a somewhat stable position in an agency to "rolling the dice" with starting a private practice. Many quality therapists combine salaried positions in agencies with a small part-time private practice, sharing expenses with several therapists, whereas some join with an established psychiatric or psychological services private practice. Few therapists ever completely "go it alone," and this is especially true these days. The heyday of the independent private practitioner has passed, and so believing or expecting that you will be someday on your own professionally is a bit naive.

It is also important to remember that it is easy to view private practice as glamorous and lucrative. In reality, it is neither for the vast majority of clinicians. To be successful in a solo private practice, you must be a very mature and competent therapist. You will need to have both the regard of enough other professionals to provide you with a sufficient supply of referrals as well as the business savvy to stay afloat in these times of shrinking client numbers and reimbursement rates dictated by managed care companies. Furthermore, you need to have an incredible will to succeed in this forum because the amount of energy you will expend taking care of the business end of things will be far beyond the normally tiring world of clinical work. We are not saying an independent private practice is an impossibility, but we are saying it is very difficult and most therapists today will not be suitable for its unique demands.

MENTAL HEALTH SERVICES: SETTINGS AND CLIENT POPULATIONS

A number of settings generally associated with the provision of mental health services also tend to service different types of client populations. There are traditional outpatient settings of community-based mental health and substance abuse treatment centers funded by county and state resources. These outpatient facilities provide what we usually think of when we refer to outpatient psychotherapy. There is most often a wide range of clients in terms of socioeconomic status, ranging from poor people with no means of payment or limited government entitlements on up to middle-class and sometimes upper-middle-class clients with insurance benefits and financial means to pay for services at full fee. The wealthy tend to frequent other types of service settings.

Clients in typical outpatient community mental health settings generally present with garden-variety problems of depression; anxiety; parent-child conflict and childhood/adolescent behavior problems; marital conflict and dissatisfaction; post-traumatic stress disorder; occasional court-mandated treatment for substance abuse, child abuse, or domestic violence; and adjustment disorders related to life transitions (death, divorce, the empty-nest syndrome). Client motivation for treatment can range from highly interested and eager, to the predictable reluctance of adolescents brought in for therapy by their parents or adults who are suspicious about social services in general, to adults who are being forced to comply with an order from a court or a child protective services agency. With the growing prevalence of managed care, there is a strong emphasis on short-term treatment that utilizes brief models of therapy.

There are similar outpatient clinics that are hospital-based and affiliated with either the psychiatric department of the hospital involved or a private corporation. These clinics are subcontracted to provide mental health services to clients referred from within and outside of the hospital. Some charitable organizations set up facilities to provide these same kinds of outpatient psychotherapy services, along with related family services such as adoptions and foster care. In addition, religiously affiliated social service organizations exist, which may or may not utilize a treatment philosophy that is spiritually based to provide outpatient therapy services. Finally, there are private practices that provide traditional outpatient services and often include a specialty area of treatment or client population as an added marketing strategy (e.g., divorce/stepfamily adjustment issues, anxiety disorders, eating disorders, child and adolescent behavior problems, geriatric clients). The variety of outpatient settings is quite wide, as you can see. Curiously, our experience suggests that clients who obtain services from a private practice are generally viewed as having a somewhat higher level of motivation and sophistication than clients receiving services from community-funded agencies.

Two related trends exist in the world of outpatient services, most noticeably with regard to private practice, that are primarily the result of the influence of managed care. The first is the trend toward mergers to consolidate resources and lower overhead to meet the financial challenges of lower reimbursement rates. Service providers across the board are having to do more—or at least as much—with fewer resources. This has given impetus to the second trend, which involves mergers or simple affiliations that allow the providers to present themselves in a unified fashion to demonstrate a stronger base of services available in marketing for contracts with a managed care company or specific provider panel. This allows an affiliated group of agencies or practices to bid for a contract to be the sole provider of services to a large group of clients in their geographical area on the same mental health managed care plan.

More serious conditions diagnosed as severe or chronic mental illness (schizophrenia and other psychotic disorders) are also served by programs within outpatient, community-based agencies. These programs are specifically designed to serve the needs of this population's long-term care through the use of ongoing medication, case management, residential services, and some psychotherapy. The problems most families face with a mentally ill member provide an important opportunity to utilize a family systems approach to helping families manage, intervene, and cope with these clients. This population, however, can engender much frustration for a therapist, as progress can often only be measured in very small, often very fragile steps. Moreover, these clients are often susceptible to relapse and decompensation in mental status. In addition, family members often have distanced themselves to minimize their own involvement and allow "the system" to provide the continuity of care for these clients. Acquiring their involvement again can be quite a challenge.

In addition to outpatient settings, there are also the traditional hospital inpatient units where stabilization through medication and psychotherapy are provided. It should be noted in this era of managed care that the cost for inpatient care is most daunting and hence subject to the most severe containment and reduction in reimbursement from insurance companies and other funding bodies. In response to this trend, there has been an increase in more cost-effective partial hospitalization or day treatment programs that allow for much of the intensity of an inpatient stay without incurring such high costs and staffing requirements.

The clients seen in inpatient and partial hospitalization programs would include clients similar in many ways to those in traditional outpatient settings. Inpatient clients may be going through a single episode of major depression in response to a specific stressor in their life (being fired or laid off from their job, the death of a loved one, a sudden marital separation, etc.), or they may be experiencing a particularly intense period of struggle. Ordinarily, some may be working in outpatient therapy and have been admitted into an inpatient setting as a result of a temporary self-harm threat or decompensation that occurred in their therapy. Inpatient and partial hospitalization programs can also serve in the frequent restabilization of the severely mentally ill population in the community. This diverse combination of clients can make for a wide range of client motivation for treatment, family involvement, and length of stay in the program.

More recently, we have seen an increase in home-based family therapy services to multiproblem "at risk" families in need of a high-intensity, time-limited treatment regiment. This might be termed as family therapy "in the trenches," as the work is very intensive (three to five times a week for at least several hours each day) and is provided directly in the clients' home and related social environment. Oftentimes, these families have been ordered to receive this treatment through the court or child protective services agency; hence, they can not only be reluctant but downright resistant and hostile toward the services. Additionally, the social contexts these families often live in are a bit intimidating, and may even be dangerous for outsiders such as therapists. Nevertheless, programs of this nature appear to be very much part of the wave of the future.

Another setting involves residential treatment facilities for children and adolescents with severe behavioral and legal problems related to violent behavior, sexual offenses, and/or chemical dependency that necessitate either their temporary or permanent removal from their families. These clients often have experienced extreme emotional neglect and/or abuse and have subsequently established a pattern of serious acting out of antisocial behavior as a result. These are no doubt some of the most challenging clients with which to work because they generally do not have a part in the decision to be placed out of the home and community, which heightens their feeling that they are the scapegoats for their family system. They may also lack some of the requisite verbal and cognitive skills and impulse controls that ordinary therapy usually requires as a result of their less-than-ideal life experience.

The overall growth of the health services field has brought with it increased opportunities for mental health services to be provided in a variety of other settings. Specialized medical service programs for patients dealing with various forms of cancer, closed head injuries, infertility, sudden infant death syndrome, organ transplants, Alzheimer's disease, and a host of other medical issues have begun to utilize mental health professionals as a built-in component of their treatment programs. In fact, medical family therapy is a professional domain in its own right (we recommend a look at *Medical Family Therapy* by McDaniel, Hepworth, and Doherty, 1992). The rise in emotional and behavioral problems impacting young people in the educational system has resulted in many grants and programs that incorporate into schools a variety of mental health services for children and adolescents. There are some programs affiliated with criminal justice systems that provide or require mental health services for various offenses, such as shoplifting, domestic violence, sexual abuse perpetration, and driving under the influence of substances. And there are also a number of specialized agencies that provide mental health services for specific problems such as teenage pregnancy, sexually transmitted diseases, HIV/AIDS, drug and alcohol abuse, domestic and family violence, and numerous other situations.

CHANGING CAREERS . . . BUT WHAT ABOUT THIS ONE I AM JUST STARTING?

Why on earth would we bring this subject up to you now? Frankly, because in this day and age, changing careers happens more often than you might think. Along with the seemingly constant state of transition occurring in the mental health field at this time, our discussion on clinical burnout should suggest to you that some therapists reach a point where the emotional wear and tear of the profession becomes a strong motivation to move on to something else. This move may be into the administrative end of the mental health business, into a different career that is closely related to psychotherapy training, or a whole departure from the field itself to a brand new career unrelated to psychotherapy.

Why would you want to be mindful of this possibility as you are in the midst of your training or having just started your first job? Because we believe you owe it to yourself and cannot afford to be naive. In the same way that you felt the need to respect and respond to some type of call or urging to become trained as a therapist, you owe it to yourself to consider that some day you may find that the job of a therapist no longer fits you very well. It is not a crime that you decided to become a therapist. Thus, it is also not a crime to heed your ongoing self-examination which some day may tell you that, for the welfare of yourself and the clients you would serve, it is time to move on. This is not meant to scare you into thinking that you ought to pack your parachute now in anticipation of bailing out of this career. It is meant to remind you that being a therapist is a very serious business with very significant implications for not only the clients you treat but for you and your family as well.

What we want you to take with you from this part of the chapter is a recognition of how your career may proceed. Few people start their graduate training with an exact *and* realistic focus about what they want to be doing for the next twenty or thirty or more years. You will have ample time to sample from the wide variety of opportunities available today, and tomorrow's opportunities, although most likely not the same as those of today, will be there for you to take advantage of as well. Do not be afraid to allow your interests and even your professional functioning to seemingly meander across the mental health services territory. You may find a particular area that interests you so much that you want to specialize in it, a process that we will turn to discuss in the next, and final, chapter.

Chapter 18

Becoming the "Master Therapist" You Always Wanted to Be

The term "master therapist" is no longer in vogue the way it was several years ago, in part because therapists as a group have tended to become a tad more humble of late and also as a result of the increasing influence of postmodern thinking. In its salad days, the term called to mind a level of expertise that was something to strive for, and conferred a status of great bearing on the therapist to reach this clinical reputation equivalent of guru. The master therapist was often a charismatic figure, someone with both the confidence and apparent skill to solve virtually any problem a client system presented, almost always using a particular approach that usually became associated with that therapist's name. Consequently, there were books to write, workshops to conduct, students (disciples, really) to teach, colleagues to impress, and a little money to be made. Although this may sound rather cynically presented, in reality the master therapist phenomenon in the marriage and family therapy field provided a great deal of impetus to the field's growth and distinctiveness from the other traditional mental health disciplines.

Master therapists still exist today, and although they may not designate themselves as such, both new and old names in the field jockey about demonstrating their techniques and theories that are claimed to warrant particular attention among the clinical alternatives. There are still books to write, etc., and a lot more money to be made. In addition, there remains no shortage of practitioners out there just waiting to leap on the next emerging "super-therapy." Who knows, you may soon be among the elite when you develop the next amazing treatment modality that works wonders. We are only half-joking when we say that. In truth, clinical innovations have always been and are essential contributions to the field, and they need to be pursued vigorously. Those professionals whose names are currently at the forefront of the field need to be listened to and their ideas and techniques critiqued so that true benefit and hype can be accurately distinguished.

In the same way, your pursuit of excellence—becoming a master therapist, so to speak—is a necessary goal for your career as a therapist. In some respects, the process of maturing as a therapist occurs naturally as a function of time and increasing experience with a wide population of clients. You learn to recognize patterns and traps that are common to some kinds of clients, you become adept at watching and listening to numerous sources of data simultaneously, you develop some interventions that seem to fit particularly well with your persona, and your overall confidence and competence grows.

In contrast, some aspects of professional maturation do not come so naturally. Rather, they need to be sought out, pursued, and "conquered," or perhaps they need to at least be recognized as areas in which no development is desired. In any case, there needs to be an awareness of what you are good at and comfortable with, and what you are not.

OBSERVING MASTER THERAPISTS
CAN BE HAZARDOUS TO YOUR HEALTH

We have mentioned earlier (in Chapter 6) the importance of learning to do "doable" therapy, and we have mentioned as well how the training videos and such of master therapists may not be very helpful in that regard. You need to learn how to make use of other people's demonstrated clinical skills in ways that fit you. Much of what the master therapists demonstrate is idiosyncratic to their own personalities and clinical styles despite the universality of their theories, and it is both what makes them seem more than just effective but actually brilliant and unteachable.

Attempting to become the next Whitaker, Minuchin, or Satir is an admirable goal, but to do so you will have to find a treatment path that has not yet been discovered. Otherwise, your emulation of one of the greats could have some untoward outcomes for you and your clients. One of the problems with becoming a disciple of a particular model and the master that teaches it is that the more convinced you are of the model's power, the less likely you are to try something else in the event that it does not produce the desired results. The connection to religious fundamentalism is real in the sense that the certainty of one's assumptions about how to treat a client situation is inversely proportional to the flexibility and creativity of the clinician in that situation. If your plan does not go as it is "supposed to," you may be more likely to do it again and more forcefully (e.g., "try a stranger paradox," or "draw more connections to the family of origin") and risk alienating your clients, and at the same time, you are less likely to hear input from another point of view. If you end up stuck, you had better switch gurus, at least for this case.

Another problem with becoming a disciple of a master therapist is that it can actually hinder the development of your own clinical personality. If you are busy emulating and practicing a master therapist's style or approach, you are doing *his* or *her* approach, not your own. Some readers may argue that no matter how much you try to emulate another, it is still *your* version; perhaps so, but being so enamored with another's theory about and way of conducting therapy that you attempt to think and act like them does not make maximal use of what is unique about you. Further, the energy you expend honing your imitated expertise means that there is that much less for exploring your own unique ways of being as a therapist.

We are not saying that you should just toss out what has been done by the masters. Quite the opposite is true—you should make use of what they have shown, but make it *yours*. It should be a tool in your box, not the entirety of your repertoire. The same advice applies to what you see and hear from less famous masters, the veteran therapists who do solid clinical work in the shadows of anonymity, and even complete novices. You can and should be able to learn from anyone who is connected to therapy, including peers, students, and clients, but it must all be mediated through your own uniqueness. At the beginning of your career, it is understandable to imitate someone (anyone?) who seems to know what they are doing, but as you mature, you must inevitably seek your own way of practicing.

As a brief but hopefully relevant aside, we wonder why new therapies seem often to attract such rabid and vociferous followers. Is it because too many therapists have not settled on their own styles that they become quickly mesmerized by the next treatment fad? Or is it that helping people in solving their problems is much more complicated and difficult than therapists like to admit and that frustrates them; thus, when someone comes along trumpeting a clinical breakthrough that promises quick and lasting results, practitioner support is not hard to find? Perhaps it is a little of both. Or maybe it is all about money generated from books, workshops, speaking fees . . . nah.

BECOMING A SOLID GENERALIST

The road to clinical maturity begins someplace—hopefully before your formal training began—but it does not ever end. No therapist, no matter how "masterful" he or she becomes, ever arrives. Even Jesus, whom is considered by some to be the most therapeutic person in history, was not successful 100 percent of the time in helping those who came to him to change. We would encourage you to avoid any unrealistic expectations, even if you someday are recognized as a famous master therapist.

The first step that must be taken in your professional development is to become a solid generalist. We mean by this that you are competent to work with most clients' problems in most circumstances. You should be well-rounded, familiar with the major treatment models and techniques, and adaptable and flexible in applying them. You should know something about medical components of treatment, biological contributions, referrals and nonsystemic tools, and you should be able to navigate through treatment with most DSM diagnoses. Having read this book and doing what is recommended within it will help point you in that direction.

The solid generalist is not an expert in everything and needs to be honest about that. There will be certain clients and situations with which you will be unqualified, or at the very least questionably qualified, to work. Actively schizophrenic or psychotic individuals, for instance, may be beyond your competence as a treatment population although you may find yourself inadvertently working with them from time to time. Persons with multiple personalities, disso-ciative disorders, or abuse histories may also be more than you are quite ready for, at least as you begin your practice career. Other clients may also prove too complicated. We would suggest you be prudent in choosing to refer based upon your own abilities. If you are unsure, we suggest falling back on the ol' standby of supervision.

A good way to think about being a generalist versus becoming a specialist or master therapist is to liken the comparison to the differ-ences between family practice physicians and medical specialists. Family physicians are the consummate generalists, often the gate-way professionals that people first consult when they have a prob-lem. Often, their skills are sufficient to help solve the problems, and so they treat the medical condition satisfactorily and that is that. However, they do have a network of specialists to whom they regularly refer patients when a given case warrants it, making that decision based upon the level of severity, complexity, or uncertainty that the generalist experiences in attempting to provide treatment. You, as the solid generalist marriage and family therapist, should occupy an analogous role, treating most of the clients that come your way, and then making referrals or alternative arrangements based on your experience of stuckness or a clinical situation that makes you uncomfortable. You should also work at developing a referral list for just such occasions.

At this point, it may be useful to refer you back to the end of Chapter 3, where a rather lengthy list of clinical competencies was presented. You should be able to gain experience with most, if not all, of the populations, problems, and aspects of "normal" treatment that are included in that list over the course of time in practice. Any gaps in your experience you should seek to fill, if necessary by seeking clients with the particular situations with which you have yet to work through soliciting the intake coordinator, your supervisor, or whomever makes case assignments. An ideal use of this competency checklist involves documentation (case notes or reports, audio- or videotape, live supervision report) of each competency as it is com-pleted. This documentation allows you to accurately assess your progress, strengths, weaknesses, areas of specialty interest, and overall exposure to clinical experiences as you develop profession-ally. It should be noted that *exposure* and *competence* are not interchangeable terms; the former is the initial step toward the latter. You may check off what you are exposed to, but it is important to remember that the development of skill and competence typically requires more than working with a single case.

DEVELOPING A SPECIALTY:
ONE WORKSHOP DOES NOT AN EXPERT MAKE

After you have become an effective generalist, you may wish to develop an area or areas of specialization. As you gain experience with a variety of clients, there probably will be areas in which your personal interest is piqued, your professional interest is encouraged, or you may find the rewards of successful work particularly stimulating. Thus, you decide you want to develop particular expertise in the area(s), and you want to go about setting up a plan to accomplish that.

One question often asked is this: How long does it take to become a solid generalist? Answer: It depends. The question is answerable from a variety of perspectives. To what standard of competence do you appeal in evaluating yourself as competent? Some therapists develop skills and experience quickly, as a result of opportunity, personal factors, motivation, and/or necessity. In contrast, some therapists take much longer to become seasoned. In any event, you and your colleagues and supervisors will be the best assessors of your development and maturity.

In the same vein, the question is also asked about how long it takes to become a specialist. Again, the answer is dependent on a host of variables, ranging from the motivational level of the therapist to the opportunities for focusing in a specific area to the variable degree of astuteness for picking up new skills that each individual has. What is consistent, though, is that developing a specialty takes deliberate and focused effort over a period of time. One workshop or class does not qualify you as an expert although it may offer you an introduction to new ideas or skills that you can make use of almost immediately. Another part of becoming an expert is the old-fashioned notion of practice. You must internalize your new skills and knowledge through their practice in a variety of situations and with a range of clients in which your specialty is focused. Only after you have developed mastery and a high degree of effectiveness can you begin to think about presenting yourself as an expert.

EXCELLENCE AND HUMILITY:
TWO SIDES OF THE SAME COIN

Whether you choose to develop a specialty or to remain a generalist, the goal of excellence should remain, drawing you much like an airport beacon focuses the course of an airplane. Expertness is a descriptive characteristic you should be able to watch develop in yourself, assuming you remain in the role of professional clinician for a sufficient length of time. Expertness connotes excellence, but it is not a haughty or arrogant excellence. If anything, it reflects a starkly different attitude that highlights both your own humble but well-founded confidence in your skills and your unmitigated appreciation and respect for the client, who ultimately bears the responsibility and credit for what takes place in treatment.

In response to a personal correspondence many years ago, the therapist/author Sheldon Kopp wrote the following words to an eager and insecure young therapist grappling with self-assessment:

> I am pleased that my writing has touched you so. I know your struggle well. The only reassurance that I can offer is that some of us outgrow our perfectionism as we grow more seasoned. Settling for more modest and attainable flawed performance, astonishingly we find ourselves at times doing work more brilliant than we had ever dreamed we might do. For this we need only be willing to fall on our asses intermittently amidst those other spectacular performances. (February 13, 1978).

Excellence as a function of maturity fundamentally requires humility on the therapist's part, as Kopp so aptly reveals, in the recognition that the therapist is only a part of successful treatment and must learn to measure performance against a realistically founded standard. The moments of brilliance are sprinkled in among the more commonly experienced normative passages, in which you do your best and see what happens. Most of therapy is unspectacular from this vantage point.

Being a therapist requires the development of an almost paradoxical self-perception. While on the one hand, you are there to accomplish something in the life of a client and are an essential component for whatever changes are to be made, you at the same time must hold your contribution to the process in perspective. You are never as powerful as you may be tempted to believe as you begin your career, but you do have considerable influence, and learning how to use it with respect and humility is at the heart of becoming the expert therapist you wish to be.

EXPERIENCE AND SUPERVISION: THERAPY FOR THE THERAPIST

One final area of relevance and also of some controversy that we wish to discuss has to do with therapy for the therapist as an end in itself and as a means to the end of becoming a master. Some professionals believe that therapy for the therapist is an essential part of training, and they would insist that no clinician should be in the position to practice without having experience in the client's chair (e.g., Pope and Tabachnick, 1994). Others debate the absoluteness of that position, stating that therapy for the therapist may be beneficial, but as an irreplaceable requirement it is problematic (e.g., Wheeler, 1991). Still others question the nature of therapy in its entirety anyway, and so the traditional view of therapist as expert has no relevance, nor does the belief in requiring therapists to undergo their own therapy.

Regardless of the position to which you subscribe, we can only argue that at the very least it cannot hurt to put yourself in the position of being a client. In doing so, you will be able to develop a keener appreciation and empathy for what the role of client may demand, and this insight should not be lost on your own clients. Your sensitivity to their experiences, their feelings, their fears, their curiosity, and even some of the more uncomfortable possibilities such as working with a therapist who is condescending or patronizing, can only increase. In addition, you will likely have the opportunity to examine some of your own ways of operating, both as a professional and as a person. In this field, the distinction between the two is understandably blurry, and so you may glean a benefit both in your own personal world and in your clinical role.

It is possible to gain some of these therapeutic benefits through the experience of good supervision. As we discussed in Chapter 3, a good supervisory relationship is a tremendous asset throughout your career. It provides you with quality and focused attention and feedback regarding your clinical practice of therapy that has very powerful implications for your own personal growth. One of the rewards available to you as a therapist is the experience in understanding and appreciating the human drama with all its depth and complexity. From these experiences, you can derive much insight and fulfillment for your own personal life. Supervision for the therapist, like therapy for the client, can be the catalyst and crucible for these types of life-enhancing experiences.

In much the same way as supervision, it is also possible to examine aspects of your self and your life within other contexts, including family and friendship relationships. Going back to our discussion of the roles of professional and social therapists in Chapter 12, you have had and will have social therapists whose presence, attention, and feedback contribute immeasurably to your life. The acceptance you feel in these relationships coupled with the trust you have in their challenges and confrontations of you provide the similar kinds of therapeutic experiences to those of good therapy and good supervision. You learn to become a more fully developed person by learning from all the teachers that life has provided for you. As a therapist, you will derive the most from your career when you access the many valuable teaching moments offered by your supervisors, your clients, your friends, and your family members.

In any case, to develop as a master therapist, you must allow your own person to be the subject under examination on a more or less regular basis with people that you respect and whose opinions and points of view you value. No book or workshop can adequately serve you in this regard. Rather, you must be able to do this in the context of an ongoing relational opportunity. It is better to seek out such opportunities proactively than to do so as remedial action. We would encourage you to begin looking for them as soon as possible.

It is our hope that now, as you have completed this book, you are in a better position from which to practice professional marriage and family therapy than you were when you started reading. We hope we have offered you some valuable information, some provocative ideas, and even some potentially uncomfortable suggestions. We also hope that you find yourself more energized and enthused about the practice of the profession as a result, and we hope that you are all the more well prepared to venture into the real world of marriage and family therapy. If you do it right, you will find that your adventure is well worth it. We wish you every blessing and the best of luck.

References

American Association for Marriage and Family Therapy. (1991). *AAMFT code of ethics.* Washington, DC: Author.

American Psychiatric Association. (1987). *Diagnostic and statistical manual of mental disorders,* third edition, revised. Washington, DC: Author.

American Psychiatric Association. (1994). *Diagnostic and statistical manual of mental disorders,* fourth edition. Washington, DC: Author.

Aponte, H. (1994). How personal can training get? *Journal of Marital and Family Therapy,* 20, 1-16.

Aponte, H. (1992). Training the person of the therapist in structural family therapy. *Journal of Marital and Family Therapy,* 18, 269-282.

Becvar, D., and Becvar, R. (1996). *Family therapy: A systemic integration,* third edition. Boston: Allyn and Bacon.

Bergin, A. (1980). Psychotherapy and religious values. *Journal of Consulting and Clinical Psychology,* 48, 95-105.

Bischoff, R., and Sprenkle, D. (1993). Dropping out of marriage and family therapy: A critical review of research. *Family Process,* 32, 353-375.

Bishop, D., and Eppolito, J. (1992). The clinical management of client dynamics and fees for psychotherapy: Implications for research and practice. *Psychotherapy,* 29, 545-553.

Boszormenyi-Nagy, I., Grunebaum, J., and Ulrich, D. (1991). Contextual therapy. In A. Gurman and D. Kniskern (Eds.), *Handbook of family therapy,* volume two (pp. 200-238). New York: Brunner/Mazel.

Brock, G., and Bernard, C. (1992). *Procedures in marriage and family therapy,* second edition. Boston: Allyn and Bacon.

Buck, J. (1970). *The house-tree-person technique.* Los Angeles: Western Psychological Service.

Budman, S., and Gurman, A. (1988). *Theory and practice of brief therapy.* New York: Guilford.

Campbell, C., Doane, D., and Guinan, J. (1983). Instant supervision: Therapy for the therapist. *Voices,* 19, 71-76.

Chalfant, H., Heller, P., Roberts, A., Briones, D., Aguirre-Hochbaum, S., and Farr, W. (1990). The clergy as a resource for those encountering psychological distress. *Review of Religious Research,* 31, 305-313.

Constantine, L. (1978). Family sculpture and relationship mapping techniques. *Journal of Marital and Family Therapy,* 4, 13-23.

de Shazer, S. (1985). *Keys to solution in brief therapy.* New York: Norton.

Doherty, W. (1994, March). *Therapeutic morality in an age of uncertainty.* Presented at 17th Annual Family Therapy Networker Symposium, Washington, DC.

Doherty, W. (1995). *Soul searching.* New York: Basic Books.

Doherty, W., and Boss, P. (1991). Values and ethics in family therapy. In A. Gurman and D. Kniskern (Eds.), *Handbook of family therapy,* volume two (pp. 606-637). New York: Brunner/Mazel.

Doherty, W., and Simmons, S. (1996) Clinical practice patterns of marriage and family therapists: A national survey of therapists and their clients. *Journal of Marital and Family Therapy, 22,* 9-25.

Duhl, F., Kantor, D., and Duhl, B. (1973). Learning, space, and action in family therapy: A primer of sculpture. In D. Bloch (Ed.), *Techniques of family psychotherapy: A primer* (pp. 47-63). New York: Grune and Stratton.

Dryden, W., and Spurling, L. (Eds.). (1989). *On becoming a psychotherapist.* London: Tavistock/Routledge.

Edwards, J. (1990). "Attrition in family and marital therapy: A decay curve approach." Unpublished PhD dissertation.

Exner, J. (1978). *The Rorschach: A comprehensive system,* volume two. New York: John Wiley and Sons.

Farber, B. (1990). Burnout in psychotherapists: Incidence, types, and trends. *Psychotherapy in private practice, 8,* 35-44.

Fee, practice, and managed care survey. (1995, January). *Psychotherapy finances, 21,* 1.

Fisch, R., Weakland, J., and Segal, L. (1983). *The tactics of change.* San Francisco: Jossey-Bass.

Framo, J. (1992). *Family-of-origin therapy: An intergenerational approach.* New York: Brunner/Mazel.

Freeman, D. (1992). *Family therapy with couples: The family-of-origin approach.* Northvale, NJ: Jason Aronson, Inc.

Goldenberg, I., and Goldenberg, H. (1996). *Family therapy: An overview,* fourth edition. Pacific Grove, CA: Brooks/Cole.

Guttman, H. (1991). Systems theory, cybernetic, and epistemology. In A. Gurman and D. Kniskern (Eds.), *Handbook of family therapy,* volume two (pp. 41-62). New York: Brunner/Mazel.

Haley, J. (1987). *Problem-solving therapy,* second edition. San Francisco: Jossey-Bass.

Haley, J. (1984). *Ordeal therapy.* San Francisco: Jossey-Bass.

Hathaway, S., and McKinley, J. (1989). *Minnesota Multiphasic Personality Inventory–2.* Minneapolis: University of Minnesota Press.

Hoffman, L. (1981). *Foundations of family therapy.* New York: Basic Books.

Huber, C. (1994). *Ethical, legal, and professional issues in the practice of marriage and family therapy,* second edition. New York: Merrill.

Kaslow, F. (Ed.). (1996). *Handbook of relational diagnoses and dysfunctional family patterns.* New York: John Wiley and Sons.

Kerr, M., and Bowen, M. (1988). *Family evaluation.* New York: Norton.

L'Abate, L. (1981). Skills training programs for couples and families. In A. Gurman and D. Kniskern (Eds.), *Handbook of family therapy*, volume one (pp. 631-661). New York: Brunner/Mazel.

Lageman, A. (1993). *The moral dimensions of marriage and family therapy*. Lanham, MD: University Press of America.

Lebow, J. (1995). Open-ended therapy: Termination in marital and family therapy. In R. Mikesell, D. Lusterman, and S. McDaniel (Eds.), *Integrating family therapy: Handbook of family psychology and systems theory* (pp. 73-86). Washington, DC: American Psychological Association.

Liddle, H. (1991). Training and supervision in family therapy: A comprehensive and critical analysis. In A. Gurman and D. Kniskern (Eds.), *Handbook of family therapy*, volume two (pp. 638-697). New York: Brunner/Mazel.

Liddle, H. (1988). Systemic supervision: Conceptual overlays and pragmatic guidelines. In H. Liddle, D. Breunlin, and R. Schwartz (Eds.), *Handbook of family therapy training and supervision* (pp. 153-171). New York: Guilford.

Liddle, H., and Saba, G. (1984). The isomorphic nature of training and therapy: Epistemological foundation for a structural-strategic training program. In J. Schwartzman (Ed.), *Families and other systems: The macrosystemic context of family therapy* (pp. 27-47). New York: Guilford.

Madanes, C. (1981). *Strategic family therapy*. San Francisco: Jossey-Bass.

Maslow, A. (1954). *Motivation and personality*. New York: Harper and Row.

McDaniel, S., Hepworth, J., and Doherty, W. (1992). *Medical family therapy*. New York: Basic Books.

McDaniel, S., and Landau-Stanton, J. (1991). Family-of-origin work and family therapy skills training: Both-and. *Family Process*, *30*, 459-471.

McGoldrick, M., and Gerson, R. (1985). *Genograms in family assessment*. New York: Norton.

Minuchin, S., and Fishman, H. (1982). *Techniques of family therapy*. Cambridge, MA: Harvard University Press.

Moreno, J. (1952). Psychodrama of a family conflict. *Group Psychotherapy*, *5*, 20-37.

Nelson, T., Heilbrun, G., and Figley, C. (1993). Basic family therapy skills, IV: Transgenerational theories of family therapy. *Journal of Marital and Family Therapy*, *19*, 253-266.

Nichols, W. (1996). *Treating people in families: An integrative framework*. New York: Guilford Press.

Odell, M., and Stewart, S. (1993). Ethical issues associated with client values conversion and therapist value agendas in family therapy. *Family Relations*, *42*, 128-133.

Phillips, E. (1987). The ubiquitous decay curve: Service delivery similarities in psychotherapy, medicine, and addiction. *Professional Psychology: Research and Practice*, *18*, 650-652.

Physician's Desk Reference, fifty-first edition (1997). Montvale, NJ: Medical Economic Company, Inc.

Piercy, F., Lasswell, M., and Brock, G. (Eds.). (1989). *American Association for Marriage and Family Therapy forms book*. Washington, DC: AAMFT.

Pope, K., and Tabachnick, B. (1994). Therapists as patients: A national survey of psychologists' experiences, problems, and beliefs. *Professional Psychology: Research and Practice*, *25*, 247-258.

Prince, S., and Jacobson, N. (1995). A review and evaluation of marital and family therapies for affective disorders. *Journal of Marital and Family Therapy*, *21*, 377 - 401.

Private practice fees, incomes, and trends. (1996, December). *Practice Strategies: A Business Guide for Behavioral Healthcare Providers*, *2*, 1.

Quinn, W., Atkinson, B., and Hood, C. (1985). The stuck-case clinic as a group supervision model. *Journal of Marital and Family Therapy*, *11*, 67-73.

Rosenbaum, R. (1994). Single-session therapies: Intrinsic integration? *Journal of Psychotherapy Integration*, *4*, 229-252.

Ryder, R., and Hepworth, J. (1990). AAMFT ethical code: Dual relationships. *Journal of Marital and Family Therapy*, *22*, 27-40.

Scharff, J., and Scharff, D. (1987). *Object relations family therapy*. Northvale, NJ: Jason Aronson, Inc.

Segal, L. (1991). Brief therapy: The MRI approach. In A. Gurman and D. Kniskern (Eds.), *Handbook of family therapy*, volume two (pp. 171-199). New York: Brunner/Mazel.

Selvini Palazzoli, M., Boscolo, L., Cecchin, G., and Prata, G. (1978). *Paradox and counterparadox*. New York: Jason Aronson, Inc.

Smith, T., McGuire, J., Abbott, D., and Blau, B. (1991). Clinical ethical decision making: An investigation of the rationales used to justify doing less than one believes one should. *Professional Psychology: Research and Practice*, *22*, 235-239.

Sprenkle, D. (Ed.). (1995, October). *Journal of Marital and Family Therapy, Special issue: Effectiveness of Marital and Family Therapy. 21*(4).

Stander, V., Piercy, F., Mackinnon, D., and Helmeke, K. (1994). Spirituality, religion and family therapy: Competing or complementary worlds? *American Journal of Family Therapy*, *22*, 27-41.

Sussman, M. (1992). *A curious calling: Unconscious motivations for practicing psychotherapy*. Northvale, NJ: Jason Aronson, Inc.

Talmon, M. (1990). *Single session therapy*. San Francisco: Jossey-Bass.

Talmon, M. (1993). *Single session solutions*. Reading, MA: Addison-Wesley.

Titelman, P. (Ed.). (1987). *The therapist's own family: Toward the differentiation of self*. Northvale, NJ: Jason Aronson, Inc.

Tjeltveit, A. (1986). The ethics of value conversion in psychotherapy: Appropriate and inappropriate therapist influence on client values. *Clinical Psychology Review*, *6*, 515-537.

Tomm, K. (February, 1992). "Ethical postures in therapy." Paper presented at a seminar titled "Presentations and Conversations with Auerswald, Tomm, and Levin," Athens, GA.

Trepper, T., and Nelson, T. (Eds.). (1993). *101 interventions in family therapy.* Binghamton, NY: The Haworth Press.

Watzlawick, P., Weakland, J., and Fisch, R. (1974). *Change: Principles of problem formation and problem resolution.* New York: Norton.

Weakland, J., and Fisch, R. (1992). Brief therapy—MRI style. In S. Budman, M. Hoyt, and S. Friedman, (Eds.), *The first session in brief therapy* (pp. 306-323). New York: Guilford.

Wechsler, D. (1991). *Wechsler Intelligence Scale for Children,* third edition. San Antonio, TX: The Psychological Corporation.

Wechsler, D. (1981). *Wechsler Adult Intelligence Scale Revised.* San Antonio, TX: The Psychological Corporation.

Wheeler, S. (1991). Personal therapy: An essential aspect of counsellor training, or a distraction from focussing on the client? *International Journal for the Advancement of Counselling, 14,* 193-202.

Whitaker, C., and Keith, D. (1981). Symbolic-experiential family therapy. In A. Gurman and D. Kniskern (Eds.), *Handbook of family therapy,* volume one (pp. 187-225). New York: Brunner/Mazel.

Whitaker, C., and Ryan, M. (1989). *Midnight musings of a family therapist.* New York: Brunner/Mazel.

White, M., and Epston, D. (1990). *Narrative means to therapeutic ends.* New York: Norton.

White, M., and Russell, C. (1995). The essential elements of supervisory systems: A modified Delphi study. *Journal of Marital and Family Therapy, 21,* 33-53.

Wiener-Davis, Michelle. (1992). *Divorce-busting.* New York: Summit.

Woods, D. (1995, November). "Forces of change in mental health care delivery." Presented at the 53rd Annual Convention of the American Association for Marriage and Family Therapy, Baltimore, MD.

Worden, M. (1994). *Family therapy basics.* Pacific Grove, CA: Brooks/Cole.

Worthington, E. (1986). Religious counseling: A review of published empirical research. *Journal of Counseling and Development, 64,* 421-431.

Worthington, E., Kurusu, T., McCullough, M., and Sandage, S. (1996). Empirical research on religion and psychotherapeutic processes and outcomes: A 10-year review and research prospectus. *Psychological Bulletin, 119,* 448-487.

FOR FURTHER READING...

The following is a very brief list of a few books and articles that we suggest as possible sources for additional information on various topics. Most of these are hot off the press, or at least fairly recent.

Chapter 1

Haley, J. (1996). *Learning and teaching therapy.* New York: Guilford.
Titelman, P. (Ed.) (1987). *The therapist's own family: Toward the differentiation of self.* Northvale, NJ: Jason Aronson, Inc.

Chapter 2

Piercy, F., Sprenkle, D., Wetschler, J., and Associates. (1996). *Family therapy sourcebook,* second edition. New York: Guilford. If you could only take three professional books with you to a desert isle, this would be one to pack.

Chapter 3

Haber, R. (1996). *Dimensions of psychotherapy supervision.* New York: Norton. Good for both sides of the supervisory experience.
Nichols, M. (1995). *The lost art of listening.* New York: Guilford. This book is useful for both the development of clinical skills as a listener and the development of general interpersonal skills that will help in personal and professional relationships.

Chapter 4

Morrison, J. (1995). *The DSM-IV made easy: The clinician's guide to diagnosis.* New York: Guilford.
Perlmutter, R. (1996). *A family approach to psychiatric disorders.* Washington, DC: American Psychiatric Press, Inc. A strong but weighty book about integrating family and individual models of treatment.
Sporakowski, M. (1995). Assessment and diagnosis in marriage and family counseling. *Journal of Counseling and Development, 74,* 60-64. This article offers a pretty good synopsis of the tension between the traditional individual model of treatment and the systemic model of treatment, and it has a good set of references.

Chapter 6

Brock, G., and Bernard, C. (1992). *Procedures in marriage and family therapy,* second edition. Boston: Allyn and Bacon.

Taibbi, R. (1996). *Doing family therapy: Craft and creativity in clinical practice.* New York: Guilford. Practical, practical.

Chapter 8

Physician's Desk Reference, fifty-first edition. (1997). Montvale, NJ: Medical Economic Company, Inc. This is an annually updated compendium of just about every drug known to humanity and their uses, misuses, half-life, side effects, etc.

Sperry, L. (1995). *Psychopharmacology and psychotherapy: Strategies for maximizing treatment outcomes.* New York: Brunner/Mazel.

Chapter 10

Aronson, J. (1996). *Inside managed care: Family therapy in a changing environment.* New York: Brunner/Mazel.

Bagarozzi, D. (1996). *The couple and family under managed care.* New York: Brunner/Mazel. Brunner/Mazel has a series of books called "Mental Health Practice Under Managed Care," of which this is one title.

Practice strategies: A business guide for behavioral healthcare providers. This is a monthly newsletter published by AAMFT—a gold mine of practical stuff.

Chapter 11

Cushman, P. (1995). *Constructing the self, constructing America: A cultural history of psychotherapy.* Reading, MA: Addison-Wesley. This is a fascinating account of the interplay between the historical development of American society and psychotherapy. Good to know where we have been, how we got here, and where we might be going . . .

Doherty, W. (1995). *Soul searching.* New York: Basic Books. A provocative and easy-to-relate-to book from one of the foremost thinkers in the MFT field today.

Chapter 12

Hepworth, D. (1993). Managing manipulative behavior in the helping relationship. *Social Work, 38,* 674-682. Pointers for the clinician who wants to avoid being fooled by manipulative behaviors of clients.

Ryder, R., and Hepworth, J. (1990). AAMFT ethical code: Dual relationships. *Journal of Marital and Family Therapy, 22,* 27-40. Provocative piece about the problems inherent in defining all dual relationships as potential ethical problems.

Chapter 13

Trepper, T., and Nelson, T. (Eds.) (in press). *101 interventions in family therapy,* second edition. Binghamton, NY: The Haworth Press.

Trepper, T., and Nelson, T. (Eds.) (1993). *101 interventions in family therapy.* New York: Haworth. Both of the foregoing contain lots of practical and creative stuff.

Chapter 15

Brock, G. (Ed.) (1994). *American Association for Marriage and Family Therapy: Ethics casebook.* Washington, DC: AAMFT.

Vesper, G., and Brock, G. (1991). *Ethics, legalities, and professional practice issues in marriage and family therapy.* Boston, MA: Allyn and Bacon.

Chapter 16

Ellenbogen, G. (Ed.) (1987). *Oral sadism and the vegetarian personality.* New York: Ballantine.

Ellenbogen, G. (Ed.) (1996). *More oral sadism and the vegetarian personality.* New York: Brunner/Mazel. Both of the above books are compilations of articles from the infamous *Journal of Polymorphous Perversity.* If you can find this journal anywhere or get these books, do so for immediate humor therapy for yourself!

Index

Order Your Own Copy of
This Important Book for Your Personal Library!

THE PRACTICAL PRACTICE OF MARRIAGE AND FAMILY THERAPY
Things My Training Supervisor Never Told Me

_____ in hardbound at $49.95 (ISBN: 0-7890-0063-6)

_____ in softbound at $24.95 (ISBN: 0-7890-0431-3)

COST OF BOOKS_____

OUTSIDE USA/CANADA/
MEXICO: ADD 20%_____

POSTAGE & HANDLING_____
(US: $3.00 for first book & $1.25
for each additional book)
Outside US: $4.75 for first book
& $1.75 for each additional book)

SUBTOTAL_____

IN CANADA: ADD 7% GST_____

STATE TAX_____
(NY, OH & MN residents, please
add appropriate local sales tax)

FINAL TOTAL_____
(If paying in Canadian funds,
convert using the current
exchange rate. UNESCO
coupons welcome.)

☐ **BILL ME LATER:** ($5 service charge will be added)
(Bill-me option is good on US/Canada/Mexico orders only;
not good to jobbers, wholesalers, or subscription agencies.)

☐ Check here if billing address is different from
shipping address and attach purchase order and
billing address information.

Signature_____

☐ **PAYMENT ENCLOSED: $**_____

☐ **PLEASE CHARGE TO MY CREDIT CARD.**

☐ Visa   ☐ MasterCard   ☐ AmEx   ☐ Discover
☐ Diner's Club

Account # _____

Exp. Date _____

Signature _____

Prices in US dollars and subject to change without notice.

NAME _____

INSTITUTION _____

ADDRESS _____

CITY _____

STATE/ZIP _____

COUNTRY _____ COUNTY (NY residents only) _____

TEL _____ FAX _____

E-MAIL_____
May we use your e-mail address for confirmations and other types of information? ☐ Yes   ☐ No

Order From Your Local Bookstore or Directly From
The Haworth Press, Inc.
10 Alice Street, Binghamton, New York 13904-1580 • USA
TELEPHONE: 1-800-HAWORTH (1-800-429-6784) / Outside US/Canada: (607) 722-5857
FAX: 1-800-895-0582 / Outside US/Canada: (607) 772-6362
E-mail: getinfo@haworth.com
PLEASE PHOTOCOPY THIS FORM FOR YOUR PERSONAL USE.

BOF96

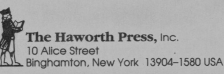

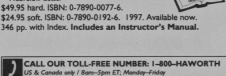